The Goths in Ancient Poland

the goths

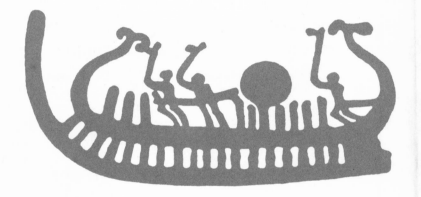

In cooperation with
The American Institute of Polish Culture

iN ANCiENT pOLAND

A STUDY ON THE HISTORICAL GEOGRAPHY
OF THE ODER-VISTULA REGION DURING
THE FIRST TWO CENTURIES OF OUR ERA

by JAN CZARNECKI

University of Miami Press
Coral Gables, Florida

Copyright © 1975 by
University of Miami Press

Designed by Anne Hertz

Manufactured in the United States of America

Library of Congress Cataloging in Publication Data

Czarnecki, Jan, 1912-
    The Goths in ancient Poland.

    Bibliography: p.
    Includes index.
    1.   Goths in Poland.   2.   Oder-Neisse area–Historical
geography.   3.   Vistula Valley–Historical geography.
I.   Title.
DK421.C88   913.363   74-20750
ISBN 0-87024-264-4

The illustration used as a decoration on the title page and elsewhere in this book is based on a prehistoric rock engraving of a boat with projecting keel that was found in South Sweden.

MEMORIAE PATRIS SVI, AVGVSTINI
LELIVVAE, IN INVASIONE POLONIAE
TRAGICA MANV BARBARICA CAESI
CHORZOVIAE DIE VNDECIMO MENSIS
SEPTEMBRIS A.D.MCMXXXIX,PAGINAS
SEQUENTES DEDICAT

AVCTOR.

CONTENTS

MAPS

FIGURES

PREFACE

This study is not just another history or story of the early Goths. It is an historical-geographical investigation of the territory occupied and the moves made by the Goths in the Oder-Vistula region during the first two centuries of our era. The term "Oder-Vistula region" describes the area comprised in the basins of the Oder and Vistula rivers. This area is almost congruent with the territory of present-day Poland, hence the title *The Goths in Ancient Poland*. The terms "Oder-Vistula region" and "ancient Poland" are strictly geographical concepts and do not imply any ancient or modern ethnic, political, or national notions.

The methodological approach to the matter investigated is different from that found in many other studies, both old and new, dealing with the same area and period. Many of these studies are based chiefly on conclusions drawn from the interpretation of archaeological finds or linguistic calculations. The testimony of contemporary historical source material has been used cautiously, hesitantly, or with insufficient historical criticism by their authors, a method that is successful if applied to prehistoric cultural districts and large historical ethnic groups, but which definitely loses its validity if the moves and abodes of one single small tribe are the subject of investigation.

General prehistoric maps, drawn by different schools of archaeology, depict the area as occupied either by one or by three archaeological cultural districts, while more than thirty peoples are recorded as inhabitants of the area in contemporary historical sources. As yet there are no archaeological criteria available that would permit the location of one single small tribe in a precise space within the limits of one prehistoric cultural district.

Linguistic evidence, like archaeology, deals with concepts broader than tribal units. The linguistic material consists of a number of tribal, personal, and geographic names, transmitted to us frequently in distorted, mutilated, or corrupt forms. These transmitted forms have been reconstructed or corrected and brought in agreement with the forms of an extinct or modern language. In turn, etymologies have been derived from these languages. Since specialists in several languages were involved in the evaluation of names, many times there are several etymologies available for each name. General linguistic maps, drawn by different schools, depict the area in different colors and have added to the confusion. Linguistic evidence may be helpful in general and comparatively broad subjects; very rarely, however, will it be helpful if a single tribe is being investigated.

For these reasons, a different methodological approach was chosen in this study. It proceeded from the assumption that contemporary writers, namely Strabo, Pliny the Elder, Tacitus, and Ptolemy, are trustworthy witnesses; therefore their accounts have been treated as primary sources. Realizing that their information is not complete and that it may contain unreliable data or errors in judgment, every bit of information was examined individually and reports of doubtful content were carefully analyzed and corrected whenever possible. No information obtained from an ancient source was rejected on the ground of conflict with modern archaeological or linguistic evaluation. Material obtained from one historical source was compared with that from another. In most cases the location of one tribe, reported by an ancient author, was not specific enough to place the tribal territory on a modern map; therefore the location of direct and distant neighbors had to be established first.

Among these neighbors there was almost always one that could be located and identified by a significant physiographic or topographic feature of the land. The coast of the Baltic Sea, the estuaries of the Oder and Vistula, courses of rivers, directions and crossing points of trade routes were excellent guides for locating several peoples. The limited vocabulary used by the ancients for the points of the compass has been a slight handicap. For example, terms such as "north," "above," "beyond" may all mean either a straight northern, a northeastern, or a northwestern direction, an inaccuracy which amounts to $90°$ between the outermost points, i.e., northeast and northwest, or to a possible maximal deviation of about ten degrees in longitude in a list of peoples living "north," etc., of each other within a distance of three degrees in latitude. It was necessary, therefore, to work with many variables, some of which could be eliminated due to conflict with another fixed point.

The graphic structure, derived from historical sources and containing many imperfect links, when placed over a modern physiographic map necessitated some minor adjustments. The adjusted structure was then placed over differing prehistoric maps produced by several schools of archaeology. Prehistoric maps which disagreed with the historical diagram were rejected, and maps showing the least conflict with the diagram were chosen as auxiliary sources for locating peoples and places. With the help of these archaeological maps, minor adjustments on broader issues and major corrections of details were made; linguistic evidence was used as further auxiliary source material.

Surprising results were obtained from this methodological approach, since it revealed the existence of two tribal territories occupied by the Goths in the Oder-Vistula region. One was situated near the Middle Oder, the home of the Goths during the first century; the other lay at the Lower Vistula, occupied by the tribe during the second century. The study would not have been complete without explaining the relationship between these two tribal territories, which apparently had some connection with the phases of the general migratory process from Sweden to the Black Sea region.

Since the migratory route of the Goths is not recorded in any dependable historical source, a few auxiliary subjects had to be discussed, namely general problems of the historical geography of Eastern Germania and Sarmatia, the character or nature of contemporary migrations in Central Europe, and the technological level of ancient Germanic watercraft. Separate publication of these auxiliary subjects would have eliminated all the deviations from the main subject, but would have then required many references to various periodicals, an impractical solution. To justify the variety of subjects included, a subtitle has been added, i.e., *A study on the historical geography of the Oder-Vistula region during the first two centuries of our era.*

The texts of the primary sources are quoted from easily accessible editions, available in almost any college library. The following editions were selected as working texts: Strabo, edition and English translation by Jones (Loeb Classical Library, 1917-1933); Pliny, edition and English translation by Rackham (Loeb Classical Library, 1938-1963); Tacitus, *Germania,* edition and commentary by Anderson (1958); Ptolemy, edition by Nobbe, reprinted with an introduction by Diller (1966).

Variants of the ancient texts and commentaries were taken from critical editions quoted in abbreviated bibliographic form; the editions consulted are listed in the bibliography (pp. 161-174), the abbreviations in a special list (p. xvi).

Material for this study was collected over a period of more than twelve years and several earlier drafts were written in the city of New York, making use of its rich library resources. The manuscript was completed many years later in Miami, with the Library of the University of Miami at Coral Gables as the only library resource. I had to rely heavily on interlibrary loans, which are an excellent if limited help, since not everything needed is available at all or available at the time needed. For this reason several essential works such as Lubor Niederle, *Slovanské starožitnosti* (1902-1925), E. Šimek, *Velká Germanie Klaudia Ptolemaia* (1930-1953), G. Müller-Kuales, "Die Goten." *(Vorgeschichte der deutschen Stämme,* III, 1940), a few Polish monographs, and some articles published in the periodical literature were either not available to me or could not be satisfactorily evaluated. I do hope, however, that these omissions do not affect basic conclusions drawn.

One deviation from common practice has been made in this study, namely that foreign language citations, as a rule, appear in the text in English translation or condensed summary while the original quotations are placed in the Notes. Bibliographic references and quotations from languages using the Cyrillic script are transliterated into the Roman alphabet, according to the system used by the Library of Congress in Washington, D.C., except that all diacritics have been omitted. It was not feasible to transliterate Greek passages since this would have led to further distortion and ambiguity of the disputed forms of personal and place names. The names of the ancient tribes are given in their current anglicized form, and the authority for this has been *The Cambridge Ancient History.* Whenever a tribal name was not recorded in this work, it has been given in its original Latin or transliterated Greek form. Diacritics are used very rarely, mostly in translated quotations. The Latin forms Germania and Germani are used to distinguish the geographical concept of Germany in ancient times from the national one of later periods, and the tribal name from the modern national name. The names of places which were not part of Poland before 1945 are entered under the present official form with older forms added in parentheses. An exception was made only in the case of Danzig because the present form Gdańsk is rarely seen in the English literature and would have caused inconsistencies between the form chosen by me and the name used in quoted English works.

Cut-off date for publications included is the year 1971; however a few later works have been consulted.

ACKNOWLEDGMENTS

For many years past I have been so fortunate as to receive help and encouragement from many colleagues and friends. It is my great pleasure to mention their names and express my gratitude.

My foremost thanks go to Dr. Gerald Govorchin and Dr. Christos Patsavos, professors of history at the University of Miami, who encouraged me to create a homogenous entity out of many unfinished drafts and papers on the Goths and on problems in the historical geography of the Oder-Vistula region in ancient times. They were both kind enough to read the entire manuscript and to make valuable comments and suggestions.

My thanks go to my colleagues at the University of Miami Library; to those in the Interlibrary Loan Section who, for many years, patiently searched for and secured works not available in the library; and to Dr. Dale Barker, Associate Director of the Library, who assisted me in many ways.

I am greatly obliged to a dear friend, Mrs. Elsie Fansler, of the Florida International University at Miami, who devoted many evenings of her invaluable time to going through the manuscript with a fine pencil and correcting obscure passages. Mrs. Cathryn Moore and my wife, Irene, typed the final manuscript, and I have relied on their judgment at many points. I am especially grateful to Jacqueline and Albert E. Marten, my first American friends, who gave me the courage to go ahead with my studies in this country.

Last but not least I should like to express my gratitude to the American Institute of Polish Culture, which provided a subsidy for the publication of this work. It was the Institute's President, Mrs. Blanka Rosenstiel, and its Board of Directors who finally turned my project into reality and moved the manuscript from the publisher's shelf to his desk and to the printing press.

ABBREVIATED CITATIONS

These are primary sources that have been used as working texts.

Pliny
Gaius Plinius Secundus, *Natural History. With an English translation by H. Rackham,* 1938-1963. Other editions are quoted as Pliny (Mayhoff), etc., with reference to Pliny's text or to the page of the commentary.

Ptolemy
Claudius Ptolemaeus, *Claudii Ptolemaei Geographia. Edidit C.F.A. Nobbe, cum introductione a Aubrey Diller,* 1966. Other editions are quoted as Ptolemy (Cuntz), Ptolemy (Müller), etc., with reference to Ptolemy's text or to the page of the commentary.

Strabo
Strabo, *The Geography of Strabo. With an English Translation by Horace Leonard Jones,* 1917-1933. Other editions are quoted as Strabo (Kramer), Strabo (Meineke) or Strabo (Stratanovskii), with reference to the text or to the page of the commentary.

Tacitus, *Annales*
Cornelius Tacitus, *The Annals. With an English Translation by John Jackson,* 1925-1937. Other editions are quoted as Tacitus, *Annales* (Halm), etc., with reference to the text or to the page of the commentary.

Tacitus, *Germania*
Cornelius Tacitus, *Cornelii Taciti De Origine et Situ Germanorum. Edited by J. G. C. Anderson, 1958.* Other editions are quoted as Tacitus, *Germania* (Much), Tacitus, *Germania* (Robinson), etc., with reference to the text or to the page of the commentary.

Tacitus, *Historiae*
Cornelius Tacitus, *The Histories. With an English Translation by Clifford H. Moore,* 1925-1937. Other editions are quoted as Tacitus, *Historiae* (Halm), etc., with reference to the text or to the page of the commentary.

ONE   ORIGIN AND EARLY HISTORY OF THE GOTHS

 Until recent times there was general agreement among historians and other scholars as to the earliest history of the Goths. It was said that their homeland lay in southern Sweden. The regions today bearing the names Öster- and Västergötland, and sometimes also the island Gotland were specifically mentioned as their original abodes. Approximately at the beginning of the Christian era, the entire tribe or its major part left Sweden, crossed the Baltic Sea, and landed near the estuary of the Vistula. The Goths subdued neighboring Germanic or other tribes and became masters of a huge territory covering almost all of Pomerania and parts of former East Prussia. The Parsęta (Persante), Pasłęka (Passarge), and Noteć (Netze) rivers were customarily mentioned as the western, eastern, and southern borders of their territory. After an approximate two centuries' stay in that area, the Goths started their march south, moving through Poland all the way to the Black Sea. The Gepids, a branch of the Goths, followed them sometime later. Between 200 and 375 A.D. the Goths built a powerful state in the Black Sea region and became an instant threat to the Roman provinces along the Danube. To the north their kingdom reached deep into Eastern and East-Central Europe: from the Don in the east to the Hungarian plain in the west, including most of Dacia. Its southern frontiers stretched along the coast of the Black Sea and the Danube. In 375 A.D. the entire structure collapsed under the invasion of the Huns.

This is, in rough outline, the traditional picture of the earliest history of the Goths. It can be found in many textbooks and special studies on the subject. For illustration, a few maps are reproduced to show the alleged states of the Goths (see maps 1-3).

Literature about the Goths is abundant and interesting. There are many examples in history of how historiographical images keep chang-

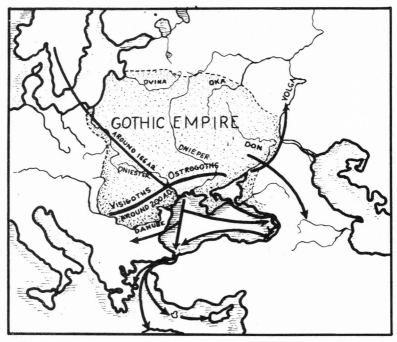

Map 1. The Gothic empire according to Smal-Stocki.

ing in time. The historical image of the Goths is one of the most colorful examples. Emotional attitudes, prejudices and distortions appear in historical writings from the sixth century until our present time. The changing image of the Goths is best portrayed in Hanno Helbling's interesting study.[1]

The Goths entered the stage of history in a distorted presentation caused by philosophical, ecclesiastical, and political ideas. In the late Middle Ages a new source of confusion appeared, a misinterpreted nationalistic factor. From then on, every once in a while a new distorting color was added to the picture, so that the present concept of the Goths is blurred and far from historical reality. This unreal picture is partially derived from some historical and prehistorical writings dating from the close of the nineteenth century until about the outbreak of World War II. Innocently at first, and later for definitely political reasons, the Goths and a few other Germanic tribes were looked upon as the ancestors of the modern German nation. This was done in spite of the fact that some of the ancient Germanic tribes were long extinct and had nothing in common with the making of the German nation.

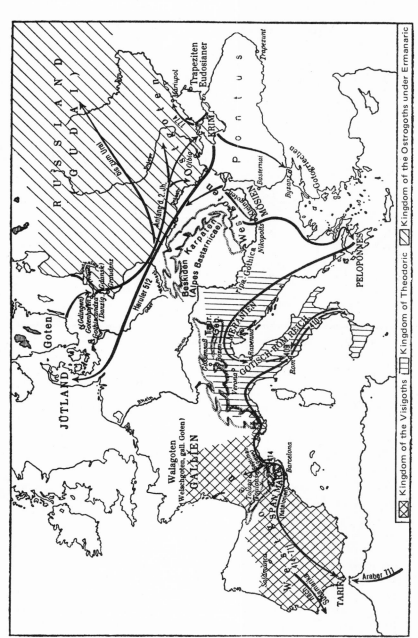

Map 2. The migrations of the Goths according to Obermüller.

The terms *deutsch* and *germanisch* (German and Germanic) were used as if they were synonyms. The importance of some Germanic peoples, even if they lived east of Germany for only a short time, was unduly magnified. Unusual talents in political and military leadership were ascribed to these primitive tribes. The early past of the German nation was made to look more beautiful, more impressive and ancient. These writings obviously reflected and boosted a certain political ideology of influence in Eastern Europe.

The period discussed in this study covers only the first two centuries of the Christian era. It is the time when the Goths lived at or near the southern shore of the Baltic Sea, an insignificant time in their history. No major development or activity involving them is mentioned in contemporary Greek and Latin sources. Most of what is known about this period comes from much later sources and from evidence laboriously put together by archaeologists and scholars in other disciplines concerned with prehistoric research.

One later work has specifically influenced historians and archaeologists in their quest for a synthesis. It is Jordanes' *History of the Goths,* written about 551 A.D.. This is not an original source, but an epitome of a work written several decades earlier by Cassiodorus, a statesman and official at the court of Theodoric the Great. Cassiodorus' aims were strictly political; history was just a means toward his goal, which was to add grandeur and legitimacy to the Gothic rule in the West. He tried to prove that the Goths were an ancient nation, equal to the Greeks and Romans in civilization and political leadership.[2] His work is lost entirely and is known only from Jordanes' compilation, which became very popular and has been quoted time and again from the Middle Ages until our days. The early part of the Jordanes' *History* is filled with many fabulous tales and inaccurate reports; modern historians do not consider the early times described in this work as historical source material. One tale, however, became part of historical evidence. This is Cassiodorus' narrative about the original home of the Goths and their migration to the estuary of the Vistula.

Though the story may be well known from many books and essays on the subject, Jordanes' report should be mentioned briefly since it is considered a basic source. He said that the cradle of the Goths stood on the island Scandza, which is modern Scandinavia (in his times the Scandinavian Peninsula was still known as an island). "From this island of Scandza," he wrote, "The Goths are said to have come forth long ago under their king, Berig by name. As soon as they disembarked from

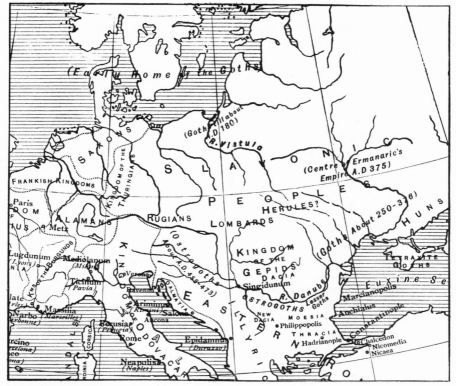

Map 3. The Gothic nations according to Bradley.

their ships and set foot on the land, they straightway gave their
name to the place. And even today it is said to be called Gothi-
scandza."[3] Shortly after their landing, the Goths conquered first the
Ulmerugi and then the Vandals. They remained in their new abodes for
a few generations, and then, under king Filimer–about the fifth in
succession after Berig–they moved from that region. "In search of
suitable homes and pleasant places they came to the land of Scythia,
called Oium in that tongue," explained Jordanes. Later, when speaking
about the Gepids, Jordanes once again mentions the emigration from
Scandinavia to the southern shore of the Baltic Sea. "You surely remember that in the beginning I said the Goths went forth from the
bosom of the island of Scandza with Berig, their king, sailing in only
three ships toward the hither shore of the Ocean, namely Gothi-
scandza." He locates the Gepids more precisely than the Goths as living
"in the province Spesis on an island surrounded by the shallow waters

of the Vistula. This island they called in the speech of their fathers, Gepedoios . . .[4]

So much for Jordanes' account of the Scandinavian origin of the Goths and Gepids, and their stay in the Vistula region. The events described were recorded by him about 550 years after they had allegedly taken place. He is the only one of the early writers to mention explicitly Scandinavia as the homeland of the Goths and the route of their migration to the mouth of the Vistula. The lapse of time and Cassiodorus' political aim in producing and constructing a history of the Goths as ancient as possible, has cast a serious doubt upon the trustworthiness of the entire account. Nevertheless, modern historians were inclined to see in his narrative a true oral tradition of the tribe, transmitted from generation to generation through heroic tales and songs. His chronology was corrected and certain details of the story were classified as legendary. The nucleus of the story, however, has been accepted as historical truth. The Jordanes account conflicted with the information given by Tacitus and Ptolemy, both of whom mention the Goths in the interior of the country. Still, the belief in Jordanes was so powerful that the testimony of these writers was generally dismissed on the ground that their knowledge of Eastern and East-Central Europe was insufficient and incorrect.

Jordanes' tale also influenced prehistorical research, because archaeologists were successful in discovering a long-lasting prehistoric culture in Västergötland that eventually spread into Östergötland and the island Gotland. They also observed that with the beginning of the Christian era the intensity of that culture gradually diminished. The logical conclusion was that either the entire tribe or its major part had left the country and settled elsewhere. A prehistoric culture, however, remains anonymous or can be named only by its archaeological characteristics, unless it is associated with peoples known from historical sources. This is where Jordanes entered the stage. He spoke of a homeland of the Goths in Scandinavia, of their journey across the Baltic Sea, of their landing at the estuary of the Vistula, and of their conquest of tribes who allegedly lived there. Archaeologists, like historians, disregarded the earlier historical sources and took Jordanes' account for reality. His narrative conveniently fitted into a projected mold. Cultural forms of the estuary of the Vistula were compared with those of Sweden, and certain similarities were discovered. Various criteria were used to prove the identity of the cultures. The archaeological territory grew larger and the Goths found themselves in possession of a large country situated on both sides of the Vistula and covering almost all of Eastern Pomerania.

The proof given by archaeologists was neither satisfactory nor complete. Even Eric Oxenstierna, whose archaeological study on the original homeland of the Goths is generally accepted, was not sure of the results of his own work. Though he was convinced that the culture at the Lower Vistula was a continuation of that of Västergötland, he had to admit that the Gothic cultures of Västergötland and the Vistula do not exhibit many similarities.[5] But he also drew a bold, direct line from Göteborg to Danzig as the alleged route of the Goths across the Baltic Sea (see map 5).

Oxenstierna's views are shared by many archaeologists. These scholars, however, hold different opinions about the ethnic structure of the Oder-Vistula region in prehistoric times. The role and importance of the Germanic peoples living in that region have been either magnified or minimized. Time and again it was stated that Tacitus as well as Ptolemy located the Goths in the interior of the country; no one, however, could explain what force had driven them away from the coast. Except for a few isolated suggestions, the possibility that they could have landed at another place was not taken into consideration. It was not supposed that they could have reached the Lower Vistula at a later time, after having left their original place of landing.

The archaeological method of direct comparison of the finds of Västergötland with those on the Lower Vistula would be valid only if Jordanes were trustworthy. If his testimony is not true, then the archaeological method cannot be considered valid. By itself it would not prove that the Goths had come to the Vistula directly from Sweden. The archaeologists worked on the assumption that the arrival of the Goths was an immediate sequel to their departure from Sweden. In discussing historical migrations, weeks, months, or years would not matter, but decades and centuries do. There is a lapse of time of at least one and a half centuries between the tentative time of the departure of the Goths from Sweden and the time when they are recorded in the Lower Vistula valley. A century and a half is a long time, signifying changes, even in a slowly progressing primitive society. Any similarities in the forms of the material cultures of Sweden and the Vistula region might as well have been the result of trade relations. As no valid objection can be raised against the archaeological synthesis of the Gothic culture in Sweden, the archaeological criteria showing the relationship between the cultures of Sweden and the Lower Vistula deserve, at least, some questioning.

Many of the critical remarks on the credibility of Jordanes' account and the traditional historical image of the Goths are based on or influenced by three studies, approaching the Gothic question from different starting points.

The first work is Kazimierz Tymieniecki's *History of Poland in Ancient Times,* written in 1951. The author maintains that Jordanes' early history up to the fourth century A.D. does not deserve much confidence. According to him, more attention should be paid to what ancient writers like Strabo and Tacitus had to say. In general, Tymieniecki disagrees with the archaeologists. Their criteria for the identification of the Gothic culture in the Vistula region do not prove that this area was settled or conquered by Goths coming directly from Sweden. It makes more sense, he says, to look for the Goths near the Elbe than at the Vistula. The Goths went first to Jutland and moved southward along the Elbe. They dwelt somewhere in the vicinity of Maroboduus' state, and not in Pomerania. In their migration toward the Black Sea they followed the traditional route of Celtic and Germanic tribes along the Danube, and not the road along the Vistula across Poland. The question whether or not Ptolemy's Gythones are identical with the Germanic Goths cannot be answered with certainty; this small tribe inhabiting part of the Lower Vistula might as well have been of Baltic origin.[6]

The second work is a study by Curt Weibull on the emigration of the Goths from Sweden, written in 1958. In a thoroughgoing manner, the author analyzes the relevant parts of Jordanes' text and compares them with the existing literature of the Late Roman Empire. He comes to the conclusion that in Jordanes' time the Goths had no clear picture about their country of origin. No tribal tradition existed in the sixth century and the tale about their homeland in Sweden is Cassiodorus' invention. Cassiodorus did not use any historical source or oral tradition but studied Christian theological writings and pagan philosophical treatises. These materials led him to the conclusion that the original homeland of the Goths must have been situated in the extreme north of the world. From two places known to him, namely Britain and Scandinavia, he arbitrarily chose the Scandian island. All the details of the story were products of his imagination. Jordanes repeated the story in his own work. The latter's presentation was then adopted in the late Middle Ages by Bishop Nicolaus Ragvaldi, who identified Jordanes' Goths with the medieval Götar and the island Scandza with Sweden. In this form, the tale survived in historical writings until our present days. Weibull concludes his study with the sweeping statement that the concept that the Goths ever originated in Sweden and lived on the shores of the Baltic Sea is based solely on Jordanes; its existence or doom depends entirely on the credibility of his account.[7]

The third work is an archaeological study of the so-called Gotho-Gepidic culture in Eastern Pomerania, written in 1962 by Jerzy Kmieciński. This author reviews the basic historical and prehistoric literature on the subject and analyzes thoroughly all elements of this culture in Pomerania. He observes that it was a continuation of the earlier Oksywia culture of the Late La Tène period. It had many indigenous forms, while some others appeared in Pomerania earlier than in Southern Sweden. The entire material shows only a minimal connection between the two regions. This can be explained by the existence of neighborly relations, but it does not prove the conquest of Pomerania by the Goths. Kmieciński comes forward with a hypothesis of his own, namely that the migration of the Scandinavian Germanic tribes started out as a gradual infiltration into the region east of the Oder—a process which is typical of agricultural peoples. Traders, small military detachments (similar to the later Viking expeditions), individual families, and larger units which may have stayed in the southern Baltic region for shorter or longer periods of time, are difficult to trace by archaeological methods. According to him, the slow and gradual integration into tribal units or peoples took place in the south of Europe. His theory explains the difficulty of tracing the Scandinavian tribes by archaeological remnants, especially during the early stage of the stay of the Goths and Gepids in the Danubian and Black Sea regions.[8]

Some of these issues, repeated from the works described, may be known from casual remarks by earlier archaeologists and historians who had discovered that not all of our present image of the Goths is correct. The virtual merit of these three studies lies in the fact that they have brought the essence of the distorted picture to the surface. This distortion is caused by the fact that Jordanes' narrative was considered as the basic source for the early migration of the Goths, a view supported by incomplete archaeological interpretation. The archaeological evidence brought to bear thus far loses its support as soon as the earliest past of the Goths is described without Jordanes' testimony. Scholars today may reject the general results of these three studies or disagree on specific points, but they cannot bypass or ignore them.

Summarizing the matter, there are five major concepts contained in these studies. These are: the elimination of Jordanes as a source for the earliest history of the Goths and their first migration; the assertion that Sweden may not have been the original homeland of the Goths; the possibility of the existence of other migratory routes than the one from Göteborg to Danzig and across Poland to the Black Sea; the theory of the gradual infiltration of Scandinavian Germanic tribes into the lands east of the Oder, replacing the theory of conquest and mass invasion; the non-existence of a powerful Gothic kingdom on the southern coast of the Baltic Sea.

Investigations conducted in this study have led to conclusions which differ in some points from the results of the above-mentioned works. A major point of disagreement is Tymieniecki's location of the Goths. He correctly observed that Strabo's report indicates a location of the tribe in the vicinity of Maroboduus' dominion. Consequently, he placed the Goths near the Elbe, which is the westernmost point where they could have lived. This location was the chief reason for his assumption that their migratory route took place along that river and the Danube. This, however, conflicts with the location of Ptolemy's Gythones at the Lower Vistula. Therefore, Tymieniecki thought it possible that these Gythones were a Baltic tribe, since he could see no geographical connection between the Middle Elbe and the Lower Vistula. This study is in agreement with Tymieniecki's basic observation that in Strabo's time the Goths lived near the country of the Marcomanni. It favors, however, a more eastern location of the Goths, which fits more readily into Tacitus' description, i.e., the region of the Middle Oder. The conclusion was drawn that Strabo's, Pliny's, Tacitus', and Ptolemy's Goths are all the same people. Ptolemy's location of the Gythones at the Lower Vistula is explained as the result of a second migration, from the Middle Oder to the Lower Vistula, which could have taken place sometime after 98 A.D.

Another point of disagreement is with Weibull's general conclusion that the Goths never lived in Sweden nor on the Baltic shore. Weibull reached that conclusion as a result of his argumentation that the narrative of both Cassiodorus and Jordanes is pure invention. But, even if a historical source is entirely forged, false, or otherwise untrustworthy, this does not imply that the entire content of the counterfeit history is untrue. Jordanes' narrative contains three separate assumptions in the following sequence: that the original homeland of the Goths was situated in Sweden; that the Goths sailed from Sweden directly to the mouth of the Vistula; and that immediately after their landing, the Goths conquered several tribes living in that area and founded a powerful kingdom on the southern Baltic coast. After rejecting Jordanes as an untrue source, the sequence of these alleged facts cannot be ascertained by archaeological or historical evidence. The ethnic character of the so-called Gotho-Gepidic culture of Pomerania cannot be identified with that of the historical Goths. This evidence does not prove that the Goths came from Sweden and lived on the Baltic coast as a tribe or a large ethnic unit. In reliable historical sources, the Goths are mentioned as inhabitants of the interior of the country, but not of the coast. They could have reached the interior of the Oder-Vistula region from an original homeland situated outside of Sweden. If they did come from Sweden, perhaps they used some other route than the one to the estuary of the Vistula.

The investigations conducted in this study aim at confirming that the Goths lived in the interior of the country as an ethnic unit and that the Baltic coast was occupied by other peoples. They are also meant to prove that a mass transfer of a whole population from Göteborg to Danzig in a direct sea crossing was impossible. Observations made in this study did not prove that the homeland of the Goths was not situated in Sweden. In this respect its conclusions differ from those of Weibull.

Weibull quotes the opinions of several Swedish archaeologists to support his statement that Sweden was not the homeland of the Goths. These quotations generally refer to the statement that no relationship exists between the forms of material culture of Sweden and those of the Vistula or Black Sea regions. However, the opinions he quotes do not deny the possibility that the Goths could have lived in Väster-götland and the adjacent districts; they refer only to the lack of rela-tionship between the different cultures. But these observations are only partially correct, and should not lead to the conclusion that Sweden was not the homeland of the Goths. There was a culture in Väster-götland that might be attributed to the Goths. If there is no rela-tionship between the archaeological forms of Sweden and the Vistula or Black Sea regions this means only that there was no such situation as that anticipated by earlier archaeologists—no conquest of Pomerania or mass invasion. The Scandinavian Goths could have arrived on or near the southern Baltic coast in a way that would not have had an imme-diate effect on the material culture of Pomerania. Nevertheless, any discussion on this subject requires a clear and definite answer to the question whether or not the Goths were aboriginal in the Oder-Vistula region.

There is general agreement among scholars that the Goths belonged

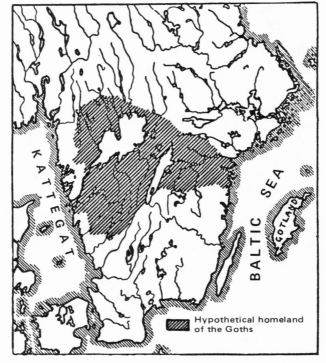

Map 4. The homeland of the Goths according to Tunberg.

to the so-called East-Germanic group, and that the homeland of most of the peoples belonging to this group was either Scandinavia or Jutland, which implies that the Goths were not aboriginal in the Oder-Vistula region. The ethnic structure of the Oder-Vistula region during the first two centuries of our era was very unstable. It favored the formation of new human groups or tribes. There were migratory movements of large and small groups: some peoples moved eastward, while others went toward the west, south or north. It is possible that tribal units separated from the main bodies and settled in diverse places. Eventually, such groups became known by different names and appeared as individual tribes. This means that certain tribes could have originated in this territory and that it cannot be ascertained whether they actually were branches of other peoples. The reverse process also took place: loose groups, clans, or petty tribes melted into larger units or peoples. This was the case of the Vandals, who consisted of a mixture of various human groups.

The Goths did not originate in this area. Strabo, Pliny, Tacitus, and

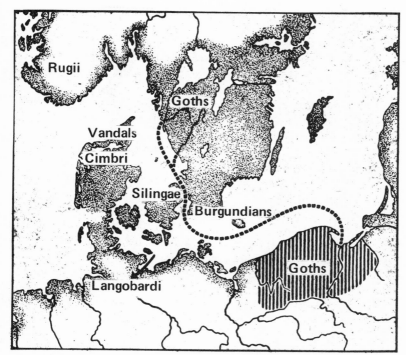

Map 5. The original homeland of the Goths in Sweden, their abodes in Pomerania, and their migratory route according to Oxenstierna.

Ptolemy mention them in almost the same fashion—as an average tribe or a small people. No extraordinary achievements or deeds are recorded as performed by them. This indicates that the Goths maintained a similar status from about 6 to 150 A.D. Apparently, there were no changes before 6 A.D. either, which means that prior to their arrival in the Oder-Vistula region they had existed as a tribe or tribal unit, and were not aboriginal in that area.

Until now, no other place than Sweden has been considered as their original homeland. They were attributed a prehistoric culture of Southern Sweden, which originally developed in Västergötland and eventually spread into Ostergötland and the island Gotland. It is not yet known how much of that territory was actually Gothic, since a prehistoric culture is seldom limited to one single tribe. According to Tunberg, the hypothetical homeland of the Goths stretched from the Kattegat to the Baltic Sea. Oxenstierna's map indicates that their abodes lay between the Kattegat and Lake Vättern (maps 4 and 5). The notion that Västergötland is to be considered the original homeland of the Goths until their emigration from Sweden is also contained in this author's later works.[9] Preference was given to Oxenstierna's conception, and this was done on account of some linguistic evidence which connects the name of the Goths with the river Göta. As a working hypothesis, therefore, it was assumed that before their departure from Sweden, the Goths lived in the region of the Göta River and between the Kattegat and Lake Vättern. Thus, they had access to the sea at the Kattegat only.

The archaeological theory of the original homeland of the Goths in Sweden gains some support from linguistic evidence provided by the etymology of their tribal name and its various forms recorded in several places by ancient and early medieval writers. In the Gothic language, their name was *Guthiuda*, 'the people of the Gut'; the root *gut* is derived from the Gothic *giutan* 'to flow, to flood,' a root present in a river name, *Gautelfr* (Göta River, Swedish *Göta alv*), a river flowing through Västergötland. Their tribal name simply meant 'the people living near the Gautelfr.' Strabo's text reads *Butonas,* but scholars generally accept the corrected form *Gutonas.*[10] Pliny speaks of *Gutones* (variants: *Gu///nes, Gniones, Guttones*). He also mentions a river *Guthalus* (variants: *Gythalus, Gothalus, Guttalus, Lutta Alus*).[11] Tacitus calls them *Gotones* (variant: *Gothones*).[12] Ptolemy records *Gutai* (variants: *Gautai, Utoi, Dutai*) in Scandinavia[13] and *Gythones* in European Sarmatia.[14] Procopius of Caesarea records *Gautai* in Scandinavia.[15] Jordanes uses the form *Gothi.* In later medieval times, Gotland was described as inhabited by the *Gutar* or *Gautar.*

For over a hundred years, the name of the Goths has been subject to interpretation and reevaluation by linguists and scholars in related fields. Kaspar Zeuss thought that Ptolemy's *Gautai* of Scandinavia and *Gythones* of the Baltic area were names denoting two different peoples.[16] Torsten Evert Karsten maintained that the linguistic root for both *Gutar* and *Goths* is contained in the name of the *Gautelfr,* and that from this river name both tribal names are derived.[17] Similarly, Rudolf Much pointed out that the names of the *Goths* and *Gautai* are closely related; he also said that the name *Goutai* is a distorted form of *Gautai.* This name, as well as that of the *Gautar,* points to the *Gautelfr.*[18] These linguistic interpretations are merely selections from an abundant literature on the subject.

A general assumption, acceptable to both linguists and nonlinguists, is necessary in order to connect the linguistic results with archaeological and historical evidence, namely, that the various names of the Goths are either identical or similar and that they all contain the same linguistic root as that of the Göta River. Applied to archaeological and historical evidence, this belief should to some extent answer the question whether there existed one human group (amassed or dispersed) known by the name of Goths, or whether there were several human groups bearing names similar to that of the Goths.

The archaeological culture of Västergötland flourished in an area of which the Göta River was a part. Ptolemy speaks of some Goths in Scandinavia. There is no reason why these Goths should not be associated with Västergötland. On the other hand, he also mentions some Goths in the western part of European Sarmatia. This provides a possible link between Sweden and the Lower Vistula. It could at the same time explain the nature of the Gothic emigration from Sweden, during which only a part of the population could have left the homeland, while the other part remained in the original abodes. This would be analogical to the emigration of the Cimbri.

Strabo's Goths ought to be placed near Bohemia; Pliny's between the Elbe and the Oder; Tacitus' between Pomerania and Lusatia or Silesia. These three locations are different descriptions of the same area, namely the region of the Middle Oder. It is very unlikely that three different peoples with names so similar lived in close proximity to each other. They must have been one and the same people. The three authors mentioned above described situations and facts pertaining to the first century of our era (from about 6 or 18 A.D. to 98 A.D.). Ptolemy, whose work was written in about 150 A.D., knows of the existence of Goths in Scandinavia and at the Lower Vistula. He does not record any Goths near the Middle Oder. The conclusion is obvious: the same people who during the first century of our era lived near the Middle Oder, moved to the Lower Vistula sometime after 98 A.D. Archaeologists estimate the time of the Gothic emigration from Sweden as having taken place at the beginning of our era or somewhat earlier. This is only a decade or two before they are known from historical sources. These data combined indicate that the chronological sequence of the abodes of the Goths was Sweden–Middle Oder–Lower Vistula.

This sequence excludes the possibility that the Goths entered the territory of ancient Poland via the estuary of the Vistula. Traders or small groups of people, sailing along the coast, may have landed there occasionally, but the mass of the Gothic population came from the west, from beyond the Oder. The arrival of the Goths in the Oder-Vistula region was not an act of conquest resulting in the founding of a powerful kingdom in Pomerania. There is not a single fact to prove its existence. Archaeological evidence fails to do so; the historical sources do not mention it, on the contrary, they rather tend to deny its existence. A few decades after their arrival in the Oder-Vistula region, the Goths became subject to Maroboduus' rule, and Maroboduus did not control the coast of the Baltic Sea.

 The Goths of the Oder-Vistula region are re-
corded in ancient sources as inhabitants of Ger-
mania and Sarmatia. Any attempt to place
them on a modern map is fruitless as long as
two problems of this area are not solved. The first is relatively simple: it
concerns the border between Sarmatia and Germania. The second is
extremely complex. It is the modern ethnological evaluation of the
area, based on prehistoric and linguistic evidence and its relationship to
ancient historical sources. At the present stage of research, a final solution to that problem has not been reached. In fact, it may be presumed
that it will take a long time before darkness and confusion will turn
into light and order in this matter.

In ancient times a part of central Europe was called Germania, which
bordered on the east with Sarmatia. The term Germania was introduced
into literature by Caesar, who speaks of it vaguely as of a country
between the Rhine and the Dacians.[1] Eventually its southern boundary
was set at the Danube, the western along the Rhine, and in the north
the country was described as reaching to the "ocean." The eastern
frontier was open. According to Strabo (before 18 A.D.), only the
portion of Germania between the Rhine and the Elbe was known; the
country east of the Elbe toward the "ocean" was an unknown land.[2]

The first to fix its boundary in the east was Marcus Vipsanius
Agrippa, son-in-law of the emperor Augustus, who planned the making
of a huge map of the world. He died in the year 12 B.C. and the project
was not finished until twenty-five years after his death. The map was
painted on a wall in the *Porticus Vipsaniae* in Rome,[3] and it showed
the Vistula as the eastern border of Germania. Agrippa was the origi-
nator of the concept that the Vistula was the dividing line between
Germania and Sarmatia.[4] The map itself, so conspicuously displayed in

the capital of the Empire, had a strong influence on the popular notion of Germania and on later cartography. Agrippa's version was repeated many times by later geographers. It was adopted by Pomponius Mela (43-44 A.D.), who said that Germania extended to the east as far as the countries inhabited by Sarmatian peoples and that the Vistula was the border of Sarmatia. The first piece of information was taken from a Roman source describing the country in a west-east direction and stating clearly that the Sarmatians lived east of the Germani. Further on Mela used a Greek source describing the area in an almost opposite direction, i.e., from the Pontus toward the north or northeast; the Vistula thus was the western border of Sarmatia.[5] Pliny (77 A.D.) mentions the Vistula three times. First, he lists it among the seven main rivers of Germania. The second time, he quotes Agrippa, who describes Germania as extending toward the Sarmatian desert as far as the river Vistula. The third time, he says that "some [people] report that the area as far as the Vistula is inhabited by the Sarmatians, Venedi, Sciri, and Hirri."[6] This sentence calls for elucidation. The Sarmatians have always lived east of the Vistula. The territory of the Venedi is controversial; some scholars locate it somewhere east of the Vistula, others on both sides of the river. The Sciri and the Hirri are usually considered to have been Germanic tribes. The listing of the Sarmatians among peoples living "as far as the Vistula" suggests that he used a report describing the country as viewed from the Pontus toward the Vistula. In this case the Sciri and the Hirri are out of place. If the report is a description of the country as viewed from Rome toward the Vistula, then, the Sarmatians are out of place. No matter how his sentence is interpreted, there are either Germanic peoples living east of the Vistula, or Sarmatians west of this river. In both cases, Agrippa's division does not work.

Although Pliny's books on geography have been criticized for inconsistencies and faulty judgment,[7] he deserves some words of defense. He was more of a historian than a geographer, a well-informed man with a good knowledge of Germania, fully aware of the faults and inconsistencies of the material he had to use. Pliny realized that there was much disagreement in the data reported by various writers; he knew that the parts of Germania known to the Romans were conquered at approximately the time of Agrippa's death, and that the country itself was explored many years later, never completely. This made him cautious about Agrippa's data pertaining to Sarmatia, Scythia, and Taurica, and he called them uncertain.[8] It was, therefore, not faulty judgment that made him use data which were not reliable.

Ptolemy's *Geography* (between 140 and 151 A.D.) mentions numerous peoples and places in the Oder-Vistula region. Among them are the Venedi who appear to have lived west of the Vistula, i.e., in Germania. The location of the Venedi is connected with the abodes of the Goths and will be discussed in chapter VII, but they are mentioned at this point because their territory is relevant to the basic concept of the border between Germania and Sarmatia. Describing the eastern boundary of Germania, Ptolemy says that it stretched from the Sarmatian mountains, "between these mountains, toward the mentioned source of the river Vistula and then, along the river itself, as far as the sea." In his description of Sarmatia he reports that the country is divided "from the West by the river Vistula and [the land] between its source and the Sarmatian mountains."[9]

The frontier between Germania and Sarmatia looks different in Tacitus' *Germania* (98 A.D.). In his words: "Germania as a whole is separated from the Gauls, the Raeti and the Pannonians by the rivers Rhine and Danube; from the Sarmatians and Dacians by mutual fear or mountains. The rest is surrounded by the Ocean which embraces spacious bays and very large islands. Some of the peoples and kings have recently become known to us—as war has disclosed."[10] The Rhine and the Danube were, for some time, the political border of the Roman Empire. It is obvious that Tacitus mentions these rivers as the western and southern frontiers of Germania for the sake of convenience; they were not ethnic limits. Some Germanic tribes lived west of the Rhine; Celts and other non-Germanic peoples lived east of the Rhine and north of the Danube. Tacitus' concept of the eastern border of the country is of extreme interest. In his opinion, it was not the Vistula that separated Germania from Sarmatia, but "mutual fear or mountains" separated the Germani from the Sarmatians and Dacians. These are the words of an ancient scholar who was concerned with the description of human groups, and not of geographical spaces. He was aware of the fact that in the eastern part of Germania or in the borderland there lived peoples of doubtful ethnic origin. Unaware of the existence of other ethnic groups in that area, he tried to class them as either Germani or Sarmatians. It was known in his time that the Sarmatians were nomads who lived on horseback and in wagons, used the bow and arrow as their chief weapon, and carried no shields. The Germani lived in permanent homes, carried shields, and fought and marched on foot. These were his criteria for classification—yet he was hesitant to use them consistently. He says: "I doubt whether I should class the peoples of the Peucini, Veneti and

Finns as Germani or as Sarmatians. Though the Peucini, who by some [writers] are called Bastarnae, are like the Germani in their language, customs, settlements and buildings. They are filthy and their chiefs apathetic: because of mixed marriages they are bad looking as the Sarmatians. The Veneti have acquired much from them [i.e., from the Sarmatians]; in their predatory raids they roam over all the forests and mountains between the Peucini and the Finns. They are, however, to be classed as Germani rather than Sarmatians, because they build permanent houses, carry shields, and take delight in marches and the swiftness of their feet, contrary to the Sarmatians who live in wagons and on horseback." [11]

The ancient historical sources thus disclose two different concepts of the border between Germania and Sarmatia. The first is Tacitus' view. He looked at this portion of Europe with the eyes of an ethnographer: the Germani were sedentary peoples, the Sarmatians nomadic. There was a border area between the areas called Germania and Sarmatia, inhabited by peoples whose ethnic origin was not known. Any sedentary non-Germanic tribe of this area appeared to him as a Germanic people; any nomadic non-Sarmatian group as a branch of the Sarmatians. In his time no ethnic border was known between Germanic and non-Germanic peoples. The second concept, considering the Vistula as the border between Germania and Sarmatia, is contained in geographical works. This concept was introduced into ancient geography by Vipsanius Agrippa at a time when very little information if any at all was available about the ethnic conditions along the Vistula. Thirty years after Agrippa's death, Strabo reported that the country east of the Elbe was still an unknown land. The Vistula as the border between Germania and Sarmatia was a strictly conventional demarcation line between two geographical areas. It had no ethnic or political meaning. It was similar to our modern conventional dividing lines between Europe and Asia, or Asia and Africa.

The actual meaning of the Vistula as the border between Germania and Sarmatia escaped the attention of many archaeologists who defined several prehistoric cultures between the Oder and the Vistula. One group of scholars believes that the Vistula was the ethnic border between Germanic and non-Germanic peoples. Consequently the local cultures of that area were attributed to the so-called East-Germanic peoples and associated with Germanic tribes known from historical sources by name, but not always by location. Another group of scholars came forth with a new theory on the ethnogenesis of the Slavs, and

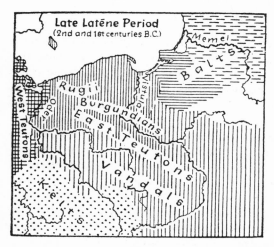

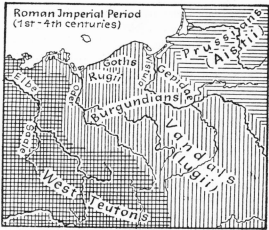

Map 6. The Oder-Vistula region between 200 B.C. and 400 A.D. according to La Baume.

attributed most of the local cultures to the Venedi—the Slavs, as known from ancient historical sources.[12] In other words, the area between the Oder and Vistula in earliest historical times is claimed for Germanic peoples by some scholars, while others consider it predominantly Slavic. These two different views are illustrated by two maps, called for lack of better terms the East-Germanic and the Venedian map.

The East-Germanic map (map 6) is reproduced after La Baume and is representative of views held by German and most Western scholars.

The territory east of the Oder, deep into Belorussia and the Ukraine, appears to have been inhabited by Germanic tribes. A huge portion of Southern Poland was occupied by the Vandals (Lugii). La Baume's text contains the customary erroneous statement that "the Vandals are cited under the name of 'Lugii' by both Tacitus and Ptolemy; in Ptolemy's map they are shown in mideastern Germany." [13] By "mid-eastern Germany" the author apparently means the southwestern part of present-day Poland or, more properly, the eastern part of ancient Germania, where Ptolemy's Lugii are usually located. The middle part of Poland, between the Oder and the Vistula, was inhabited by the Burgundians. The Gepids lived east of the Lower Vistula, in the present provinces of Olsztyn and Warsaw. The Goths and the Rugii shared the space on the Baltic coast, between the Oder and the Vistula. The Baltic tribes are called Prussians (Aistii); there is no space reserved for the Venedi.

The Venedian map (map 7) is reproduced after Konrad Jazdzewski [14] and is representative of views held by many Polish and a few other Slavic scholars. They claim that the area covered by the prehistoric Pit-Grave (also called Venedian) culture ought to be attributed to the ancient Slavs. Consequently, they consider the entire Oder-Vistula region and farther to the east and south as a territory inhabited mainly by Slavic tribes. According to them, the Carpathian mountain area shows some traces of Thracian and Celtic peoples. The area east of the Oder, approximately up to the ancient trade route between the Adriatic and Baltic coast (the so-called amber route) running through Wrocław-Kalisz-Toruń to Danzig and portions of the province of Olsztyn, had a mixed Slavic and Germanic population. East of the Pasłęka and north of the Narew the country was inhabited by Baltic tribes.

There is no agreement at all between these two maps. Even if there were, the results of prehistoric research can be used as general guidelines only, as they are not specific enough to permit the exact location of a single tribe. Districts of prehistoric cultures deal with spaces larger than those occupied by single tribes. Many sedentary tribes could have lived within one prehistoric cultural district but such a district cannot be considered the cultural area of a single tribe. Whether archaeologists subdivide the area into two or five local cultural districts, there are more than thirty different peoples recorded in ancient sources as its inhabitants.

According to the East-Germanic map, most of the Oder-Vistula region was inhabited by the Rugii, Goths, Gepids, Burgundians, and Vandals (Lugii). Of these five peoples, only the Rugii appear in their

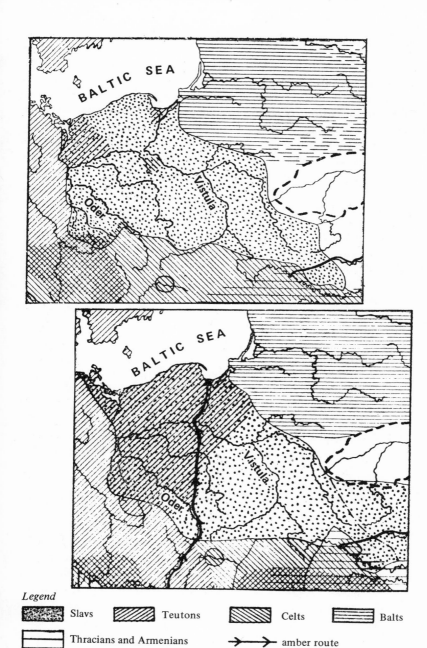

BALTIC SEA

Vistula

Oder

BALTIC SEA

Vistula

Oder

Legend

Slavs   Teutons   Celts   Balts

Thracians and Armenians   → amber route

Map 7. The Oder-Vistula region between 150 B.C. and 200 A.D. according to Jażdżewski.

proper location, which can be verified in Tacitus' and Ptolemy's texts. The Goths are located in the interior of the country, and not on the Baltic coast. The location of the Gepids in the Oder-Vistula region is still a controversial issue. They were unknown to the writers of the first and second centuries of our era. No historical source (with the exception of Jordanes) ever recorded them on the Baltic coast. Reliable sources mention them for the first time in 260 A.D., in which year they entered Dacia at an unknown point. [15] Their stay in the Oder-Vistula region is a matter of archaeological speculation, investigated and proven wrong by Kmieciński. [16] Today, the general opinion prevails that the division of the Goths into several branches took place after they had left the Oder-Vistula region. The Gepids, being a branch of the Goths, could not have existed as an independent tribe in the Lower Vistula region. The dwelling places of the Burgundians at different times have not yet been definitely established. [17] The opinions of scholars about the space occupied by this tribe vary widely. Some of them visualize the Burgundians as spread over the huge area stretching from the Oder to the Vistula, while others reduce them to the size of an average tribe, dwelling west of the Oder. At the present stage of research it is impossible to speak of a final solution; moreover, it is not only a matter of difference between views held by two archaeological schools or between the archaeological and the historical interpretation, but also a question of interpreting the historical source material itself. This material contains ambiguous information which may easily lead to erroneous conclusions. While discussing the territory of the Goths, it is not irrelevant to define two Burgundian territories, one situated near the Middle Oder and occupied by the Burgundians in the times of Pliny (probably also in those of Strabo), and the other located at the Lower Vistula around the estuary of the Narew, where the tribe dwelt during the second century A.D. I do not claim that this is a final solution. The last people in the East-Germanic map are the Vandals (Lugii). They are the most controversial people of those that lived in the area. The identity Vandals = Lugii is an archaeological speculation, defying and disregarding all historical evidence. In ancient writings, the Lugii and the Vandals always appear as different human groups at different times. There is not the slightest hint of an indication that they referred to the same human group. Since the location of the Lugii is essential in determining the territory of the Goths, this problem is discussed further on in greater detail.

The East-Germanic map contains many features that disagree with the reports of ancient writers or lead to fantastic conclusions. The Goths are placed at the Baltic shore, thus contradicting the reports of Tacitus and Ptolemy who locate the tribe in the interior of the country. Ptolemy says that the Goths lived south of the Venedi, but on the East-Germanic map the Venedi cannot be placed north of the Goths. According to Ptolemy, the Venedi were a numerous people living in the western part of European Sarmatia. On this map, the area east of the Vistula is occupied by the Gepids, Prussians (Aistii), and Vandals. There is no space at all provided for the Venedi. Ptolemy also mentions the existence of a Venedian Gulf. He certainly did not invent this gulf in Alexandria—it must have existed in reality, at the shore of the Baltic Sea. The name indicates that some Venedi lived somewhere along the coast, while on this map the country along the coast is divided between the Rugii, Goths, Gepids, and Prussians (Aistii). Strabo reports that Maroboduus had conquered the Lugii, the Goths, and a few other tribes outside of Boihaemum. If the Lugii were identical with the Vandals and the Goths lived at the Baltic coast, it would mean that Maroboduus ruled over the Vandals and that his empire reached deep into the Ukraine and Belorussia, and to the Baltic Sea. Pliny said that the Burgundians, the Varinnae, the Charini, and the Goths were part of the Vandili. Although many historians explain that the name Vandili is a collective appellation for a group of Germanic tribes, some archaeologists insist that the Vandili were an individual people, identical with the Vandals = Lugii. If the Vandili = Vandals = Lugii were an individual people, and the other tribes mentioned by Pliny were part of them, then the latter should be considered either as branches of the Vandals, or as conquered by them. In both cases the implication is that almost the entire Oder-Vistula region was Vandalic. German and other historical maps place the Sciri and Hirri recorded by Pliny, and the Bastarnae recorded by several writers, in the region south of the Vistula toward the Ukraine. According to the East-Germanic interpretation, this was a purely Vandalic territory.

Many more arguments could be raised against the composition of this map. Its evaluation looks like a collection of negative statements, which was certainly not intended. This map, like many others, is the result of ethnological interpretation by one school of archaeology. Some of the arguments brought against this interpretation reflect perhaps views held by other schools of archaeology. The adherence to views held by one school should not be used as arguments against ethnological maps composed by archaeologists belonging to other schools. In a geographical-historical study of this type, however, one cardinal question must be raised and firmly answered. If there are two ethnological-archaeological maps contradicting each other, it has to be decided which of the two maps agrees with the earliest historical records and which fails to do so. Although full agreement cannot be expected, as the knowledge of the ancient writers about the Oder-Vistula region was incomplete and not always accurate, the cumulation of disagreeing facts proves that an archaeological map is wrong; the testimony of the ancient writers could not have been erroneous all the time.

These examples demonstrate that there are several serious contradictions between archaeological interpretation and facts recorded in the earliest historical sources. Modern historians, regardless of whether they are German or not, cannot rely on the content of the East-Germanic map with its doubtful location of early historical tribes. It divides the Oder-Vistula region into five tribal territories, while the earliest historical sources record about thirty peoples or human groups in the same area. Neither this map, nor others of the same kind, can serve as an archaeological-ethnological guide to the geographical study of the earliest historical times. The rejection of the East-Germanic map, however, does not make the Venedian map fully acceptable either. It is a very general map, trying to solve the broad issue of the geographical distribution of the Germanic and Slavic peoples, and does not outline any specific tribal territories. Due to its general character, it is bound to contain fewer contradictions with the earliest historical sources. Its basic assumption is the hitherto disputable notion that during the first two centuries of our era the Oder-Vistula region was chiefly inhabited by Slavs, and that its western and northern parts had a mixed Slavic and Germanic population. Its composition allows a few general conclusions to be drawn. If a Germanic tribe, whose exact territorial limits are unknown, is recorded in the area, a tentative location west of the ancient amber route should be preferred. If a tribe of unknown ethnic origin is placed by ancient writers in the country east of the amber route, it could be assumed to be a Slavic people. If such a tribe is placed west of the amber route, it could be either Germanic or Slavic. These are vague guidelines only. Neither the Vistula, nor the amber route can be considered as strict ethnic borders. It is my aim to prove that two Germanic tribes, the Goths and the Burgundians, had crossed the Vistula and lived in Sarmatia during the second century A.D.

The Venedian map is acceptable in its general structure, but cannot be considered as the result of a final synthesis. The scholars who contributed to the development of the autochthonous theory of the Slavs, or who agree with it, have not yet offered a satisfactory explanation of the relationship between the Germanic and Slavic populations in the mixed area. The notion of "mixed population" covers several forms of coexistence. There may have existed many small territorial units whose population consisted of members of one tribe or one ethnic group only. On the other hand, the territorial units may have been larger, which would imply that more than one tribe or ethnic group shared a common territory. There are two ways in which such a symbiosis could come into existence. It could have been the result of conquest, whereby the population of such a territory would be divided into two social classes, the masters and the slaves, of different ethnic origin, which would account for the difference in the forms of the material culture obvious in archaeological remains. Another form of symbiosis could have been the result of an agreement between the sedentary population and a migrant or semisedentary group. The nonsedentary population could have lived in groups dispersed over the entire territory of the sedentary population, or they could have lived together with the native population, in the same villages or in separate areas, as agreed upon. This form of symbiosis would not have affected the social structure of either group, and would have been of a more or less temporary nature. All these forms of coexistence would appear on a general map in the same way. The map would show only an area of mixed population.

Prehistorians and historians have not paid much attention to the possibility of several forms of coexistence. The relationship between the Germanic and Slavic groups is generally explained by the theory of conquest, whereby the invading Germanic group became the ruling class, while the autochthonous Slavic population was reduced to serfdom. Such an interpretation, however, does not solve the question of the simultaneous expansion of the Slavs in the west. In the territory east of the Oder, the Slavs allegedly became the victims of Germanic aggression, while, consequently, they must be regarded as aggressors in the lands west of that river. The theory of conquest has not been proven either by historical, or by archaeological evidence. The writers of those times do not record large-scale conquests in the Oder-Vistula region (except for Maroboduus' temporary acquisitions). The assumed expansion of the Lugian tribes is still subject to discussion. It is not yet known whether the name Lugii meant a political federation of several tribes, or whether it designated a group of unrelated tribes living in one specific geographical area. Archaeological remains do not prove large-scale invasion and settlement by Scandinavian tribes in the area along the southern Baltic coast. Until a final solution has been reached, the safest way to deal with the location of the peoples of the Oder-Vistula region is to treat them as the ancient writers have seen them. From writings of the latter, it appears that the area was inhabited by a large number of small tribes, and only very few larger ethnic groups. The general picture of the area should be likened to a mosaic consisting of two colors only, and not to a painting using these two colors in high light, deep shade, and halftones.

The Venedian map is otherwise in very minute disagreement with the early historical sources, if at all. On the contrary, it adds meaning to some ancient reports. Ptolemy's Venedian Gulf can be safely identified with the present Gulf of Danzig or its environs. The land along the Baltic coast was inhabited by some unknown Venedian tribes. Ptolemy's report that the Goths lived south of the Venedi appears to be correct. The Goths can be located at the Lower Vistula, in an area in which the prehistoric map indicates traces of Germanic settlements. The Burgundians of Ptolemy's times lived south of the Goths. In this study, an attempt is made to place them at the Lower Vistula, around the estuary of the Bug. This location does not agree with the Venedian map, which shows no traces of Germanic settlements in that area. The Goths of Strabo's times can be placed at the Middle Oder, in an area where traces of both Slavic and Germanic elements are found. Tacitus' location of the Goths as living north of some Lugian tribes and south of the Rugii and Lemovii points to the same area where Strabo's Goths lived, i.e., the Middle Oder. The location of the Goths near the Middle Oder explains the size of Maroboduus' conquests. The Oder was not far from the border of Boihaemum, the country of the Marcomanni. Pliny's Vandili occupied part of the territory between the Elbe and the Oder in an area which was partly pure Germanic and partly mixed Germanic-Slavic (cf. the detailed discussion in chapter VI). It is true that these locations take away the splendor from the ancient great Germanic empires, but their alleged heroic deeds are a problem of historiography, and not of historical geography.

Generally speaking, the first dawnings of history in the Oder-Vistula region unveil a picture clouded by ancient concepts and followed by a chain of misinterpretations which turned it into a completely distorted image. The territory is rich in traces of human life and activity. It was not a peaceful area; war and fear were well known to its peoples. Frequent shiftings of human groups took place, dictated by economic factors, pressure from neighbors, and aggressive invaders or raiders. The ancient civilized world did not have a clear picture of the area. Describing the unknown world that stretched beyond the imperial frontiers, the ancient writers relied on the reports of merchants, sailors, or slaves. Geographers and historians worked with incomplete or unreliable data, and supplemented them with their own speculations. Vipsanius Agrippa placed landmarks through the middle of an unknown land and divided it into Germania and Sarmatia. Strabo made its peoples look like gypsies. Tacitus used the wheels of a cart and the walls of a house as criteria for ethnographic classification.

In modern times the efforts of historians and scholars in kindred disciplines have succeeded in drawing only a general picture of the area in the earliest historical times. The lane that unites archaeology and history leads into a labyrinth of dead-end streets and crossroads on both sides. Before the texts of the ancient writers were sufficiently evaluated by historians, archaeologists and linguists tried to solve intricate problems in history. Some of their suggestions and results furthered historical research, others did not. Frequently, improper criteria were used in order to reach a general conclusion. Archaeologists replaced Tacitus' wagons and permanent homes by spearheads, broken vessels, and other objects found in graves, in order to determine an archaeological culture and its spatial extent. There would be nothing wrong with this method, if it were not for the fact that archaeological spatial units were identified with ethnic or tribal territories. In the case of the Goths, for example, this generalization does not prove true, as there is absolutely no connection between the forms of material culture traced in Scandinavia and at the Black Sea. This generalization could have led to valid conclusions only if the number of archaeological districts had been identical or approximately equal with the number of peoples recorded in the area. As it is, they do not approach each other.

Linguists tried to solve the ethnological problems of the area by investigating place and tribal names. Not all of these etymologies can be correct, owing to the fact that the historical source material is not accurate enough to draw proper linguistic conclusions. It is seldom known whether a recorded tribal name is the form of self-denomination of a given tribe, and whether a place name is the form used by the local population. In both cases, they could have been transmitted in the form used by a direct or distant neighbor who spoke a different language. It is not certain whether the original aural perception of a foreign name is in agreement with the graphic reproduction by Greek or Roman writers. The holographs of all ancient texts were lost long ago; present editions are based on medieval manuscripts that were copied and corrected time and again. Misspellings of ordinary words can be successfully corrected or interpreted, but this is not possible in the case of place or personal names. Quite frequently there is no way of distinguishing the true form from the variants in the manuscripts; the least reliable text may have preserved the original form of a name. Linguistic criticism may fail; what appears as corrupt to a specialist in one modern language, may sound correct to the specialist in another language. Linguistic research, therefore, which has to work with incomplete data and unreliable forms recorded in ancient sources, cannot claim to reach infallible conclusions.

Using written testimony as a basis for locating peoples and places, historical geography cannot claim that it works with infallible sources either. The Oder-Vistula region was not sufficiently explored by the ancients. Many data recorded in their writings were obtained from unreliable accounts. Moreover, the ancient writers were limited by the geographical terminology they used; various directions are expressed only in terms of the four basic points of the compass. If the location of a specific place is described as being situated south of another place, this southward direction may mean south, southeast, or southwest. When only one place is described in this manner, there are at least three possible variants. When several places are involved in such a description, the amount of variants increases substantially. A sequel of places reported in ancient sources in a straight north-south direction may have to be corrected to a general northwest-southeast direction describing an irregular line swaying from southwest to southeast at each possible point.

The dimensions given by Marinus of Tyre and Ptolemy contain an error in general computation. Although the cardinal error is known, there is no mathematical formula available to correct distances which were part of the general computed dimensions. Ptolemy was aware of the discrepancies between the general dimensions and the totals of their sections. Whenever he discovered a discrepancy, he adjusted the distances of the sections. This means that his text contains locations which he corrected and locations which he did not change. Each of his locations requires individual evaluation. The evaluation of such individual cases may result in establishing either a firm point or a set of variant locations.

Many uncertainties have to be taken into account in historical-geographical investigation. It is known that the ancient writers used many merchants' itineraries and reports. The vision of a merchant moving along a trade route is similar to that of a modern traveler speeding through a foreign country on highways. He registers data pertaining to situations existing along the trade route and its environs rather than to the interior of the country. This uneven distribution of the information has to be taken into consideration. Tribal and place names are a problem not only in linguistics, but also in historical investigation. It is to be anticipated that certain human groups were recorded by more than one name. The self-denomination of a human group is not always identical with the form used by an outsider to describe it. This circumstance could have been overlooked by ancient writers. As a result, the amount of tribal names recorded is greater than the amount of human groups that actually lived in a given area. In addition to that, the recorded forms vary not only in the different manuscripts of one historical source, but also within a single text of an ancient writer. It is not always possible to distinguish clearly between similarity and identity. The physiographic features of the country were not known to the ancient world in the same way as they are known today. The Sudeten and the Carpathians were not recognized as two big orographic units, and were described by names referring to individual sections only. The Oder was known by more than one name, and the designations recorded in ancient sources are different from the one used today.

Protohistoric times frequently raise many problems. The appearance of the first written record referring to a particular area does not mean that the area can be described on the basis of such a record, as it reveals only a minute portion of what actually existed. Information is restricted to fragmentary bits; unless these pieces can be put together, the entity remains unknown. Fortunately, in most cases additional information is available. Prehistoric archaeology, linguistics, and other disciplines investigating the past on different levels and with different aims come close at certain points, though the final results of one discipline are not congruent with those of another. Investigators in one branch of knowledge realize that their evidence contains gaps and feel the need of filling them with information obtained from another discipline. They know that such a procedure may solve a particular issue, and that other disciplines in turn may profit from their solutions or suggestions. If facts missing in the evidence of one discipline are supplemented with indisputable facts established or synthesized by another discipline, the method is legitimate and proper. If, however, the investigator selects from another discipline only items that fit accidentally into his own theory, the method must not be considered valid.

In the past this method was heavily misused, contributing to the distortion of the ethnographic and geographic picture of the area under discussion in protohistoric times. Some of the distorting features have been removed since, but the gradual change of general maps is a long process, retarded by disagreement on an acceptable synthesis, if only a temporary one. The greatest impediment is the almost contradictory evaluation by the various archaeological schools, less contradictory as regards archaeological evaluation than ethnological applications. A second impeding factor is a certain lack of coordination of the results of the individual disciplines dealing with the past; they all carry different weights of argumentation improperly balanced. A third impeding factor is the wide range of personal opinions among scholars in various disciplines, which in fact is but the logical outcome of the two preceding factors.

Until an unbiased general picture of the conditions in the Oder-Vistula region is available, any student of ancient geography will have to labor under the disadvantages resulting from incomplete evidence transmitted to us in ancient sources, and from distortion caused by modern interpretation. The geographical location of the Goths is heavily affected by the problems described in this chapter. The difficulty in discussing the history of the Goths is caused not so much by the inaccuracy of the ancient authors, as by modern evaluations frequently based on preconceived ideas and biased opinions.

THREE MIGRATIONS IN CENTRAL EUROPE IN THE LAST TWO CENTURIES B.C.

The migration of the Goths was not a unique phenomenon in the history of Central Europe during the last two centuries before the beginning of our era. In fact, the ethnic pattern of this area was very unstable in those times. Shifting of human groups from place to place was quite common, and occurred in various forms ranging from conquests of large tribal territories to moves on a very small scale. Ancient sources contain fragmentary information on some of these migrations, especially if they interfered with or affected the interests of Rome.

The migration of the Helvetii in 58 B.C. is described by Caesar, who led the campaign against them and their allies. This migration was well planned and organized, and preparations for it were begun two years before. Every possible stretch of land was tilled to increase crops. Draft animals and carts were bought wherever possible to provide sufficient means of transportation. Food supplies for three months were ensured for the entire population. Friendly relations were established with neighboring tribes and their participation solicited. As a result, the Rauraci, Latobrigi, Tulingi, and Boii decided to join the Helvetii. When the day of the scheduled departure arrived, the people set fire to their villages, thus shattering any hope of return. First, they tried to force their way through the country of the Allobroges. Their assaults were beaten back by Caesar, who had fortified the entire west bank of the Rhone. The Helvetii turned then in another direction. After some negotiations they obtained permission for unobstructed passage from the Sequani, with whom they came to an agreement sealed by an exchange of hostages. Their march through the country of the Sequani proceeded in an orderly manner, but, as soon as the moving masses reached Aeduan soil, they began to spread terror by their acts of violence. Not only the Aedui, but also the Ambarri and Allobroges suffered from their invasion. Caesar met and defeated the invading tribes near Bibracte, thus bringing the migration to an end three months after it had started.

In the captured camp the Romans found records of a census taken prior to the departure, written in Greek. The names listed amounted to a total of 362,000 participants, of whom 92,000 were men capable of bearing arms. This figure is high and probably incorrect. Caesar himself estimated that 130,000 of the invaders survived the battle. Before the migrants were allowed to return home, the Romans took another census which showed a total of 110,000 people.[1]

Well remembered in history is the migration of the Cimbri, which created a state of emergency in Rome. This migration is described by Posidonius of Apamea, who lived either between 135 and   50 B.C. or between 125 and   40 B.C. His work is lost and is known only from quotations in later writers. Another ancient source is Plutarch's biography of Marius wherein the Roman military operations are described, providing a few interesting details about the Cimbri and their allies. Modern historians set either the year 120 or 115 B.C. as the starting point of this migration. Several Roman armies were defeated between 113 and 105 B.C. and the battle of Arausio (modern Orange), in which the Cimbri annihilated an entire Roman army, was one of the most dreadful disasters Rome had ever suffered. The Cimbri and their allies the Teutones were finally defeated at Aquae Sextiae in 102 B.C. and at Vercellae in 101 B.C., which means that these peoples had been on the move for almost fifteen or twenty years.[2]

Allegedly a storm tide had torn away part of the shore and the cultivated soil of the country of the Cimbri, which lay in northern Jutland, and this loss gave the impulse for their leaving the country. If this was the true cause, it means that the Cimbri could not have prepared their journey as thoroughly as the Helvetii did. Two tribes, the Teutones and Ambrones, went with them; however, not all of the Cimbri and Teutones left the country, since in Tacitus' times some of them were still living in Jutland. The fate of the Ambrones is not known; their name does not appear in later sources. They are currently considered to have been one of the North Germanic tribes.[3]

These three tribal groups moved southward, very likely along the Elbe. In the Hercynian Forest they were repulsed by the Celtic Boii, who at that time lived in Bohemia. The details of this battle are unknown. It could have taken place as early as 120 or 115 B.C. During the following years, the migrants lived among Celtic tribes in Pannonia and Illyricum. In 113 B.C. they appeared in Noricum and defeated a Roman army near Noreia. The way to Rome was now open, but the invaders turned toward Gaul instead. Their numbers increased, since the Helvetian Tigurini and Toygeni decided to join them.[4]

Not much is known of the situation in Gaul between 113 and 102 B.C.; there is not enough evidence to evaluate it. Most of the country seems to have been in general uproar. Military raids are recorded extending as far as the country of the Celtiberi in the Pyrenees, and of the Belgae in the north. Three Roman armies were defeated in the south of the country. The victories won by the Cimbri and Teutones on the battlefield were a great military achievement. It is no wonder that some modern historians consider them to have led to the complete conquest of Gaul and are full of praise for the talent and leadership of these tribes. There are, however, arguments speaking against this interpretation. To justify terming the event a conquest, it should first be demonstrated that the idea of conquest was present in the mind of the invaders, i.e., that they intended to acquire by force of arms a territory for their own abode or for permanent use. This, however, cannot be inferred from the actions of the Cimbri and their allies. The fact is puzzling that they did not penetrate into the heart of Italy when they had the opportunity to do so. Victorious on many battlefields, they constantly renewed their petitions to settle in a territory assigned to them by Rome—they fought Rome in order to live under its protection. Was the entire migration a senseless enterprise, or did these barbarians have a definite goal in mind?

This question has been answered by Bühler, who pointed out that the Cimbri and their allies were agricultural peoples interested in the possession of fields, cattle, pastures, and permanent settlements. It is easy to invade a foreign country, devastate it, and then retreat, carrying away the loot; but it is difficult to settle permanently amidst a hostile and numerous people. This may be why the Cimbri may not have wished to penetrate into Italy. Instead, they repeatedly renewed their request to settle in a territory assigned by Rome. The latter was not willing to grant such permission, because this would have attracted more barbarians from the north. The final attack on Italy in 102 B.C. was an act of despair. The Cimbri and Teutones simple could not stay any longer among the hostile tribes of Gaul, and were worn out and tired from endless wandering.[5]

The Helvetii left their country for a strictly political reason. It was Orgetorix's ambitious idea to achieve dominion over all of Gaul. He realized the disadvantages of the geographical location of his native country; well protected by natural boundaries, it was an ideal place for a peace-loving people, but the very natural boundaries that protected it created conditions unfavorable for political expansion. Orgetorix knew that in order to control Gaul, the Helvetii had to leave their homeland and establish a new center for future operations. Though he did not live to see the day of departure (he died in 60 B.C.), his observation was correct. Since Caesar was successful in defending the bank of the Rhone, the future rulers of Gaul could not get out of their own country without bargaining with the Sequani for a free passage.

The migration of the Cimbri had a different cause. Whether the story of the destructive storm tide is true or not, there is behind it an economic factor. It was the need for more arable land that caused the emigration. In any primitive agricultural society, an increase in population determined a situation in which the available tillable land could no longer satisfy the growing needs of the population. Tribal societies were not advanced enough to undertake large-scale cultivation of unused land. Territorial expansion was a solution, but it was not possible if the neighbors had the means to resist it. The only answer was total or partial emigration. Migratory routes pointed toward Rome—the magic center of wealth. In its proximity, the barbarians expected to find better fields, more abundant crops, and richer pastures. They had no political illusions, and cherished no dreams of becoming a great power; these are all ideas attributed to them later. The causes of the early migrations were the economic conditions in the homeland; their goal was economic improvement under the protection of Rome, or settlement in countries where conditions were more favorable.

The economic concept visible in the move of the Cimbri is more representative of the early Germanic migrations than the political concept of the Helvetian move. It is not irrelevant to discuss here Caesar's account of the campaign against the Helvetii. His description contains many interesting details about the technique of migration: the preparation for the march, the need for equipment and supplies, the conditions that changed an itinerary, and the kinds of agreements reached with other peoples either before or during the march. Most of these important technical aspects are unjustifiably neglected in historical studies dealing with migrations. After all, one does not cross a sea without a ship, and the manner in which a group of armed horsemen travel is different from that of a group of farmers with their families, cattle, and carts. These secondary technical aspects deserve consideration in any historical study that aims at completeness.

The migration of a sedentary agricultural people was apt to cause drastic changes in their way of life. The entire economic system came to a complete stop when people changed their abodes from one place to another. They could not till the soil and wait for the season of harvest while they were traveling, but had to live on the supplies they carried with them, on food gathered along the road , and off their flocks. Their life became similar to that of the nomads. This is how Strabo's description of the peoples of Germania should be understood. He says that "it is a common characteristic of all these peoples in this part of the world that they migrate with ease, because of the meagerness of their livelihood and because they do not till the soil or even store up food, but they live in small huts that are merely temporary structures; and they live for the most part off their flocks, as the Nomads do, so that, in imitation of the Nomads, they load their household belongings on their wagons and with their beasts turn whithersoever they think best."[6] Scholars today argue whether the Germanic society in the time of Christ was agricultural-pastoral, or mainly pastoral with some agriculture. In either case, it meant the possession of permanent homes, tillage of the soil, and storage of crops. Strabo's account obviously refers to a temporary migratory phase, and not to the permanent sedentary stage of Germanic society.

Climatic factors had a great influence on the migratory process. In most parts of Central Europe, winter was not suitable for travel, and all major moves were delayed until the spring. This appears from Plutarch's remark that the Cimbri and Teutones "had left their homes and moved westward, not in a single march, nor even continuously, but with each recurring spring they had gone forward, fighting their way, and in the course of time had crossed the continent."[7] The people had to be sheltered and cattle had to be kept under cover. A small group of travelers could find temporary quarters in villages situated along the roads, but a huge mass of wandering people faced a serious housing problem.

It is extremely difficult to evaluate statistical data obtained from ancient historical sources. The census taken by the Helvetii amounted to a total of 362,000 people, while Caesar's figures show a total of from 110,000 to 130,000. In the estimate of Polish archaeologists and historians, the population of the area corresponding to present-day Poland did not exceed the hypothetical number of 375,000 in the second century A.D.[8] In Germania or Gaul, population density may have been higher, but under no circumstances could a group of about 100,000 people be absorbed by any local population. Temporary quarters had to be constructed, and this must have required a considerable length of time. It is very likely that four or five months of each year of migration were spent preparing for the hibernating season and waiting for it to pass.

Integration with larger human groups was a feature frequently seen in the migrations of those times. The host of the Helvetii consisted of five different peoples, and that of the Cimbri of either four or five, depending on whether or not the Toygeni can be counted as a separate tribe. Boihaemum, the country of the Boii, was invaded by two tribes, the Marcomanni and the Quadi. The group of the Hasdingi, who invaded northern Hungary, was a mixture of various peoples and tribal units that assumed the collective name of Vandals. There lay an advantage in increasing the size of a migrating body: it provided a greater striking force in case of an armed conflict, and gave an enhanced feeling of security. But actually it worked against the real purpose of the migration, since there is no doubt that the greater the number of participating peoples, the more land had to be conquered or otherwise obtained for permanent agricultural settlement. Outside groups joining a migrating body were an additional burden, creating organizational and transportation problems.

The caravan of a migrating agricultural people cannot be likened to the march column of an army. A population of about 120,000, with six persons, two draft animals, and one wagon per household required 40,000 draft animals and 20,000 wagons, to which a great number of domestic animals of all kinds should be added. Such a conglomeration of men, beasts, and equipment could not be kept in perfect marching order. There were no organized columns, the caravans were broken into many hundreds of parts, and each of the individual parts stopped many times a day. The motion was thus slow and uneven. In a migration of the size mentioned above, many days were bound to pass between the moment when the first scout rode past a given point and the time when the last wagon passed it.

The slow movement and the length of time required for the passage of such migratory groups can be illustrated by examples taken from the accounts of Caesar and Plutarch. The first is the crossing of the Saône by the Helvetii. It took twenty days, and only three-fourths of the people had made it by the time Caesar approached. His army crossed the river within a single day.[9] No exact figures are available to compare these two crossings. The number of Helvetii who managed to reach the west bank of the river can be estimated to range between 90,000 and 120,000, but the total number of Roman soldiers cannot be established. In the battle near Bibracte, Caesar led an army of six legions with auxiliary troops; however, his legions very frequently were not at full strength, and the size of the auxiliary forces was always fluctuating. In this particular case, a total of 30,000 men should be a fairly accurate guess. These two estimates show a daily rate of 30,000 soldiers against 4,500 to 6,000 civilians. This comparison is not a fair one, however, since the structure of the organized Roman army was different from that of a migrating barbarian people. In addition to the difference in structure, different levels of technological progress were involved. To cross the river, the barbarians used rafts and boats tied together, while the Romans had constructed a temporary bridge. The only valuable information obtained from Caesar's report is the fact that the Helvetii needed twenty days to transport three-fourths of the migrants across the river. His information can safely be generalized and applied to almost any migration of this type and time: a large migratory group, similar in size to that of the Helvetii, would need almost four weeks to cross a medium-sized calm river, if no bridges or natural fords were available.

The second example is taken from Plutarch's description of the size and movement of the Teutones. After unsuccessful attempts to capture the fortified Roman camp at the estuary of the Rhone, the migrants withdrew. From the wall of their camp, the Roman soldiers watched the columns of migrating Teutones described by Plutarch as follows: "then, indeed the immensity of their numbers was made specially evident by the length of their line and the time required for their passage; for it is said they were six days in passing the fortifications of Marius, although they moved continuously." [10] In view of the figures on the crossing of the Rhone by the Helvetii, Plutarch's report does not seem exaggerated.

Most of these technical problems and political or armed conflicts were characteristic of mass migration only. Such movements of peoples were hazardous enterprises which could end in disaster even if no armed conflicts took place. On the other hand, danger could lessen almost to the point of nonexistence if people moved in small groups only. Single families or other incidental small human groups were no menace to any sedentary population. They could move along all possible routes and were easier to feed and shelter. They were, so to speak, part of the local or commercial traffic in the area. In the course of several decades, a whole tribe or any larger human group could reach a set destination in this way, and could settle in an uninhabited or thinly populated area without any conflict with the peoples whose lands it traversed. The gradual shifting of people from one country to another never made headlines in ancient writings, as only the final results of these transplantations of men came to the attention of contemporary writers.

Such peaceful migration of small groups is a theory which cannot be proven by the testimony of ancient writers. It is, however, not a unique phenomenon in history. Many similar movements took place in later centuries without preceding conquests. The peaceful immigration of German settlers into medieval Poland or the landing of the Pilgrim Fathers in Plymouth may serve as random examples. It is an acceptable explanation in cases when conquest has not been recorded in historical sources, or when prior conquest was entirely impossible. The migration of the Goths could have taken place in this way. Like any other Germanic or Celtic tribe, they were capable of organizing a large-scale migration, in the course of which the whole tribe or its major part would leave the homeland in a single move, but they could have chosen, just as well, to migrate in small groups which would have left the country at various times over a period of several decades.

Yet, in one respect, their migration was different from those of the Cimbri, the Helvetii, and many other tribes. The Goths had to cross the sea in order to settle in the Oder-Vistula region. They could have reached it by land, marching through Scandinavia, Finland, and Northwest Russia; but this was a long route, with many physiographic obstacles, impractical, and probably not known at all in those times, since, in the belief of the ancients, Scandinavia was an island. A boat was needed to leave this island, and only a well-constructed vessel could take people to faraway shores.

The Gothic emigration from Sweden is a typical example of a situation in which the movement of man depended entirely upon the tools he made. This dependence on technical equipment has not been taken into consideration in studies dealing with the migration of the Goths. Knowledge of the means that enabled them to cross the sea, however, is apt to throw light on the circumstances of their appearance in the Oder-Vistula region.

FOUR   ANCIENT GERMANIC WATERCRAFT

 Between the estuaries of the Göta and the Vistula there is a stretch of sea of about 700 kilometers that meant a very long journey for an ancient voyager. It required daring, experience, and a seagoing vessel to take a group of sailors from one point to the other; a large fleet of such vessels would have been needed to transport an army or a large human group to their destination.

The emigration of the Goths from Sweden took place in the middle of the first century B.C. If archaeological finds or historical sources can produce evidence that adequate seagoing vessels existed in the area at that time, it can be assumed that fleets consisting of such vessels were available. If, however, archaeological and historical evidence should prove that such vessels did not exist in the area at that time, the existence of large fleets would naturally be precluded.

Archaeological finds show that trade relations between Scandinavia and the opposite shore had existed for centuries. A number of Roman imports have been unearthed in Sweden. This, however, does not prove that large cargo vessels were used. The type of goods imported into Sweden could have been brought over in small fishing boats sailing through the Danish islands, which are located in close proximity to each other.

One of the boats used in Scandinavia was found in the small Hjortspring bog on the island of Als. Its construction has been dated at around either 200 or 100 B.C. It is a double-ended boat of a shape characteristic of many other vessels in the area, and also of the later Viking ships. It has an internal length of ten meters, but the double beaks at bow and stern bring it to an overall length of about seventeen and a half meters, and it weighs 530 kilograms. The boat consists of a flat bottom and two planks on each side. Steered by a large oar at the

Fig. 1. The Nydam boat (4th century A.D.).

stern, it was propelled by paddles, and had no mast or sail. Its structure was extremely light and elastic, and it could carry about twenty men.[1] J. G. D. Clark calls it a war canoe.[2] It was not a sea-going vessel; its use was restricted to short trips along the coast, according to the opinion of Ole Klindt-Jensen, who says that the construction "would enable it to stand up to battering by the waves of the more sheltered parts of the Danish coast."[3]

A few ships were recovered from the Nydam bog in Southern Jutland. One of them has survived until our day in an almost perfect condition. It is commonly called the Nydam boat, and it was constructed either in the second half of the third, or during the fourth century A.D. (figure 1). Its shape is similar to that of the Hjortspring boat, in that both ends are pointed, but instead of the two beaks or rams, it has stemposts at bow and stern. Made of oak, it has a keel plank, five planks on each side, and a gunwale. The clinker-built sides are fastened together with iron nails. The boat was propelled by oars and steered by means of a large oar or rudder suspended from the stern. The rowlocks are affixed to the gunwale; they are reversible and could be adjusted so that the boat could be rowed in an opposite direction without making a turn.

The studies describing this boat contain many discrepancies regarding its exact measurements, the size of its crew, and its loading capacity. According to Haakon Shetelig and Hjalmar Falk, the length of the boat from post to post is 22.84 meters, the length of the bulwark 21.38 meters, the maximum width 3.26 meters, and the depth from under the keel plank 1.09 meters. According to W. Vogel, the length from post to post is approximately 24 meters, the maximum width 3.4 meters, the height at midship 1.28 meters, and at bow and stern 2.14 meters, the sheer not less than 1.14 meters. Rudolf Much says that the oars are 3.6 meters in length.[4]

More disturbing than the minor differences in measurements are discrepancies in descriptions of the equipment and estimates of the loading capacity. Some scholars count fifteen rowlocks on each side, and consequently fifteen pairs of oars (Clark, Klindt-Jensen, Shetelig, and Falk).[5] Others count only fourteen rowlocks on each side, i.e., fourteen pairs of oars (Romola and R. C. Anderson, Piggot, Schmidt, Vogel, Wahle), while Oxenstierna maintains that the boat had "room for thirty-six oarsmen," which would imply that there were eighteen pairs of oars (if all men worked the oars at the same time).[6] From photographs of the original boat and its reconstructed model, it is impossible to find out whether the boat had twenty-eight, thirty, or thirty-six oars. The number of oars would indicate the size of the crew. Counting one man per oar and one at the rudder, the crew would amount to twenty-nine, thirty-one, or thirty-seven men. Schmidt's calculation of two men per oar and at least two for working the rudder brings the total of the crew to no less than sixty men.

It is also difficult to estimate the approximate loading capacity of the ship. Schmidt, relying on the content of a letter sent to him, has a highly exaggerated image of the boat's cargo capacity. Besides the extremely high number of crew members, he thought that on short trips an additional one hundred men could board the ship, which makes a total of one hundred sixty passengers, including the crew. Vogel estimates that with forty people aboard, the boat had a displacement of fourteen tons and a draught of 0.7 meters. Wahle says that the boat could carry forty-five people.

There is greater agreement among scholars as to the boat's technical value and quality. It was a strong boat, propelled by oars and not by paddles, so that the crew's energy was more efficiently employed. Vogel stresses the high quality of the construction and the boat's usefulness at sea: "at any rate, the superb construction seems to point to not inconsiderable seaworthiness and long nautical development" he says.[7] In Klindt-Jensen's opinion, "the vessel was tall and comparatively strong, and would have stood up to the battering of all but the highest seas. It was, however, not yet strong enough in construction to stand an ocean passage in the manner of the later Viking ships."[8]

Archaeologists and historians generally speak of the Nydam boat as a strong, well-built, and seaworthy vessel. Modern sailors, to whom the description and measurements have been shown, are less enthusiastic about its seaworthiness. It was a heavy, narrow, seventy-six-foot long rowboat, difficult to manage at sea. With forty men aboard, it had a draught of two feet and nine inches. At midship the gunwale was less than two feet above the water level. On a breezy day at sea, the wind speed reaches fifteen to twenty miles per hour, which means waves of two feet and above. A light thunderstorm or gale can bring winds of forty to fifty miles per hour with waves over three feet high. On windy days, the Nydam boat could sail only against or with the waves, since it could not bear the impact of waves higher than two feet against its sides. A storm would easily have flooded the vessel. Caught in a storm, a fleet of Nydam boats would have been exposed to disaster. A large group of people could not even dream of making a long sea voyage in the Nydam boats.

There are also some later finds of ships: the Kvalsund ship (sixth or seventh century A.D.), the Oseberg ship (about 840 A.D.), and the Gokstadt ship (850-900 A.D.).[9] They are all Norwegian and belong to the Viking age. They were built many hundreds of years after the Goths had left Sweden, and at a time when Gothic might and power had ceased to exist and had gone into oblivion. The Viking ships, however, cannot serve as models for the watercraft used by the Goths in the last century B.C. As yet, there is no archaeological evidence as to the type of vessels used during their migration; however, such a boat can be reconstructed theoretically. The Hjortspring boat was built about a hundred years before the migration, the Nydam boat approximately three hundred years after it. Granting an even rate of technical development in ship building, the structure and quality of such a ship should be situated somewhere between the Hjortspring and the Nydam boat. From historical sources, it is known that the Germanic tribes of the first century A.D. knew the method of propelling a boat by oars. Consequently, the imaginary vessel used by the Goths must have looked like the Hjortspring boat with some technical improvements: it must have had stronger construction and oars instead of paddles. This assumed quality and construction is in agreement with Germanic boats described in ancient historical sources.

When Germanicus was preparing his campaign against Arminius in 16 A.D., he ordered the construction of a large fleet. It consisted of 1,000 vessels that were built at great speed. The fleet was not intended for use in naval warfare, but for logistic purposes only: it was to carry the Roman army from the estuary of the Rhine along the seashore to the mouth of the Ems, and bring it back the same way. The actual military campaign was conducted overland, from the Ems to the Weser. The cargo was heavy. In this campaign, Germanicus commanded eight legions and auxiliary troops. The total number of men easily exceeded 40,000, which means an average of forty men and their supplies per vessel. There is a detailed account of the military operations in Tacitus' *Annals*. It contains the war report, a description of the fleet, and some details that can help to elucidate some problems of migration.[10]

The fleet consisted of various types of vessels. This is how Tacitus describes them: "some were short craft with very little poop or prow, and broad-bellied, the more easily to withstand a heavy sea; others had flat bottoms, enabling them to run aground without damage; while still more were fitted with rudders at each end, so as to head either way the moment the oarsmen reversed their stroke. Many had a deckflooring to carry the military engines, though they were equally useful for transporting horses or supplies. The whole armada, equipped at once for sailing or propulsion by the oar, was a striking and formidable spectacle, rendered still more so by the enthusiasm of the soldiers."[11] The question arises why ships of so many types were built, if Germanicus only needed transportation for his army. Was there a real need for constructing short, broad-bellied ships, useful in heavy seas, if the other vessels of the same fleet did not have this quality? What was the practical use of the double-ended ship which could move in the opposite direction without turning, and of the flat-bottomed boat which could run aground without damage, when the entire fleet was used only for one specific transportation job? The answer is obvious. The fleet was built at great speed; every type of skill or manpower available was turned to account in building it. It is easy to recognize the ships equipped with deck flooring and sails as large cargo vessels built by, or under the supervision of, Roman military or naval engineers. The construction of these ships was time-consuming and, therefore, all the other boats were probably built by local Celtic or Germanic craftsmen. These people could produce only boats similar to the ones they used to build for themselves. Certain features remind one of the Hjortspring and the Nydam boats, such as the double-ended shape, which have the ability to move in the opposite direction without turning.

The proud armada had an unhappy end. In midsummer of the same year, after a successful campaign, the greater part of the army was returning to its base at the Lower Rhine.[12] Leaving the Ems and sailing westward between the Continent and the Dutch Islands, the fleet was caught in a hailstorm, high seas, and strong winds. The vessels were not fit and strong enough to withstand the vicissitudes of a heavy storm. Many boats were flooded by the high waves and leaked through their sides faster than the water could be bailed out. Horses and supplies were thrown overboard to lighten the weight of the hulls. Many ships sank, or were wrecked, or damaged. Some boats managed to reach the shore, but the anchors were not strong enough, and the boats were driven back by the tide and winds blowing from the land. Many lives were lost. People were stranded on remote, unpopulated islands, and survived on the carcasses of horses washed up on the same shore. Some were driven by the waves as far as the coast of Britain. During the days following, crews who had survived the storm landed at the place of destination in damaged boats, with oars missing. Germanicus, whose Roman-built trireme had brought him home safely, directed the rescue operations for several days and nights.[13] Though losses in lives and equipment must have been heavy, the Roman army was not destroyed. During the same summer, Germanicus or his generals conducted several expeditions, and 30,000 men took part in them. The entire strength of the Roman army of Lower and Upper Germania was only eight legions. Therefore, many veterans of the first campaign must have participated in the later expeditions. This story proves the obvious weakness of the watercraft. The small and light barbarian-built boats were the ones that suffered most from the storm. Such boats would have to have been useless in longer voyages, even when sailing along the coast, and in the summertime.

In 47 A.D. the Chauci, whose abodes were situated at the shore of the North Sea near the Weser, harassed the coast of Gaul with a piratical fleet consisting of light vessels.[14] Describing the vessels of the Germanic pirates, Pliny says that they were primitive dugouts, some of which could carry as many as thirty men.[15]

In 70 A.D., during the Batavian rising, Civilis, the leader of the rebellion, engaged the Romans in a naval battle in the Rhine delta. Prior to that, protected by the darkness of night, he had attacked the Roman camp and captured some of their vessels. Tacitus describes the Batavian fleet, in a fragmentary but restored text which reads: "Civilis was now seized with a desire to make a naval demonstration; he therefore manned all biremes and all the ships that had but a single bank of oars; to this fleet he added a vast number of boats [putting in each] thirty or forty men, the ordinary complement of a Liburnian cruiser; and at the same time the boats he had captured were fitted with particoloured plaids for sails, which made a fine show and helped their movement." [16] The "vast number of boats" were the vessels of the Batavi. If Civilis put thirty to forty men in a boat, he really packed it with people, since no machinery or supplies were to be carried. These vessels were thus not bigger than those described by Pliny. They were small boats, and not galleys or merchantmen, temporarily adjusted for warfare.

Tacitus' account of the Suiones, who were neighbors of the Goths in Scandinavia, is also of interest here. His information has been subject to many interpretations. He says: "Next are the communities of the Suiones, at the Ocean itself, who besides in men and arms are known for their fleets. The shape of their ships is different in so far that prows on both ends act as the front, always ready for landing. They are not propelled by sails, neither is a tier of oars fastened to their sides; the rowing gear is loose as on some [boats used on] rivers, movable and can be used here and there." [17] In the second part of the *Germania,* Tacitus records many details pertaining to individual peoples living in various parts of the country. His information was based on incidental observations of varying interest. Modern scholars have studied the text carefully, and have offered elaborate interpretations. Here and there, a new meaning has been attributed to Tacitus' words. These new meanings created new concepts, that did not always agree with the rest of the evidence. As a result, Tacitus has been accused sometimes of inaccuracy. Two new concepts were introduced into the passage of the *Germania* quoted above, i.e., that the Suiones were a sea power, and that their ships were superior to those of other Germanic tribes.

Speaking about ancient seafaring peoples, Schmidt quotes *Germania* 44 to prove that Tacitus had already emphasized the sea power of the Scandinavian Germani. Later he describes the dugouts of the Chauci and Batavi, and quoting *Germania* 44 once again, reaches the conclusion that the ships of the Suiones were of superior quality. [18] This conclusion is based solely upon the fact that Tacitus described these ships in more detail. Much, always very enthusiastic about the heroic Germanic past, emphasizes Tacitus' words "praeter viros armaque classibus valent," and concludes that "*viros armaque* refers to land power in contrast to *classibus,* maritime power, though ships also require armed crews." [19] He thus deduces from Tacitus' text the definite notion of the land and sea power of the Suiones. In his edition of the *Germania,* J. G. C. Anderson is more cautious in his commentary, as, for example: "*classibus valent.* The reference is primarily to ships of war. Their sea-power is doubtless exaggerated, but they were seafaring and trading people, whose commercial connexions were mainly with the mouth of the Vistula." [20] He suggests a more liberal interpretation of the word *classes,* by including trade vessels. His suggestion is most judicious. As Tacitus' description goes on, the Suiones do not appear as a very warlike nation. They liked wealth, and probably also the comfort it brings. The "Ocean" protected them from invaders. Unlike other Germani, they did not carry arms all the time. Their weapons were kept in storehouses, whose safekeeping was consigned to slaves. [21]

Not only the alleged sea power of the Suiones and the type of fleet they had, have been discussed, but also the method of propelling the ships. Much and Anderson were concerned about the meaning of Tacitus' words "nec remos in ordinem lateribus adiungunt" and "solutum remigium." Both scholars come to the same conclusion, that since the oars were not permanently secured to the gunwale, the boats must have been propelled by paddles. In Anderson's words, this is "an impossible method of propelling sea-going craft." [22] Interpreting the same passage, Much is more critical about the credibility of Tacitus' account. First, he assumes that Tacitus had propelling by paddles in mind. Then he speaks of the impossibility of using paddles on "large sea-going ships with high sides." As a result, he accuses Tacitus of misjudging the whole matter and of giving erroneous information. [23] However, the interpretations of Anderson and Much contain the same errors: a mistaken concept about the size of the ships, and the wrong conclusion that movable oars mean paddles. Most likely, Anderson had the Nydam boat in mind when he spoke of seagoing craft. Much uses some measurements of that boat to prove that Tacitus was wrong. Indeed, it seems impossible to work the heavy Nydam boat with paddles. Its oars were 3.6 meters long, and a paddle of this size is very difficult to handle. However, this boat was built about 150 to 250 years after Tacitus wrote the *Germania,* and its measurements cannot be used as an argument against Tacitus, nor should this boat be taken as a sample of the ships of the Suiones.

Nevertheless, Tacitus' words "hinc vel illinc" require some explanation. English editions of his works often render these words by "from side to side," meaning that the oars could be used either on the right or on the left side of the boat. [24] Anderson's commentary reads: "hinc vel illinc, 'can be shifted, as circumstances require, from one direction to the other' (i.e., are reversible), so that the vessel may be rowed either way." Explaining the same term in a description of some Pontic boats, he says that " 'oars which can be shifted from side to side' is a possible translation, but gives no suitable meaning in relation to the propulsion of the boat: there is no question of turning it."[25] Tacitus' "hinc vel illinc" refers only to the direction in which the boat could move, and not to the change of oars from side to side. The boat of the Suiones was similar to the double-ended ship described in Germanicus' fleet. It moved in the opposite direction without having to make a turn; it was propelled by oars, and not by paddles. Tacitus' description itself indicates the method of propulsion. A boat propelled by paddles does not need any rowing gear at all. The fact that some kind of a movable rowing gear is mentioned proves that the boat must have had oars, and not paddles.

All the above-mentioned concepts, starting with the alleged sea power and ending with the paddle that was not permanently fastened to the side of the boat, are due to the fact that only Tacitus' words were interpreted and no thought was given to the source of his information. As in many other cases, his information was based on a merchant's report. It was the report of a man who was interested in trade, profit, personal safety, and future transactions. He may have never been in Sweden. The ancients feared the sea, and there was no need for him to make this dangerous trip. He could have met Swedish traders in any primitive harbor or trading post at the Oder or Vistula. The Roman merchant, naturally, learned some details about the people he traded with. They could have told him that their homeland was a peaceful country, protected from invaders by the "Ocean." There were no wars, there was no need to carry arms. Weapons were stored in a special place. The people liked wealth; they could produce many goods the Roman merchant was interested in, and had plenty of ships to bring the products to the hither shore. The ships of the foreign traders would strike the merchant's attention, because their construction was different from that of the ships he had seen at Ostia or at any other Roman harbor. The Roman ships were differently shaped at bow and stern. The galley had openings in her side; her oars were permanently installed in these openings, and were not taken off when she was anchored or pulled ashore. The merchantman had mast and sail. The boats of the Suiones were double-ended; Tacitus' informant must have seen the practical value of such construction; the boat could move in either direction without making a turn. He saw that the oars were taken off and placed on benches, or were leaning against the ship's side. They were not permanently installed. Yet, he certainly saw oars and not paddles. Had he seen paddles, he would have noticed their extreme shortness.

This, very likely, was the content of the report that reached Tacitus, who spoke another language, that of a Roman scholar and historian. The report left with him the impression of the existence of a human group profuse in number, with great stores of arms and many ships. He described the vessels of these people as they were described to him. He made no judgment as to their quality or superiority: he only repeated some of their features and technological details. There is nothing in his description which could prove that the boats of the Suiones were bigger and better than those of other Germanic tribes. In fact, his description shows that their ships were similar to contemporary boats used by other Germanic tribes. The experience of Germanicus' campaign showed that the Germanic watercraft was not safe for navigation in coastal waters, if used for transportation of large numbers of people. It is needless to stress that they were useless as cargo vessels in voyages across the open sea.

Information obtained from historical sources agrees with the existing archaeological evidence that the watercraft used by the Germanic tribes during the first century of our era, as well as that of the first century B.C., was not advanced enough to be used as cargo or passenger vessels in long voyages across the open sea. The Goths may have possessed large fleets at that time. Their ships, however, were not capable of carrying a large number of people from Göteborg or Karlskrona to Danzig in a nonstop crossing of the Baltic Sea. If the Goths finally arrived in the Oder-Vistula region, they must have come in a way other than across the open sea.

FIVE THE ROUTE OF THE GOTHS FROM SWEDEN TO THE ODER

 "To cross the Baltic was an easy and natural attempt. The inhabitants of Sweden were masters of a sufficient number of large vessels with oars and the distance is little more than 100 miles from Carlscroon to the nearest ports of Pomerania and Prussia. Here, at length, we land on firm and historic ground. At least as early as the Christian era and as late as the age of the Antonines, the Goths were established towards the mouth of the Vistula, and in that fertile province where the commercial cities of Thorn, Elbing, Königsberg and Danzig were long afterwards founded."[1] These words were written by Edward Gibbon in 1776. A number of basic assumptions regarding this migration have not changed much since then. It has been taken for granted that the voyage across the sea was a simple task, and that fleets consisting of large vessels were available. The crossing of the sea became so obvious, that sometimes it was totally ignored. Henry Bradley's evaluation is an example. This is what he wrote a hundred years after Gibbon: "whether the Goths did originally come from Scandinavia is a question that has been much disputed. The traditions of a people contained in its songs are not to be lightly put aside, and there is no reason to doubt that the Goths once inhabited the northern as well as the southern shores of the Baltic. But it cannot be said that apart from tradition there is any real evidence of the fact."[2]

Historians have been more or less concerned with the route of the Gothic migration, but never with the method of crossing the sea. Schmidt thought of a voyage from the southern tip of Sweden to the estuary of the Oder, instead of to that of the Vistula, since a great mass of migrating people would prefer a shorter rather than a longer sea journey.[3] Christoph Obermüller had a very sweeping concept of the homeland of the Goths and their heroic role in history, and drew on his map a route from Kristianstad, or from Karlskrona, to Danzig.[4] Discussing the expansion of Germanic tribes or tribal units from Scandinavia, Mikołaj Rudnicki stressed the importance of the chains of islands that acted as natural bridges between the Scandinavian and the other shores of the Baltic Sea. The most important of these bridges was, in his opinion, the route from Southwestern Scandinavia through the Danish islands and islets to Jutland, Schleswig, and Mecklenburg.[5] Although the author does not mention the fact, it is to be assumed that this is the route the Goths must have taken. Tymieniecki speaks of Jutland as a place of sojourn in the course of the migration of the Goths (see p. 8). According to Tunberg's map, the territory of the Goths in Sweden stretched from the Kattegat to the Baltic Sea, with very little access to the sea on either shore (see map 4 on p. 12). This suggests two possible points of departure from Sweden; either from Söderköping in the east, or from Göteborg in the west. Oxenstierna's map shows a concentration of Gothic territory between the Kattegat and Lake Vättern. The sea route he assumes to be a bold, direct line from Göteborg and Falkenberg, around the southern tip of Sweden, and through the middle of the open sea, to Danzig.[6]

The foregoing presents quite a choice of routes and distances. The voyage to Jutland through the Danish islands, as vaguely indicated by Rudnicki or Tymieniecki, required a series of short trips covering distances that varied from one to thirty-five kilometers. Gibbon speaks of a journey of "little more than one hundred miles." The crossing from Söderköping to Danzig would more than double the distance given by Gibbon; that from Göteborg to Danzig would quadruple it. But it has just been demonstrated that neither in the last hundred years B.C., nor in the first century of our era did the Goths possess adequate means of transportation to cross the open sea in a single, uninterrupted voyage. In unusual cases war vessels may have covered this distance, but the transfer of a large mass of people with all their goods and chattels was not possible. With their primitive watercraft the Goths could reach the Oder-Vistula region only via the Danish islands.

For many centuries these islands had been a natural bridge between Scandinavia and the rest of Germania. They were ideal for coastal navigation and brief sea voyages. The islands are in close proximity to one another, many of them visible from the neighboring shore. They offered overnight resting places for tired sailors, and fresh water supply for the next day's journey. Many disasters at sea could be averted as there was no need of sailing if the weather did not permit it. The short distances from island to island could be managed by primitive water-craft. The longest crossing in the area is from Sweden to Northern Jutland, a distance of about 70 kilometers. This is a long journey, yet daring sailors could have made it between daybreak and nightfall in summer and in favorable weather conditions. Otherwise, Jutland could be reached in two days with an overnight stop on the island Läsö. The longest distance in the southernmost part of the "bridge" is from the island Falster to the shore of Mecklenburg, approximately 35 kilo-meters, but this crossing could be avoided by sailing from Falster to Lölland and Fehrmarin, reducing the longest sea routes from Sweden to Mecklenburg to distances of not more than 20 kilometers each.

Since such a convenient route was known and available, it seems unrealistic to consider the technologically impossible direct route from Göteborg to Danzig. The use of the route through the Danish islands leads to the unquestionable conclusion that the Goths landed either in Mecklenburg, or in Schleswig, but not in Danzig. The estuary of the Vistula may safely be excluded from their itinerary. Its inclusion would be justified only by the assumption that the landing led to a subsequent settlement in Eastern Pomerania, which was not the case.

There is still a long way from the landing place to the alleged new abodes. The straight distance between the coast of Mecklenburg or Schleswig to the Middle Oder is approximately 350 kilometers. The destination could have been reached either overland, or by waterway. It is not known which was the choice of the Goths. Considering the kind of equipment needed for a long journey by land, they should have preferred the water. They must have arrived in Mecklenburg or Schles-wig in boats with very limited cargo capacity. With oarsmen, women, children, supplies, and household goods aboard, very little room was probably left for wagons and draft animals. A long overland journey was hardly possible without vehicles. On the other hand, they had boats that could be used for sailing along the coast, as well as on rivers. Waterways could take them to, or close to, their destination. It is very likely that they continued sailing eastward and turned south at the estuary of the Oder, ascending the river until they reached their new abodes in Lusatia or Southern Brandenburg. The trade route along the Oder was well known to the ancient Germanic tribes. During the time of the Gothic migration, the lower part of the river was a kind of borderland, an inviting feature for traveling in smaller or larger groups.

A comparison between maps 8 and 9 show that during the Late La Tène (150-1 B.C.) and the Early Roman (1-200 A.D.) periods, the

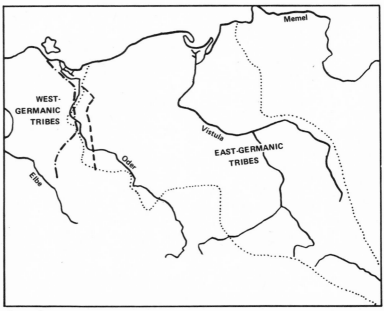

**Map 8. Archaeological culture in the Oder-Vistula region during the Late La Tène
and Early Roman periods according to some German archaeologists.**

lower part of the Oder was a demarcation line between two different
archaeological cultures, and that there was some later shifting of this
line to the east and then to the west. (Maps 8 and 9 are adapted from
Gustaf Kossina and Jażdżewski, and represent two different archaeological and ethnological interpretations; however, only their geographical aspect will be discussed in this chapter.) If such displacement
of prehistoric cultural borders took place, it points to an unstable ethnic situation along the lower part of the Oder. No archaeological culture radiated from that river in any direction. On the contrary, the
cultures approached the river from the east and from the west. The
conclusion is that at the Lower Oder there was no major tribe or people
controlling both sides of the river and capable of obstructing the passage of small or large migrating groups.

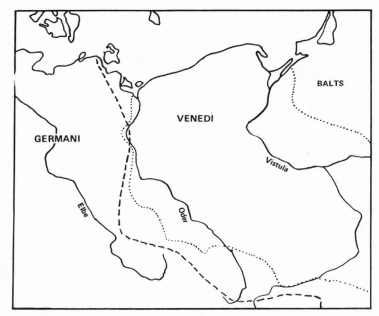

BALTS

VENEDI

GERMANI

Vistula

Elbe

Oder

Legend

.... boundary of the Venedian culture during the Late La Tène period (150-1 B.C.)

— — — — western boundary of the Venedian culture during the Early Roman period (1-200 A.D.)

Map 9. Archaeological cultures in the Oder-Vistula region during the Late La Tène and Early Roman periods according to some Polish archaeologists.

The frontier role of the Oder is expressed by the several names the river has had. As a rule, river names are permanent and do not change easily. If a river flows through an ethnically uniform territory and its name has once been established, it is usually retained, even if the ethnic environment has changed. For example, the name of the river Rhine is either of pre-Celtic, or of Celtic origin. The Celts used it during the long period of time when they occupied the country on both sides of the river. Later, Germanic peoples moved into the Rhine basin, and crossed the river but continued to use its old name. On the other hand, rivers flowing through several ethnic territories may be known by more than one name. This is the case of the Danube, which to the ancients became known as the Danubius from the river's source downstream, and as the Ister from its mouth upstream. Historical sources mention the Oder also as the Viadua, the Suebos, and the Guthalus.

The present name Oder, Polish *Odra,* is known only since the tenth century, and is not recorded in ancient sources. Linguists, however, maintain that it is very ancient, and they derive its etymology from Slavic, Veneto-Illyrian or Indo-European roots.[7] In other words, the name could have existed at the time in which the migration of the Goths took place.

The names Suebos and Viadua (Viaduas, Viados) are known only from Ptolemy's text.[8] Ptolemy thought that the two names referred to two different rivers, and recorded their estuaries at different longitudes; the Suebos at 39°30′ and the Viadua at 42°30′ east of the Fortunate Islands, i.e., about 160 kilometers apart.

In the literature on the subject there are many disagreements as to whether these two names refer to one or to two rivers. In the latter case, opinions are divided as to which of the two rivers is the real Oder. The variety of interpretation is not surprising, considering the fact that Ptolemy's data give a distorted picture of the Baltic coast. This has prompted scholars to approach the question of the Oder from the linguistic and other viewpoints; the problems of mathematical geography, so basic to Ptolemy's work, were seldom chosen as the starting point of argumentation. Since the appearance in 1937 of Theodor Steche's work on Germania in Ptolemy's *Geography* the disputed question could have been solved in an easier way. Some of his conclusions will be discussed later, in connection with Ptolemy's location of the Goths (pp. 105-106). Let it only be pointed out here that his distortion of the Baltic coast and the Oder-Vistula region was caused by a basic error in general computation, but that, within the range of that error, many of Ptolemy's locations are correct.

Let us then, using a very simple mathematical analysis, take Ptolemy's total distance between the estuaries of the Elbe and the Vistula, compare it with the same distance measured on modern maps, and investigate the location of all estuaries recorded between these two points. It is known that for the Baltic Sea and the Oder-Vistula region, Ptolemy did not have any data obtained from astronomical observations. His figures were compiled at Alexandria from nautical charts, itineraries, and similar material. Thus, if any of his sources contained an erroneous location of a place, it could have resulted in the incorrect location of the next one. Under certain circumstances, such an error could have influenced the total distance.

To make the comparison easier a chart has been drawn which lists Ptolemy's reported longitudes of the estuaries between the Elbe and the

Modern rivers (east of Greenwich)

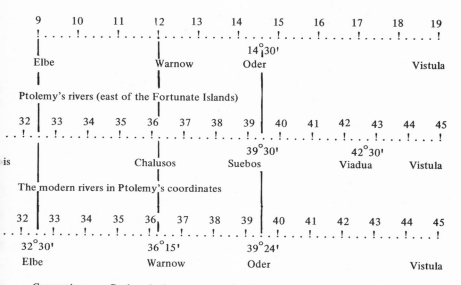

Conversion: one Ptolemaic degree equals 48 minutes of a modern degree,
one modern degree equals one degree and 15 minutes of Ptolemy's

The assumption was made that the location of the estuary of the Vistula at 19°
east of Greenwich is identical with Ptolemy's locations at 45°east of the Fortunate Islands. The difference in the location of the estuary of the Albis is due to
an error in his sources or computation.

**Figure 2. The estuaries of the rivers between the modern Elbe and Vistula com-
pared with Ptolemy's locations.**

Oder, the individual distances between these estuaries, and the corresponding modern rivers in the same area. The formula Steche has suggested for Middle Germany was used for the conversion of the data, i.e.,
one Ptolemaic degree in longitude equals 0.8 of ours, and consequently
one of our degrees is equal to 1.25 of Ptolemy's (see figure 2). According to Ptolemy, the total distance between the estuaries of the Elbe and
the Vistula is 14° which amounts to 11°12′ of ours. The actual distance, according to modern maps, is only 10°. Despite the difference of
1°12′, Ptolemy's figures are fairly accurate, after correcting the error in
his computation.

Between the Vistula and the Suebos Ptolemy counted 5°30′ (i.e.,
4°28′), while the actual distance between the Vistula and the Oder is

The assumption that Ptolemy had two locations for the Albis is a working theory, which may gain support from a revision of his map of Jutland. It is based on the observation that he located Cape Skagen three degrees farther to the east than the actual location. The following locations were checked and converted. The figures are taken from the Latin text in Müller's edition (II,11,1 and II,11,2).

Ptolemy's figures (east of the Fortunate Islands)			Conversion to locations east of Greenwich	
1 The Albis	31°	56°15'	9°	54°15'
2 Extending point after the Albis	32°	56°50'	9°48!	54°50'
3 Northernmost point	38°	59°30'	14°	57°30'

The converted locations were identified as:			Conversion to locations east of Fortunate Islands	
1 Elbe	9°	54°15' or 53°15'	31°	56°15'
2 Dagebüll	8°40'	54°50'	30°45'	56°50'
3 Cape Skagen	10°45'	57°45'	34°30'	59°50'

Ptolemy's locations and the converted locations compared (longitude only)			
Location	Ptolemy's data	Converted data	Difference
1	31°	31°	0
2	32°	30°45'	− 1°15'
3	38°40'	34°30'	+ 4°10'

Total + 2°55'

The 2°55' rounded up to 3° were responsible for the inaccuracy in the location at 31° and 34°.

Figure 3. Chart explaining the theoretical location of the Albis (I) at 31° and the Albis (II) at 34°.

4°30'. One could not find better proof for the conclusion that the Suebos and the Oder are one and the same river. Ptolemy has a distance of 2°30' (i.e., 2°) between the Suebos and the Chalusos. The distance between the Oder and the Warnow is 2°30'; thus, his distance is shorter than ours by 20% (see figure 2).

The total distance between the Elbe and the Vistula is fairly acceptable. The distance between the Chalusos and the Vistula is either accurate, or shorter than our computation. However, his distance between
the Chalusos and the Albis is much longer than that between our Elbe
and Warnow. Ptolemy placed the Albis at 31°, and the Chalusos at 37°,
leaving a distance of six degrees between them (i.e., of about 4°48 ').
The actual distance between the Elbe at 9°, and the Warnow at 12°, is
three degrees only. Consequently, Ptolemy's dimension should be reduced by about two or three of his degrees. This would shorten his
total distance from the Albis to the Vistula to about twelve degrees,
and would be in almost complete agreement with the modern measurement of ten degrees. At present, it is not known whether the Albis
should be located at 33° or at 34° and the Chalusos at 34° or at 35°. A
proper correction of his coordinates will be possible only after revising
the data pertaining to Jutland.[9] A temporary arbitrary decision would
be no solution. In this study, therefore, Ptolemy's location of the
Chalusos at 37° has not been changed; the distance between the Albis
and the Chalusos is treated as if it were either six or three Ptolemaic
degrees. This distance bears some influence upon the location of that
mysterious river, the Viadua.

Generally speaking, Ptolemy's location of the Chalusos, Suebos, and
Vistula fairly agrees with that of the modern Warnow, Oder, and Vistula. The estuary of the Viadua is incorrectly placed at 40°30 '. The
erroneous location must have been the result of a combination of data
obtained from two sources; though the assumption that Ptolemy used
more than one source can be supported by indirect evidence only, since
no direct evidence is available, it is not unreasonable to suppose that he
consulted several sources.

It is known that for the description of the northwestern and northern coasts of Europe, Ptolemy used the works of earlier Greek geographers and supplemented their information with material collected
from sailing charts. These charts were guides compiled for practical
nautical purposes. In that part of the world, navigation was predominantly coastal; the charts, therefore, contained fewer distances across
the open sea and more detailed descriptions of the shore. They recorded exact distances between such fixed points as were useful for
orientation and for estimating the length of a voyage. Estuaries of
major rivers, natural harbors, trading centers, and certain characteristic
features of the shore were excellent orientation points. General physiographic or ethnographic features were of secondary value. No sailing

chart describing a voyage eastward to the Vistula would have omitted the estuary of the Albis. This river was well known to the Greeks and Romans; it was a trading center, and marked a basic change in the course of the voyage. From here on, ancient sailors would start sailing around Jutland, changing their course from east to north. At the cape of Skagen they would turn south until they reached the southwestern corner of the Baltic Sea. The estuary of the Chalusos or its environs was of equal significance. It marked the end of the trip around Jutland, and indicated another change in the course, this time from south to east. The following two places, the Suebos and the Vistula, were estuaries of notable rivers and terminal points of trade routes. There was no remarkable point at $42°30'$ (i.e., $17°$ east of Greenwich), other than the estuary of the Słupia (Stolpe), a small and insignificant river. The ancient sailors must have passed dozens of such rivers. The obvious conclusion is that the Viadua was not recorded in the sailing chart Ptolemy presumably used, and that its location was inserted from another source. This other source must have been either a second sailing chart or an itinerary (see figure 4).

If it was a sailing chart, it could have contained either the correct or the erroneous distance between the Albis and the Viadua, assuming in this case that the Viadua and the Oder are one and the same river. The distance between them was either $5°30'$ (Ptolemaic degrees), if measured from $34°$, or $8°30'$, if measured from $31°$. Ptolemy must have been aware of the fact that he had two locations for the estuary of the Albis, one at $31°$, the other at $34°$. He favored the location at $31°$; however, having fixed the location of the Chalusos wrongly at $37°$, he realized that to eliminate contradictions, he would either have to add or to subtract the distance of three degrees, and compute a proper location. In this particular case, the second chart included the erroneous three degrees, counting $8°30'$ from $31°$ to $39°30'$. Nevertheless, Ptolemy suspected an error, since at $39°30'$ he had a valid location for the Suebos; by no means could he have known that the Viadua was just another name for the Suebos. Since two rivers could not have existed at the same geographical point, it was obvious to him that one of the figures was wrong. The location of the Suebos was fixed already, therefore he added the three degrees to $39°30'$ and established the location of the Viadua at $42°30'$. This is a possible solution to the problem of Ptolemy's computation. However, manipulation of distances of two or three degrees to a total of fourteen, which may be reduced eventually to twelve, and a comparison of these distances with another system of coordinates that totals only ten degrees, may lead to a coincidental

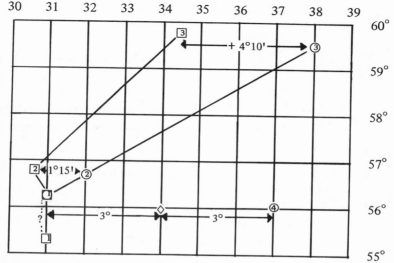

Figure 4. Diagram illustrating Ptolemy's distortion of tne west coast of Jutland, responsible for the elongated distance between the Albis and Chalusos.

Ptolemy's locations:
① Albis ② the extending point after the Albis
③ the northernmost point ④ Chalusos

Modern locations:
1 Elbe 2 Dagebüll 3 Cape Skagen
◊ tentative second location of the Albis at 34° (i.e., Ptolemy's error of three degrees corrected either from 31° to the east or from 37° to the west)

figure that does not reflect the historical truth. Ptolemy may have combined data from two sailing charts, but this possibility cannot be satisfactorily proven (see figure 5).

The assumption that the location of the Viadua was taken from an itinerary stands on firmer ground. Itineraries in the Oder-Vistula region followed a general south-north direction. They were not the safest tools to describe the east-west location of a point. Let us suppose that Ptolemy possessed an accurate description of the trade route along the Oder, and that this itinerary had correct distances from place to place, but the directions were not always precisely indicated. The directions between northeast and northwest, for example, could have been expressed in broader terms, such as generally northern, slightly toward the north, etc., causing a possible dislocation ranging between forty-five and ninety radial degrees. Under these circumstances, the partial distances from the Moravian Gate, or the crossing point of the ancient amber route at the Oder near Wrocław, added in degrees to the final

General assumption: the location of the Albis was fixed before Ptolemy located any other place at the Baltic Sea.

First source for the Baltic Sea
A sailing chart with correct distances between the Vistula-Suebos-Chalusos and an unknown or misinterpreted point (perhaps the Albis at 34° or 35°)

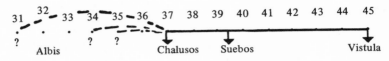

Second source for the Baltic Sea, if another sailing chart was used
A second sailing chart containing additional information about the Viadua, with a wrong distance of 8°30' between the Albis at 31° and Viadua at 39°30'

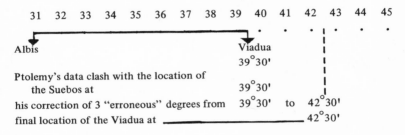

Figure 5. Diagram illustrating Ptolemy's use of possible sources leading to the wrong location of the estuary of the Viadua at 42°30'.

place on the Baltic shore, could account for a deviation of several longitude degrees at the terminal point. It is interesting to note that this crossing point at the Oder and Ptolemy's location of the estuary of the Viadua have the same geographical longitude, i.e., 17° east of Greenwich. The comparison of these two points shows a shifting of direction from northwest to north.

There are some indications that Ptolemy used such an itinerary describing the trade route along the Oder, since he mentions a few Lugian tribes who lived in the territory of modern Silesia, and who are otherwise unknown (see figure 6). Unfortunately, not enough information is available at present to figure out the progressive deviation toward the east. His description contains very little about the Viadua. It is limited to a small area near the coast. But, scanty as it is, it contains enough evidence to demonstrate that an itinerary was used as a source of information, and that the location of the estuary is wrong.

Ptolemy reported two tribes living near the estuary: the Sidinoi, west of the Rugikleioi (a name corrected from Rutikleioi) on its east

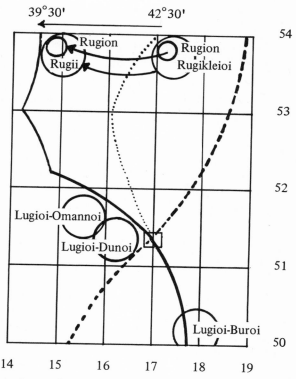

The Rugii are known from Tacitus' text; the Lugioi-Buroi, Lugioi-Dunoi, Lugioi-Omannoi, Rugikleioi, and Rugion are peoples and places near the trade route along the Oder known to Ptolemy.

Legend

─────── general course of the Oder and the trade route along it
▬ ▬ ▬ general course of the ancient amber route
······· Ptolemy's gradual deviation from northwest to north
☐ crossing point of the amber route at the Oder near Wroclaw

Figure 6. Diagram illustrating Ptolemy's use of possible sources leading to the wrong location of the estuary of the Viadua at 42°30'.

side. At a distance of twenty minutes south of the estuary (i.e., about 75 kilometers) he recorded a place called Rugion. The distance of about 75 kilometers inland favors the conclusion that an itinerary, and not a sailing chart, was used. The names Rugion and Rugikleioi are related to the name Rugii. In Tacitus' time the Rugii lived at the seashore, close to the Oder (see pp. 96-98). Since Ptolemy placed Rugion and the Rugikleioi east of the Viadua, and not east of the Suebos, the relocation of the estuary of the Viadua from 42°30′ to 39°30′ is justified. The conclusion is quite apparent that the Suebos and the Viadua are one and the same river, identical with the modern Oder. This conclusion is suggested as a final solution of the controversial issue of the Oder in ancient times.

Complex linguistic evaluation will shed more light on this complex geographical issue. The name Suebos can be interpreted either as the 'river of the Suebi,' or emendated to Swikos, Swibos, Swinos, and in its last form recognized as the Germanic name of the Oder. The name Viadua (Viasduas, Viados) is considered to be a name of either Germanic or Slavic origin. [10] The name Guthalus, mentioned by Pliny as a river east of the Vistula, and by Solinus as west of this river, is discussed later in connection with Pliny's information about the Goths. The origin of this name is similar to Suebos: as Suebos meant the 'river of the Suebi,' Guthalus was the 'river of the Goths.'

The four names of the Oder can be divided into two groups. The first group contains the forms Oder and Viadua, apparently very old names used by local populations. It is not certain whether they were of Germanic, Slavic, or other origin. The second group consists of the forms Suebos and Guthalus, which were foreign appellations, invented by the Greek or Roman merchants. The etymologies of the names of the Oder do not reveal whether during the first two centuries A.D. the region along the Oder was inhabited by Germanic or Slavic peoples. The variety of etymological explanations, however, indicates that several peoples knew the river by different names, and this indication fits in with my earlier geographical interpretation.

The ethnic picture changed approximately at the estuary of the Lusatian Neisse. At this point, the border of the eastern culture crossed the Oder, embracing a sizable portion of the country in the west. There is no doubt that this was the territory of the Lugii, a group of tribes who occupied modern Silesia and parts of Great Poland. Here, at the Middle Oder, the first migration of the Goths came to a stop. The Goths were either stopped by the Lugii, or decided to settle north or west of them. This area became their new homeland for over a century.

To summarize, their migratory route started at various points of departure on the west coast of Sweden, and proceeded southward, heading toward the Danish Islands. There were, probably, many ways of sailing through this group of islands. From their southern tips, the route went toward the shore of Mecklenburg (or Schleswig), then eastward along the Baltic coast to the estuary of the Oder, and from that point south to the region of the Middle Oder (see Map 10).

Map 10. The migratory route of the Goths from Sweden to the Middle Oder according to the author.

The exact time of the Gothic migration is not known. Scholars today are inclined to assume and almost unanimously agree that this event took place at the beginning of our era. This time has been set by archaeologists and historians who were under the impression that the Gothic migration was an invasion that ended in the conquest of Pomerania. However, it has been established that the Goths did not conquer Pomerania, and that their migration might not have been a single thrust of the entire tribe or its major part. Large-scale naval operations, mass invasion, and conquest may be excluded in view of many factors. It is more plausible that the migration was carried out by small groups and took place in several waves. This type of migration required many years or even decades. In Maroboduus' time the Goths are mentioned as one of the tribes or tribal units of the Oder-Vistula region. This means that their migration started earlier than the year 1 A.D., probably during the second half of the first century B.C.

 Assuming that the Goths entered East-Central Europe via the Oder river, their first settlements lay in less populated areas near the Oder and modern Bohemia, the homeland of the Boii, which was invaded at a later period by the Marcomanni and other Germanic tribes. Some Lugian tribes, which had stopped the Goths in their march southward, were now their neighbors.

In the beginning all worked well; the migration was a success. The number of settlers and the size of the territory gradually increased. During the first two decades of the first century of our era the group of newcomers grew large enough to be recognized as a tribe. The year 19 A.D. is given as the first undisputed date of their presence in the new homeland as recorded in Tacitus' *Annals*. Actually, they had been known to be there several years earlier. Strabo mentions them in describing a situation prevailing between the years 1 and 18 A.D. (The reference to Strabo was purposely omitted previously because the form of the tribal name found in his texts available at present needed some clarification.)

The theory that the second homeland of the Goths was situated near the Middle Oder and Bohemia is based upon the fact that most of the historical data recorded in or pertaining to the first century of our era point to that region, and the other sources of the same period that do not do so, do not contradict this location.

The Goths of the first century are mentioned in four geographical or historical works: Strabo's *Geography* (written sometime before 18 A.D.), Pliny's *Natural History* (completed in 77 A.D.), Tacitus' *Germania* (98 A.D.) and his *Annals* (ca. 116 A.D.).

The earliest writer is Strabo, who lived in the time of Augustus and Tiberius. His *Geography* is a summary of knowledge about the entire world as it was known in his day. It is, as Bunbury writes, "not only the most important geographical work that has come down to us from antiquity; but it is unquestionably one of the most important ever produced by any Greek or Roman writer."[1] It does contain errors and faulty judgments in general concepts, as well as in the description of some individual parts of the world; nevertheless, Strabo was a scrupulous and critical writer who did his best with the material available to him. His description of Germania and the countries farther north and east is the most defective part of his work. He should not be blamed for this, however, since he wrote it at a time when the Romans were only beginning to gain direct knowledge about that part of the world. Roman armies penetrated the interior of Germania, reached the Elbe, and crossed it, but never advanced farther east. Strabo made use of all the material and discoveries brought back by these military expeditions. He had very little information about the country east of the Elbe, and said that it is an unknown land; at least, he knew of no traveler who had explored this region, and the Roman armies had not advanced beyond the river.[2] Although he called it an unknown land his information on it was valuable though scanty. His description of the country of the Marcomanni, ruled by Maroboduus, contains important data regarding the Oder-Vistula region.

Maroboduus was a Marcoman, a man of remarkable ability and organizing power. Gaius Velleius Paterculus calls him a "barbarian by birth rather than by his way of thinking."[3] Maroboduus spent his youth in Rome, was educated there, and served in the Roman army. After returning to his native country, he became the leader of his tribe. In 9 or 8 B.C. he led the Marcomanni and the Quadi into Boihaemum (modern Bohemia and Moravia). This country was inhabited by the Celtic Boii (part of whom had moved out earlier), and by some Germanic tribes who had settled in its northern part. By the first year of our era the conquest of Boihaemum was completed. The Marcomanni settled in Bohemia, the Quadi in Moravia. During the following years, Maroboduus extended the frontiers of his country by subduing several tribes living north and east of Bohemia. He became one of the most powerful Germanic leaders, differing from the others, in that his goal was not merely vain military glory and conquest. He tried to organize his country in a more advanced fashion, improving its economic level and encouraging trade. Many foreign merchants took up residence in his country, and its capital became a prosperous trade center between Rome and the countries of the North.[4]

The sudden power and ambitions of Maroboduus were not regarded with favor in Rome. The existence of a well-organized state at the periphery of the Empire interfered with Rome's idea of how Germanic affairs should be handled. The Roman dislike grew to such an extent that in 6 A.D. two Roman armies—one from Carnuntum, and another from the Rhine—were ready to march against Maroboduus. The campaign was prevented only by unrest in Pannonia and Dalmatia that kept the legions busy for a few years.

Despite all good intentions, the political situation worked against Maroboduus. He tried desperately to maintain friendly relations with Rome, from which his country would profit economically, and, at the same time, to remain neutral in any Germanic-Roman conflict. After the battle in the Teutoburg Forest he was approached by Arminius, chieftain of the Cherusci, who tried to convince him of the necessity of joint action against the Empire. Maroboduus rejected this proposal by Arminius. The following year the Romans asked for his participation in a campaign against some western Germanic tribes. Once again, Maroboduus refused. His policy in foreign affairs had dangerous consequences; he gained no friends on either side. As soon as Germanicus was instructed to abandon all plans for further campaigns into Germania, Arminius turned against Maroboduus. Armed conflict took place in 17 A.D. and Maroboduus lost the battle. He had requested aid from the Romans, but now it was they who refused. Some of the tribes and people in his own camp revolted and deserted him. During the following year, or in 19 A.D., he was overthrown by Catualda. Escaping to Rome, he was granted asylum at Ravenna where he lived until his death in 41 A.D.

His successor was another Marcoman, although some authors think of him as a Goth.[5] According to Tacitus, Catualda was a young man whom Maroboduus had driven into exile. He found refuge among the Goths, who, resenting their own submission, gave him armed support against Maroboduus. It was not the Gothic army alone that caused Maroboduus' downfall, as Catualda had won the support of the corrupt Marcomannic nobles.[6] If the exact time of Catualda's exile were known it would be an invaluable aid to our study. It would seem that his exile was of short duration, since he was still a young man when he took over the leadership of the Marcomanni. More than likely, the date of his exile should be placed sometime after the battle against Arminius. He may have been, so to speak, the victim of a general purge. It may have happened at a time when Maroboduus' star was rapidly falling, a circumstance which encouraged the Goths to give Catualda the necessary support. While Maroboduus was still at the peak of his power, they would not have dared to offer asylum to Catualda. Therefore, it may be assumed that his exile lasted from approximately 17 to 19 A.D.

Scholars disagree as to the proper spelling of the name of the Goths in Strabo. The text reads *Butonas*.[7] Many authors believe that this spelling is a corrupt form of *Gutonas*; Ludwig Schmidt alone strongly objects to this emendation. According to him, the only proof that the Goths ever were subject to the rule of Maroboduus is the spelling *Gutonas* instead of *Butonas*; the fact that Catualda had found refuge among them and that they aided him in the overthrow of Maroboduus speaks against any relationship of dependence. Instead of the Goths, one should rather think of the Ptolemaic Bateinoi, or the Burgundians as subject to his rule.[8]

Schmidt's argument is not convincing. Between the forms *Butonas* and *Gutonas* there is a difference of only one letter, a common mistake in dictation or transcription, which is more plausible than the corrections of some modern scholars. Perhaps Strabo's informant erroneously heard a *b* sound instead of a *g* sound. Schmidt's correction is certainly farfetched. He was probably led to his conclusion by the common belief that the Goths ruled over a large kingdom at the Lower Vistula. Had this been the case, Maroboduus' influence would have reached the shores of the Baltic Sea, which is an impossibility. On the contrary, Strabo's account of the Goths is one of the strongest arguments against the idea that the tribe ever possessed a large state on the Baltic shore. Schmidt's correction is typical of other scholars of this period. If a known fact, reported by a reliable ancient author, does not fit into the generally accepted pattern, the text of the ancient author is corrected to fit the pattern.

There is no contradiction between the location of the Goths and the relationship between them and Catualda or Maroboduus. One should certainly look for the Goths where they lived, i.e., in the proximity of Maroboduus' state, and not on the Baltic shore. Their submission to Maroboduus' rule, and the fact of Catualda's exile, are two elements which differed in time. Tiberius was not ready to go to war because a certain Maroboduus ruled over a certain land called Bohemia. When he intended to lead his armies into Bohemia in 6 A.D. this meant that Rome was alarmed at Maroboduus' rapid rise in power and wanted to prevent further expansion. The conquest of the tribes in Silesia and Lusatia had taken place before 6 A.D. Catualda's exile lasted from about 17 to 19 A.D.

An interesting emendation of the name *Butonas* was made in Wolf-gang Aly's study. At first sight it appears daring but it is based on solid ground. Aly noticed the absence of the Burgundians from Strabo's text, and instead of the form *Butones* he suggested the reading *Bu(rgun-diones kai Gu)tones*.[9] Aly's emendation gives rise to much discussion. In later times, the Burgundians and the Goths were neighbors. It is possible that such a relationship might have existed already in Strabo's time. This would mean that the Burgundians too had been subject to Maroboduus' rule.

Strabo's *Geography* describes the country of the Marcomanni as being enclosed by the arch of the Hercynian Forest; that is, south of it.[10] By the Hercynian Forest he understood all the ranges of mountains extending from the sources of the Danube to the Carpathians, which also encircled Bohemia to the west, north, and east. His description agrees with the later location of the Marcomanni and Quadi in Tacitus.[11] In addition, the *Geography* mentions the peoples outside Bohemia whom Maroboduus had conquered. These were "the Lugii, a big nation; the Zumi, Gutones, Mugilones, Sibini, and the Semnones, a big nation of the Suebi."[12] If there is any order in the sequence of the names in Strabo's listing, it can only be geographical. The Lugii, listed first, lived near the Oder; the Semnones, who dwelt near the Elbe, are the last people mentioned. Thus, the beginning and the end of the listing indicate a general east-west or southeast-northwest direction, following the curve of the Hercynian Forest. Consequently, the four remaining small tribes must have lived between the Lugii and the Semnones. This may not be a strict geometrical order, but it can be assumed that the Zumi lived closer to the Lugii than to the Semnones, and the Sibini closer to the Semnones than to the Lugii. As little as may be gained from such an assumption, it does add some details to Strabo's scarce information.

Maroboduus' goal of organizing the country may account for his territorial expansion. He attempted to improve economic conditions by promoting trade, by inviting merchants from abroad, and by establishing centers for trade with the north. Trade routes and their safety were essential factors in promoting commerce. The more trade routes he controlled, the more prosperous the country would become.

Several arteries of traffic traversed Boihaemum. There was the ancient amber route linking the Adriatic with the Baltic. It entered the country of the Marcomanni at Vindobona (Vienna), went north to Eborodunum (Brno?), turned east, and passed the Sudeten through the basin of Kłodzko. At Wrocław the road forked; the old branch headed toward Kalisz (the ancient Kalisia), and a more recent branch led down the Oder. Another road branched off the ancient amber route north of Eborodunum and led down the Elbe. Two roads, coming from Carnuntum and Brigetio in Pannonia, met at Carrodunum. From this point, the route passed through the Moravian Gate, where it forked; one branch went along the Vistula, the other along the Oder (Map 11).

This network of roads running through Maroboduus' domain indicates the intent of his conquests, the direction of which coincides with the direction of the roads. He was not interested in the traffic through the Moravian Gate, as the Quadi would profit from that trade route more than the Marcomanni, but he was very much concerned with the roads along the Oder and the Elbe. His conquest of the Goths, eventually also of the Burgundians, and of the Semnones, extended his influence to the farther reaches of the two rivers.

Two major military campaigns, one along the Oder and another along the Elbe, and other acts of political pressure were necessary to control the two vital trade arteries. Maroboduus' main object was the control over the Lugii and Semnones; the subjection of the smaller tribes was a matter of secondary importance. He did not intend to conquer all Lugian tribes who lived as far as the Middle Vistula. A territory of such extent was beyond his reach. He was interested only in the most western portion of Lugia, which probably comprised the present provinces of Wrocław and Zielona Góra. The eastern parts of Lugia and Upper Silesia were of little economic value to him.

In Strabo's text the Lugii are called "a big nation." About eighty years after Strabo, Tacitus mentions the Lugii again, saying that their name is widely spread and applies to many tribes, and he lists the names of the five most powerful ones. [13] Several decades later, Ptolemy records three individual Lugian tribes, different from those mentioned by Tacitus. [14] Between about 50 and 180 A.D., Lugian tribes were involved in many wars between the Germanic tribes, or against the Roman Empire, and fought in the Danubian region. According to Slavic historians, they occupied the huge territory between the Oder, Vistula and Noteć, almost a third of present-day Poland. [15] During the prehistoric period discussed in this study the Lugii should be placed within the cultural district of Przeworsk, which is a local subdivision of the Venedian or Pit-Grave culture. Accordingly, they should be classified as Venedian or Slavic peoples, which will evoke sharp protests on the part of the followers of the East-Germanic theory. These scholars do not like to use the name Lugii, and prefer the term Vandals instead. They

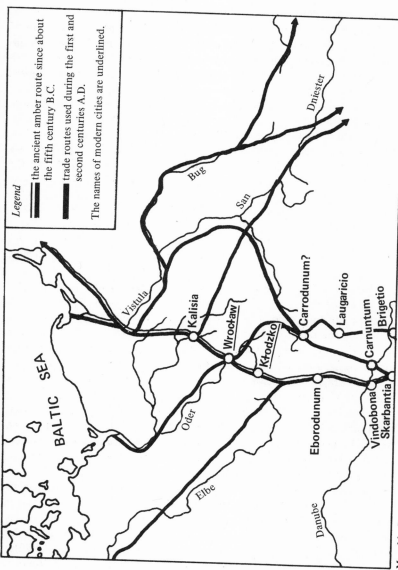

Map 11. Trade routes of the Oder-Vistula region.

Legend

━━━ the ancient amber route since about
the fifth century B.C.

━━━ trade routes used during the first and
second centuries A.D.

The names of modern cities are underlined.

BALTIC SEA

Vistula

Kalisia

Wrocław

Kłodzko

Carrodunum?

Laugaricio

Carnuntum

Brigetio

Eborodunum

Vindobona

Skarbantia

Oder

Elbe

Danube

San

Bug

Dniester

speak of an independent tribal culture, which they call Vandalic. Territorially, the Vandalic culture agrees with that of Przeworsk, with the exception that the northern part of Przeworsk has been split off and called Burgundian. The tribal culture in this area was ascribed to the Vandals, who allegedly came from Scandinavia before the Rugii and the Goths.

Among German historians only Steche has disagreed absolutely with the terminology used by archaeologists and has objected to the improper use of historical names. It is his opinion that it is not correct to use the name Vandals instead of Lugii. Prior to the Marcomannic wars there existed no Germanic people with the name Vandals. Pliny's Vandili was a collective name, equivalent to the modern term East-Germani. It included also the Burgundians and the Goths, who were of different origin than the so-called Silesian Vandals. After 170 A.D., the name Vandals referred only to the group of tribes who entered northern Hungary under the leadership of the Hasdingi. They revived the old collective term Vandili in the variant Vandali. No written ancient source confirms the forms *Vandili* or *Vandali* in Silesia. [16]

Many historians followed the lead of Kossinna and other archaeologists who were responsible for the concept of the Vandalic culture. Despite Steche's objection, general and special reference works keep repeating the old story in variously modified versions. First, there is the thesis that the Vandals were an individual tribe that immigrated from Scandinavia, and that their name originated in their Scandinavian homeland, where it must have been a true tribal name. Pliny is quoted in support of another theory. The name Vandili, as he is supposed to understand it, is a collective appellation for the East-Germanic tribes. This means that no Vandili ever existed as an individual tribal unit. The terms Vandili and Vandals are treated as if they were synonymous by other authors, who do not take into consideration the consequences of their interpretation. In the light of their theory, the Goths, the Burgundians, and two smaller tribes were part of the Vandals or subject to their rule. Some scholars have been puzzled by the fact that the ancient historical sources from Strabo to Ptolemy did not mention the Vandals as an individual tribe. They were, however, easily satisfied with the explanation derived from archaeological theories that the Lugii and the Vandals were the same people. Soon, they agreed that the form Vandals was of ethnic nature, while the form Lugii was a sacral name, denoting a regional cult. [17]

Combining these interpretations, the following picture emerges.

Prior to Strabo's time, the Vandals used the old tribal name Vandali, which in prehistoric times is not recorded in Scandinavia or anywhere else. During the period from about 18 to 150 A.D., a time when historical evidence is available, they changed their name to Lugii. After 150 A.D., about three generations later, the old forgotten name of Vandali was revived, after it had not been used for one hundred and thirty years. One circumstance was overlooked; the invaders who appeared in northern Hungary under the leadership of the Hasdingi were not a single tribe, but a mixture of peoples. Steche's straightforward explanation of the name seems to be the only logical account of the matter.

Some Polish and other Slavic prehistorians and historians tend to disbelieve the fantastic history of the metamorphoses of the Vandals. Indeed, it is easy to question it. It is unrealistic to believe that a group of farmers who in their original Scandinavian homeland occupied a score or maybe a hundred settlements would have been able within a short time to control an area larger than present-day Poland. Cases have been known in history when expansions were carried out with unusual speed, but as a rule, colonization is a long-drawn-out process stretching over many generations. Granting that the expansion of the Vandals was extraordinarily rapid, the fact has to be considered that a small number of conquerors would have had to spread over a huge territory. They could not have engaged in the production of tools and articles of daily use, and would have had to rely entirely on the production of the enslaved native population. The forms of material culture in the new homeland were bound to be different from those of Scandinavia. It would be impossible to trace the Vandals in the new country by archaeological methodology. The Vandals and the Lugii must have been two different human and spatial groups.

For some time the Lugii were considered to have been a purely Germanic people. Long ago, Polish historians suspected that they were not. Wojciech Kętrzyński spoke of them as Slavs as early as 1868, and so did Edward and Wilhelm Bogusławski in several works published between 1886 and 1902; however, their arguments failed to convince. The issue of the Slavic origin of the Lugii was raised again by Niederle, who derived their name from a proto-Slavic root. Ardent discussions have been conducted ever since to decide whether the name is of Slavic origin or not. They are almost exclusively in the field of linguistics; no final solution has been reached as yet. Highlights of this controversy were summarized by Tymieniecki and Henryk Łowmiański.[18]

Linguistic explanations of the name of the Lugii range widely. In

Schmidt's opinion, the provenience of the name is uncertain.[19] Hans Krahe thinks that it is Illyrian, while Łowmianski defends its Celtic origin.[20] Much, Niederle, Max Vasmer, and others do not exclude the possibility of its Celtic origin, favoring at the same time a Germanic or Slavic interpretation.[21] The issue is, however, whether the name is Slavic or Germanic.

By linguists who favor a Germanic etymology, the name Lugii is derived from several formative elements. Much mentions the Germanic *lugja–, (German lügnerisch 'deceitful, lying'), and the Irish luige (H*lugio–), (German Eid 'oath'), which could have had the meaning of Eidgenossen 'companions bound by an oath')[22] Schönfeld's explanation is similar. He derives the name from the Gothic root liugan, (German heiraten 'to marry'), Old Irish lu(i)ge (German Eid 'oath'); Lugii, therefore, would mean Genossen 'companions'.[23] Schönfeld's interpretation was adopted recently by Vasmer who, like Much, also thinks of the possibility of a Celtic origin.[24] A different explanation is offered by L. Schmitz, who says that "their name contains the root lug, which in the Old German signifies a wood or marsh, and still has the same meaning in the Slavonic; it seems, therefore, to be descriptive of the nation dwelling in the plains of the Vistula and Oder."[25]

The name of the Lugii has been discussed also by several scholars who incline toward a Slavic etymology,[26] and a conclusion was formulated by Lehr-Spławiński, who tried to integrate linguistic with archaeological evidence by placing the Lugii in the territory of the Pit-Grave culture. According to him, the name is derived from the proto-Slavic root lugŏ ‖ lagŏ (or *logŏ ‖ lugŏ), 'marsh, brushwood, grove, meadow,' with the suffix -ones = Slavic -ane, i.e., *Logiane ‖ Lugiane, Latin abbreviated form Lugii.[27] Thus, the name Lugii would indicate 'people of the lowland, forests,' etc. After a thorough analysis of the source material, comparing it with linguistic and archaeological evidence, Tymieniecki came to the conclusion that the Lugii were Slavs. The name itself is of Slavic origin, and applied originally to the Slavic tribes inhabiting the Polish Lowland. In time, with the gradual expansion of the Slavs, it came to denominate the tribes of the submontane and montane Sudeten and Beskid regions. It was, so to say, the Slavic linguistic counterpart of the foreign name Venedi, and contained the concept of an intertribal organization or federation of tribes.[28]

Tymieniecki's view is not shared by all Polish scholars. In his History of Poland Gieysztor writes: "The assumption is that the tribal name of the Lugii may refer to those Celtic groups. Other scholars, however,

place them among Slavic tribes," and "the name of the Lugii was eventually extended to include all Celtic, Germanic, and Slavic tribes which,
no matter what their origins, lived in this area."[29]

The question of the ethnic origin of the Lugii is not easy to solve,
since it concentrates chiefly on linguistic evaluation. The ancient historical sources are too vague to contribute to a valid solution. Archaeologists will stand on firmer ground only after it has become known
what peoples produced the Pit-Grave culture. At the present stage of
research, the Slavic provenance of this culture seems credible. If so, the
Lugii, who lived in the ambit of this culture, should have been Slavs. As
a consequence, etymologies derived from Slavic languages should gain
strength, the more so because etymologies derived from other languages
refer to peoples that were not the chief inhabitants of this cultural area;
otherwise the meanings derived etymologically are not descriptive of
the Lugii as a large ethnic group. The Celts never advanced as far as the
Lower Vistula, and Germanic peoples would have had strange names,
such as "liars," "companions," "married people," etc. The commonly
accepted Slavic etymology describes the Lugii as the "people of the
lowland," etc. This, in itself, is a geographical term, which should not
be rigidly applied in an ethnic sense, i.e., with the meaning that all the
Lugian people were Slavic. In the mosaiclike ethnic composition of the
area during the first two centuries of our era, it is possible that among
the Slavic Lugian tribes there were also Lugian tribes of non-Slavic
origin. As the peoples of the Polish Lowland gradually expanded toward the west, this regional name widened its range to include also
areas which were neither plains nor lowlands. These tentative solutions
did not, however, put an end to the debate, and the question of the
ethnic origin of the Lugii is still open and subject to further discussion.

The absence of a final solution to the Lugian controversy calls for
the statement of a few facts and working hypotheses which should help
delineate the tentative frontier of the Lugian territory, especially of its
western part. These are:

1. The fact that ancient writers placed the abodes of the Lugii in an
area situated between the Elbe and the Vistula. According to Strabo,
they lived in the vicinity of the Marcomani; Tacitus' text suggests a
location near the Middle Oder and the country east of it; Ptolemy
mentions three Lugian tribes inhabiting the country of modern Silesia,
and one of them living in the foothills of the Sudeten.

2. The fact that Strabo's account of the Lugii and other tribes
subdued by Maroboduus refers to a situation existing before 6 A.D. The

territory of the Lugii should be placed therefore within the limits of the Przeworsk (Pit-Grave, East Germanic) culture of the Late La Tène period (150-1 B.C.). This is the western part of present-day Poland.

3. The assumption that the most acceptable etymology of the name *Lugii* is derived form the proto-Slavic *lugъ*. According to it, the Lugii were peoples of the lowlands, forests, and marshy districts. The name agrees with the physiographic structure of the Oder valley and the plains of northern Silesia and Great Poland.

To a certain extent, the assumption that the Lugii lived in the lowland is confirmed by Tacitus' report. "The name of the Lugii is widely known and spreads over many tribes (*civitates*). It is sufficient to mention the most powerful ones: the Harii, Helveconae, Manimi, Helisii, Naharvali," he wrote. [30] There are only two ways in which Tacitus could have learned about the Lugii and their more important tribes or units. The names could have been selected from a general survey on the Lugii, which is an entirely impossible assumption. The only acceptable explanation is that he repeated information obtained from merchants' reports. These reports probably did not cover the entire territory occupied by Lugian tribes, and would most likely be restricted to the parts of the country that were visited by Greek or Roman merchants. They would be observations made along a trade route. In this particular case, Tacitus might have used an itinerary of the ancient amber route through Kalisz. This conclusion is drawn from the fact that he mentions the Helisii among the more important Lugian tribes.

The Helisii (variants: *Helysii, Haliosnae,* etc.) [31] have been associated with Ptolemy's Kalisia, the modern Kalisz. Bronislaw Biliński has thoroughly analyzed and investigated these names. As he reports, among the several variants, the emended form *Halisii* is preferred by Schütte, Perret, and others. They drew attention to the resemblance between Tacitus' *Helisii – Halisii* and Ptolemy's *Kalisia*. The phonetic value of both names is the same, since the Gothic *h* corresponds with the Dacian *k*. Consequently, Schütte tried to derive the name *Kalisia* from the Germanic form *Halisii*. Disagreeing with them, Biliński proved that the form *Halisii* should be corrected to the proto-Slavic *Kalisii*, [32] which is a more acceptable etymology. Kalisia was an important trading center along the amber route, and there are many place names derived from the Slavic root *kal-* 'mud, marsh, dirt, filth,' meaning a "marshy place." [33] Kalisia was such a marshy place, and the people living in its vicinity were the Kalisii.

If Tacitus did not change the order mentioned in the itinerary, it may be assumed that the Harii, Helvecones, and Manimi lived near the amber route between Kłodzko, or Wrocław, and Kalisz, and the Naharvali between Kalisz and the lower Vistula. With a few exceptions, the ancient amber route between its course west of Wrocław and the Lower Vistula lay through lowlands, marshy places, and lake districts. It may be concluded that the Lugian territory corresponds with the present lowland of Silesia, the Oder valley, and parts of the plain of Great Poland. Its western border was close to the submontane zone of the Sudeten. Maroboduus did not conquer all of Lugia; this was beyond his reach. However, he must have acquired a sizable portion of it. He must have ruled at least over the present-day provinces of Zielona Góra and Wrocław. This was a territory large enough for its inhabitants belonging to Lugian tribes, to appear to Strabo as members of a numerous people.

The first of the smaller tribes mentioned by Strabo are the Zumi, who probably lived north or northwest of the Lugii. This would place them in the northeastern corner of the Sudeten. The tribe is not mentioned in any other source, and is otherwise unknown. Traditionally, the name is considered a corrupt form. Steche is very positive about it, pointing out that the sound z is unknown in the early Germanic languages.[34] He was, of course, convinced that the Zumi were of Germanic origin, believing that most of the tribes between the Elbe and the Vistula were Germanic. On the other hand, the sound z would not exclude the possibility of a Slavic origin. Vasmer is very positive that "in any case, the Zumoi are not Slavs," but he does not substantiate his statement.[35] The Slavists have not insisted that the name is of Slavic provenience. There is a possibility that it has something in common with the Ptolemaic Lugioi-Dunoi or Lugioi-Didunoi, who lived in exactly the same place as the Zumi.[36] The change from Dunoi to Zumoi requires the substitution of two letters in a short name, and this is a risky correction.[37] It would be justified only by the geographical congruity of the location of the Zumi and Duni. The Ptolemaic Duni (or Diduni) lived northeast of the Askiburgion mountains (by which Ptolemy understood the Sudeten, from the Jeseniky in the south to the Lusatian mountains in the north), and several scholars think that they were a Slavic people.

For the time being, the third tribe in Strabo's listing, the Goths, shall be omitted, since the next one, the Mugilones, is more easily located. Again, the form found in Strabo's text is considered corrupt by some scholars. The name, however, is strikingly similar to the proto-Slavic *mogyla, which means a 'high flat terrain' or 'small hill.'[38] The word *mogyla* appears in place names such as Mogilno, Mogila, Mogilev, etc. The Mugilones could have been a Slavic tribe with a name like *Mogylane,* meaning 'inhabitants of a hilly country.' Geographically, this makes sense, since they lived in the foothills of the Sudeten. In Slavic etymology, the name is traced as *Maguljane* ≥ *Mogyljane, Mogilanie,* which is based on the proto-Slavic *magula* ≥ *mogyla* (Polish *mogiła,* 'hill').[39] Phonetic objections were raised by Vasmer, who prefers a relationship between the tribal name *Mugilones* and a Gallic personal name *Mogillonius;* he thinks that the tribe was Celtic, and that its name was derived from the Irish *mogh* (German *gross,* 'great, big').[40]

The first to claim that the name of the Strabonian Mugilones is of Slavic origin was Niederle. He pointed out that Dietmar mentioned a *pagus Mogelini* and a *Mogilina urbs* near Meissen as early as the tenth century.[41] His suggestion that the Mugilones could have been Slavs was attacked by those specialists who prefer to reject a name as mutilated rather than accept a Slavic etymology that does not fit into the traditional pattern. Other scholars, however, endorse Niederle's thesis. Among them is Tadeusz Lehr-Spławiński, who wrote that the name is most likely Slavic, and to such extent resembles a Slavic form corresponding to the Polish *Mogilanie,* that it is difficult to doubt its Slavic origin. Phonetic objections raised against this interpretation are merely illusory.[42]

The Slavic origin of the name does not make a Slavic tribe of the Mugilones. However, Jazdzewski and Tymieniecki are positive that they were Slavs.[43] Considering the geographical location of the tribe, Slavic provenance is possible. Its northern, western, and, to a certain extent, southern, neighbors were all Germanic tribes: Goths, Semnones, Sibini, (or Silingae), and Marcomani. Only along its eastern and part of its southern border were the Lugii and Zumi, who could have been Slavs. It would be very strange if a Germanic tribe, almost surrounded by other Germanic tribes, should have been known only by a Slavic name.

Niederle's observation concerning the existence of a *pagus Mogelini* and a *Mogilina urbs* does not mean that the Mugilones have to be located near Meissen. The physiographic environment of Meissen is similar to that of Bautzen or Görlitz. The Mugilones, 'inhabitants of a hilly country,' can safely be placed in the northern slopes and foothills of the Sudeten, where their southern neighbors would have been the Zumi, and their eastern ones some Lugian tribes.

Fifth in the list of the tribes conquered by Maroboduus are the Sibini. The name *Sibinoi* is also considered a corrupt form, and is the subject of discussion. Schönfeld rejects earlier attempts to identify this tribe with Ptolemy's *Sudinoi,* a people who lived south of the Marcomanni, and with another tribe of the same name, living south of the Galindi. He suggests instead that they be identified with Ptolemy's *Seidinoi* (variant *Sideinoi*) corrected to **Seibinoi,* who lived at the estuary of the Oder. He maintains further that these Sibini were the most northern tribe under Maroboduus' rule. [44] His solution, however, is not quite acceptable, as it contains the idea that Marboduus' empire reached as far as the Baltic Sea.

A very daring but sound correction of the text was made by Steche. He thinks that the transmitted form *Sibini* is the result of errors made by copyists, and that the original form was *Silingi.* Written in Roman letters, the graphic picture looks like a drastic correction, but it is less so when written in Greek capitals. [45] His correction is based on a geographical observation. He noticed that in Strabo's list, the Sibini are mentioned directly before the Semnones, and should have been, therefore, their immediate neighbors. Ptolemy, on the other hand, places his Silingae below, i.e., south of the Semnones. [46] The locations of the Sibini and Silingae point to the same place. [47] Very frequently, the Silingae were placed in Lower Silesia, but some scholars, among them also Tymieniecki, favor a location of the tribe in Lower Lusatia, where Ptolemy had placed it. [48] It follows that Steche's correction is justified. The Sibini must have been the southern neighbors of the Semnones; they lived in Lusatia, on both sides of the Elbe; south of them was the country of the Marcomani, and east of them, that of the Mugilones.

Next mentioned in Strabo's text are the Semnones, a numerous people. They are well known from Tacitus' *Germania* 39 as the most ancient and renowned branch of the Suevi. Their territory lay in modern Brandenburg and Lusatia, [49] and the Elbe was its western border. [50]

The location of the Goths is now easy to determine. They occupied the land in the Middle Oder valley, situated on the west side of the river; a smaller part of their abodes may have lain east of the river. The Semnones were their neighbors in the west, the Mugilones and perhaps also the Sibini in the south, the Burgundians in the north, and Lugian tribes in the east, beyond the Neisse and the Oder (Map 12).

An additional remark should be made at this point regarding Aly's suggested reading of the name *Butones* as *Bu(rgundiones kai Gu)tones* (see above p. 71). If his correction is accepted, it would mean that the Burgundians were also subject to Maroboduus' rule. This finding would not contradict the results of our geographical investigation, since the

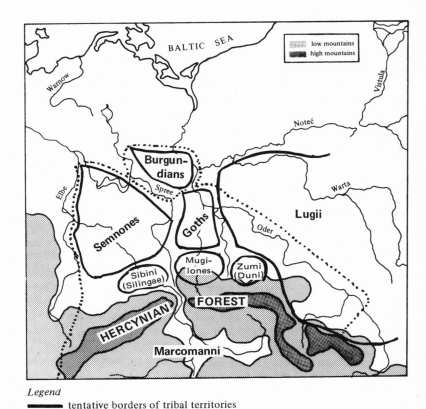

Legend
━━━━━ tentative borders of tribal territories
• • • • • tentative limits of Maroboduus' conquests

Map 12. Location of the Goths according to Strabo.

Burgundians were neighbors of the Goths in later times, a fact which has been concluded from the analysis of Pliny's text.

The source next in time to Strabo's *Geography* is Pliny the Elder's *Natural History*. Pliny was born in 23 or 24 A.D., and perished during the great eruption of Vesuvius in 79 A.D. He was a high official in the Roman administration and, among other assignments, served at the Upper and Lower Rhine. Being a prolific writer, he was the author of a history of his own time, as well as a history of the Germanic wars. Unfortunately, both works are lost to posterity. Only his main work, the *Natural History,* has survived. It consists of thirty-seven books, completed in 77 A.D. and edited later with some additions. Books

III-VI are devoted to geography. Modern historical geographers have found many faults in his work, and do not think as highly of him as of Strabo.[51] Nevertheless, Pliny's work contains valuable information about Germania, since many new discoveries had been made since Strabo's times. Pliny collected his data from both old and new sources, quoting in an almost modern fashion the authors from whom he took his information, or else introducing the data by the phrase "some people report" (*quidam . . . tradunt*). In his official capacity Pliny doubtlessly had access to information which otherwise was not available. The *Natural History* also contains some original observations of his own contributing to knowledge of Germania. Schmidt calls him "an excellent expert on Germanic affairs."[52]

Historical geographers may be right in criticizing Pliny's vague concept of the outer regions of Europe. In itself, it is not an accusation, and does not diminish the value of his reports on areas about which he had more complete information. In his description, the northern and western parts of the European continent are surrounded by the "Ocean," from the Ripaean mountains (the Urals) to Gades (Cadiz). Between these two points, he mentions several seas, islands, and rivers that cannot be identified. He was probably aware of the inexactitude of his reports, since he admits that more reliable information is offered in the description of the abodes of the Ingaevones, who lived on the "Continent," in the northern part of Germania. In what he calls "continental Germania" he distinguishes five major peoples: the Vandili, Ingaevones, Istaevones, Herminones, and Peucini-Bastarnae.[53] This obviously is not a systematic ethnographic description of Germania or a valid geographical division of the country. He also mentions, besides these five major groups, the Hilleviones of Scandinavia, a sizable people possessing 500 settlements *(pagi)*, and several small tribes at the Lower Rhine, such as the Nemetes, the Triboci, etc.[54]

Of the five major groups, the names Ingaevones, Istaevones, and Hermiones have a supratribal or regional character, covering many individual tribes. These three groups are generally placed in Jutland and the part of Germania between the Rhine and the Elbe.[55] The Peucini and Bastarnae are two branches of a people whose ethnic affiliation is still being disputed.[56] The majority of scholars consider them to have been of Germanic origin, while others think of them as Celts. According to Bühler, the Bastarnae cannot be classed as a purely Germanic people, because already in Tacitus' time they were to a large extent mixed with other peoples.[57] They are generally located along the eastern slopes of the Carpathians. Tymieniecki objects to this location for geographical reasons, and, reviving an old theory of their Celtic origin, places the Bastarnae west of the Carpathians.[58] Without disagreeing with either of these locations, it may safely be said that the Bastarnae lived in the southern part of the Carpathian region.

The name Vandili, like Ingaevones, Istaevones, and Herminones, is the collective appellation of a regional group, whom Pliny describes as "the Vandili, part of whom are the Burgodiones, Varinnae, Charini, Gutones."[59] The text clearly indicates that the Vandili were not a single people, but consisted of several tribes. The Vandili also appear in Tacitus' *Germania*, where they are mentioned in the general part of the work, but omitted from the description of individual tribes or groups of peoples.[60] It is hard to comprehend how Tacitus understood the name; all attempts to find a solution have been fruitless thus far. His usage of the term must have been different from Pliny's, since he calls the peoples of the same area by the name of Suebi.

There have been attempts to connect the Vandili with the Vandals and the Vandals again with the Lugii; however, as obvious from my discussion of Strabo's text, the interpretation Vandili-Vandals-Lugii as the names for the same people is not acceptable. According to Schönfeld and Steche, the name Vandili is to be interpreted only as the collective appellation of the East-Germanic tribes.[61] In other words, one should not look for the land of the Vandili, since the territories occupied by the four individual tribes will automatically constitute the territory of the whole Vandilian group.

The location of the Vandili does not present any difficulty. The Ingaevones, Istaevones, and the Herminones are usually placed in the western part of Germania, i.e., in Jutland and the country west of the Elbe. The Hilleviones lived in Scandinavia, and the Peucini-Bastarnae in the Carpathian region. In the opinion of historians, the Vandili thus filled the vacant place between the Elbe and the lands occupied by the Venedian tribes.[62]

Pliny's Burgodiones are identical with the Burgundians, who later migrated to the Main region and to Gaul. Their original homeland has not yet been ascertained. Historical sources reveal that during the first two centuries of our era the Burgundians lived in the Oder-Vistula region, but the exact location of their abodes is still doubtful. Some archaeologists have tried to trace them in the area south of the Noteć, between the Oder and the Vistula, an area which they called the district of the Burgundian culture, while others have endeavored to prove that

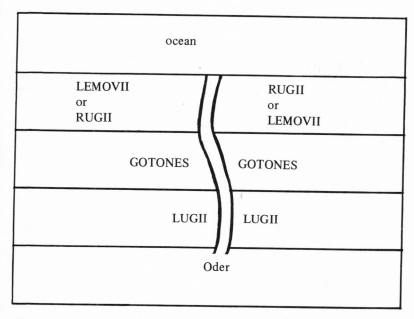

ocean

LEMOVII or RUGII	RUGII or LEMOVII
GOTONES	GOTONES
LUGII	LUGII

Oder

Figure 7. Schematic location of the tribes near the Oder after Tacitus.

the "Burgundian culture" is nothing other than a subdivision of the Przeworsk culture, which was not Germanic at all.[63]

The conflicting archaeological evidence is of little avail in seeking a geographical location for the tribe; on the other hand historical evidence, though fragmentary, might be of assistance. Pliny does not record the location of the Burgundians, but it can be safely assumed that, in his opinion, they lived east of the Elbe and close to the Oder. The vicinity of this area was described twenty years later by Tacitus. He says that "beyond (i.e., north of) the Lugii are the Gotones . . . immediately next to them, at the Ocean, are the Rugii and Lemovii."[64] These three tribes lived along the Oder (figure 7). Fifty years after Tacitus, Ptolemy, in describing the same area in a general north-south order, mentions the Semnones as living across the Elbe toward the Oder, and the Burgundians close to them toward the Vistula. South of the Semnones were the Silingi, south of the Burgundians the Lugii-Omanni, followed by the Lugii-Duni toward the Askiburgion Mountains, and the Lugii-Buri toward the source of the Vistula.[65] The accounts of the three ancient sources are slightly contradictory. It was assumed that Pliny's Goths and Burgundians dwelt in a tract along the Oder, the Burgundians living north of the Goths. Tacitus records the Rugii and Lemovii as immediate northern neighbors of the Goths; in other words, according to him, there were no Burgundians between the Goths and the two tribes occupying the belt along the Baltic shore. It is possible that the existence of the Burgundians could have escaped Tacitus' attention. This could have happened only if the Burgundians were an obscure or very small tribe. He could not have missed them if they were an important people, since the observations of merchants were fairly accurate.

According to Ptolemy, the Burgundians stretched from the Oder (or perhaps the Spree) to the Vistula (see figure 8). This is a distance of more than 250 kilometers, or 160 miles. Assuming a proportionate width to that length, the Burgundians would have occupied an immense territory, which no ancient writer could ever have missed. It follows that the territory occupied by the Burgundians must have been much smaller than the one described by Ptolemy, and the Burgundians a small rather than a large tribe. The answer is obvious, since they are known before Tacitus and after him: in Tacitus' time they no longer lived at the Oder and north of the Goths. Consequently, when Ptolemy speaks of the Burgundians as the neighbors of the Semnones, at the same time mentioning them near the Vistula, he must have pieced together two bits of information dating from different times: one was the statement that the Burgundians lived near the Oder, and the other, that they lived near the Vistula. He took it for granted that the first fact applied to the western, and the second to the eastern boundary of their tribal territory. It did not occur to him that the tribe could have moved in the meantime. Since the general direction of the migration of Germanic tribes into the Oder-Vistula region proceeded from the west or the north, and not from the east toward the west, the answer seems clear. The stay of the Burgundians near the Oder and close to the Semnones is the older information, and the one Pliny also had. Between 77 and 98 A.D., the tribe had moved eastward, toward the Vistula. Tacitus' informant had the more recent information about the peoples living along the Oder. The Burgundians were not there any longer; the Rugii and Lemovii became the direct neighbors of the Goths. The information about the location of the Burgundians near the Vistula is the later information (some time after 98 A.D.). Ptolemy had both reports at hand, and, unaware that they related to different times, he believed that he had found the western and eastern frontiers of the Burgundian

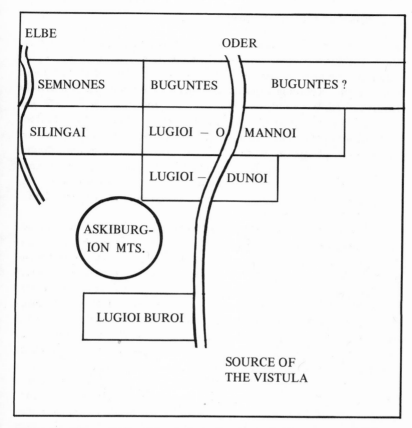

ELBE

ODER

SEMNONES | BUGUNTES | BUGUNTES ?

SILINGAI | LUGIOI – O / MANNOI

LUGIOI – / DUNOI

ASKIBURG-
ION MTS.

LUGIOI BUROI

SOURCE OF
THE VISTULA

Figure 8. Schematic location of the tribes between the Oder and the Elbe after Ptolemy.

territory. Consequently, he placed it in the huge area between the Semnones, the Oder, and the Vistula. If this analysis of Ptolemy's report is correct, it proves that in Pliny's time the Burgundians were direct neighbors of the Semnones. Not being a large tribe, the Burgundians would fit into the space between the Spree and the Oder. This is the same place where Tymieniecki has located them.[66]

The location of the next tribe, the Varinnae, is to a certain extent also hypothetical. They are certainly the same people as Tacitus' Varini, who, together with six other tribes, belonged to the Nerthus-cult group. All these tribes lived in Jutland, Holstein, and Mecklenburg. Tacitus places them north of the Langobardi and lists them in the following order: Reudigni, Aviones, Anglii, Varini, Eudoses, Suarines (or Suardones), Nuitones.[67] In his commentary of the *Germania,* Anderson says that "they are apparently enumerated in a geographical order from the Elbe northwards but, as there is hardly room for all of them in Schleswig-Holstein and Jutland, the last two are perhaps to be placed in Mecklenburg." The Varini were neighbors of the Anglii. "If Tacitus is strictly following the geographical order," Anderson continues, "their home would lie to the north of the Anglii." He consequently places the Varini in the northeast corner of Sundeved, which would agree with the place name "*Warnaes,* i.e., *Varna naes,* 'the promontary of the Varni', mod. Warnitz."[68]

The next tribe of the Nerthus-cult group, the Eudoses, should be placed north of the Varini. Anderson maintains that the Eudoses and the Eudusii are one and the same people, who lived in the south of Jutland. They were neighbors of the Harudes (*Charydes,* Greek: *Chalybes* in the *Monumentum Ancyranum,* V, 26), and he finally reaches the conclusion that "the Eudoses appear therefore to have dwelt on the east of them [the Harudes]."[69] (See figure 9.) The Harudes are not mentioned by Tacitus, and it is difficult to say whether the Eudoses were the northern neighbors of the Varini, since one would expect the Harudes north of them, and the Eudoses east of the Harudes. Somehow the straight geographical order seems to have been interrupted in this place. It is difficult to draw a diagram showing the location of the Nerthus-cult peoples. Though Anderson proposes a south-north geographical order, he omits the Suarines and Nuitones, placing them in Mecklenburg—perhaps separated from the Reudigni. Also, it is not certain whether the Eudoses were immediate northern neighbors of the Varini, or whether the Harudes were somewhere between these two peoples (figure 9). The fact that several tribes shared a regional cult should indicate that they would be direct neighbors, and this scheme seems to be interrupted. Yet, in general, Anderson's observation is correct, but the south-north column should be broken at another point and the two parts of the column placed parallel to each other. By dividing the column after the Anglii, instead of after the Eudoses, two south-north lists are obtained. The first consists of the Reudigni, Aviones, and Anglii; the second of the Varini, Eudoses, Suarines, and Nuitones. Both lists start just north or northeast of the Langobardi. The first contains the names of tribes who lived in the western part of Schleswig and Jutland; the second, the tribes living in Mecklen-

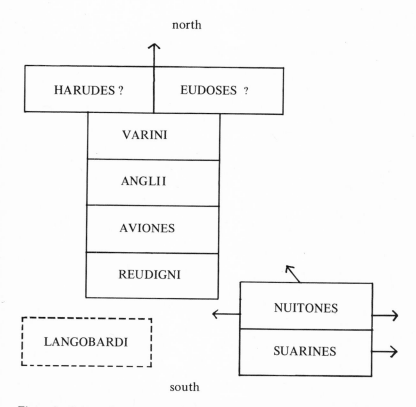

north

HARUDES ?   EUDOSES ?

VARINI

ANGLII

AVIONES

REUDIGNI

NUITONES

LANGOBARDI

SUARINES

south

Figure 9. Schematic location of the Nerthus cult peoples (Tacitus, *Germania* 40) based on Anderson's interpretation.

burg and the eastern part of Schleswig or Jutland (figure 10). Splitting the list after the Anglii instead of after the Eudoses allows the placing of the Varini in Mecklenburg, in the vicinity of the other Vandilian tribes. Had they lived in northern Jutland, they would have been separated from the main body of the Vandili, and Pliny's grouping would then make little sense.

The location of the Varini in Mecklenburg is justified by Ptolemy's recording of the Virunoi and Virunon, a people and a place situated somewhere between the Elbe and the Oder, close to the Baltic coast. [70] This particular region is described in the *Geography* as crowded with many petty tribes, and there is good reason to suspect that some of them are listed by more than one appellation. Thus, the Virunoi have been associated with Ptolemy's Auarpoi and Farodeinoi, and with the

north

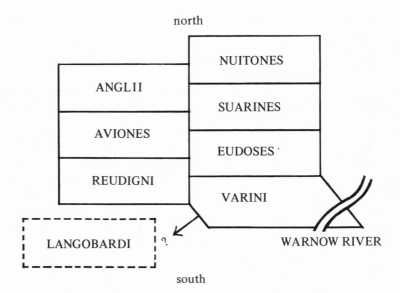

Figure 10. Tentative location of the Nerthus cult peoples after the geographical interpretation of Varini–Varinnae–Warnow River.

Varini.[71] Ptolemy's recording of the Virunoi between the Saxons, who occupied a part of southern Jutland, and the Suebi, i.e., the Suebi-Semnones who lived toward the Oder, indicates a location in the region of the Warnow.[72]

The place Virunon lay in the same area. Its location at 40°30′ and 55° east of the Fortunate Islands has to be corrected taking into account Marinus of Tyre's error and Ptolemy's double recording of the Oder. The latitude of 55° must be changed to 53°, i.e., about one degree south of the Baltic coast. The longitude coordinate of 40°30′ is a point situated two degrees west of Rugion. Earlier in this study the coordinate of Rugion was corrected from 42°30′ to 39°30′, since this place was situated on the right bank of the Oder (see p. 97). Consequently, the longitude coordinate of Virunon has to be changed from 40°30′ to 37°30′ i.e., to a location two degrees west of Rugion. Virunon was thus a place situated approximately 110 kilometers south of the Baltic coast, and 90 kilometers west of the Lower Oder: this means a location in the region of the Warnow. The names Varini, Virunoi, and Virunon point to the same geographical area, and the name Varinnae undoubtedly refers to the same people. The conclusion can be drawn that Pliny's Varinnae lived north of the Semnones and northwest of the Burgundians and their abodes centered around the Warnow.

The third tribe of the Vandilian group are the Charini (variants: Charinni, Carini), who are not mentioned in any other source. Schmidt draws attention to the possibility that the name *Chari(n)i* could be identical with that of Tacitus' Harii, a view shared by Anderson and Cüppers.[73] Much tried to elucidate it etymologically deducing the form *Harii* from the Gothic *harjis, das Heer* 'army, host', and the form *Charini* from the Lithuanian(?) *karinis, zum Kriege gehörig* 'pertaining to war'. His comment is a slightly fantastic story declaring the name of mythical origin, signifying an 'army or host of ghosts,' *Geisterheer,* a solution not endorsed in later articles on the subject.[74] The resemblance of the forms *Harii* and (C)hari(n)i in itself does not constitute sufficient proof for geographical location of the tribe. According to Tacitus, the Harii were one of the major Lugian tribes, who must have dwelt either near the Middle Oder, or between the Oder and the Vistula. This location is outside the territory occupied by the peoples of the Vandilian group. The Harii and the Charini, therefore, must have been two different tribes; the first belonged to the Lugian, the second to the Vandilian group.

The Charini could not have dwelt south of the Burgundians, since this area was occupied by the Goths. They could not have lived west of the Burgundians either, because the country there was occupied by the Semnones. East of the Burgundians there were the Venedian peoples pushing toward the west; the only possible place for the Charini was the country north of the Burgundians. This would make them inhabitants of the area between the Varini, the Oder, the Baltic coast, and the country occupied by the Burgundians.

After establishing the location of these three Vandilian tribes, it should be possible to trace the space occupied by the Goths in Pliny's times. Their name is recorded in manuscripts as *Gutones, Gu////nes, Gniones, Guttones.*[75] The Gothic tribal territory can be tentatively set south of the Burgundians. The correctness of this tentative location can be fairly well proven. In Strabo's time, the Goths lived near the Middle Oder and north of some Lugian tribes. Most likely, the Burgundians had been their neighbors. Tacitus records the Goths as living north of the Lugii, a description that agrees with Strabo. In Pliny's time they must have lived in the same area as they did in Strabo's and Tacitus' times. The bulk of their territory lay on the west side of the Oder, but it may be supposed that they also occupied a stretch of land on the east side, and that the Oder flowed through their territory (see figure 7). This is the conclusion that may be drawn from Pliny's recording of the Guthalus (variants: Gythalus, Gothalus, Guttalus, Lutta Alus),[76] as one of the major rivers in Germania, a river name that is strikingly similar to that of the Goths. By the Guthalus Pliny means the Oder and no other river of this area. As long as historians searched for the abodes of the Goths in Pomerania, east of the Parsęta, the connection between the form Guthalus and its variants, and Gutones and its variants did not make much sense, because the Guthalus-Oder was outside of the territory of the Goths. Since it has been proven that the Goths can be placed near the Oder, it would be illogical to identify the Guthalus with one of the small rivers in Sarmatia, instead of associating it with a notable river in Germania.

The name of this river is not found in any other source except in Solinus, a third-century writer who in general follows Pliny.[77] Pliny lists the important rivers of Germania in the following order: "the notable rivers which flow into the Ocean are the Guthalus, Visculus or Vistla, Albis, Visurgis, Amisis, Rhenus, Mosa."[78] His listing follows a strict east-west order. All these rivers, with the exception of one, are known by modern names and in the same order. In Pliny's text the first three rivers appear in a sequence: Guthalus; Vistula; Elbe. Since in the belief of the ancients the Vistula was the dividing line between Germania and Sarmatia, the Guthalus was not a great river of Germania but of Sarmatia, for it is located east of the Vistula. Pliny mentions the Elbe as the next river west of the Vistula; the Oder is omitted. Solinus, who relies heavily on Pliny, lists these three rivers in reverse order, i.e., from the west toward the east. In his words: "very wide rivers such as the Alba, Guthalus, and Viscla flow from the interior of the country into the Ocean."[79] The Guthalus (variants: Guttalus, Gutthalus) is placed between the Elbe and the Vistula, and certainly refers to the Oder, which is missing in Pliny's text.

The debate over whether the name Guthalus refers to the Oder or to some other river has been going on ever since Cluverius wrote on this matter in 1616. E. H. Bunbury favors the identification of the Guthalus with the Oder. He says that "it seems more probable that the name had been misplaced by Pliny and really referred to the Oder, than that he had no notion of that great river, and yet mentioned the Pregel or any other obscure stream east of the Vistula, with which the Guttalus has been identified by German writers."[80] In recent literature on the subject the view prevails that the Guthalus is either the Pregoła (Pregel), or the Niemen (Memel).[81] An ardent defender of the latter identification is Biliński, who writes that "today, however, the identity *Guthalus* = Oder is only of historical value, and almost generally the view is held that the *Guthalus* is not the Oder, but the Pregoła or Niemen."[82]

Biliński's solution cannot be accepted as final; the problem of the Guthalus is still open and worth discussing. According to Lehr-Spławiński the etymology of the name Guthalus is not certain, but the name is probably of Germanic origin.[83] Attention has been drawn to the fact that the recorded forms of this name and that of the Goths are strikingly similar. It has also been mentioned that the identification of the Guthalus with the Oder is difficult as long as the opinion prevails that the territory of the Goths lay east of the Parsęta. Since proof has been presented in this study that the Goths lived at the Middle Oder, the name Guthalus acquires a new meaning, which is simply "the river of the Goths," and should be classed in the same category as Ptolemy's "river of the Suebi." These must have been names made up by foreign visitors. It is, indeed, difficult to explain why merchants or other informants would not have known of the existence of the Oder, an important stream along one of their trade routes, and should have remembered instead names of obscure rivers flowing through a country inhabited by Baltic tribes. The conclusion is that Bunbury's identification of the river is more credible than Biliński's, though it should be adopted with a correction. He was quoted earlier as saying that "it seems more probable that the name has been misplaced by Pliny." While Pliny may have overlooked the fact that he was placing a great river of Germania in Sarmatia, if he had done so, Solinus would have used the incorrect order too (see map 13). Since Solinus copied Pliny, and Pliny's order is wrong while Solinus' is right, the answer is clear. It was not Pliny who misplaced the Guthalus, but the copyists of later times. Originally Pliny's text must have read: *Visculus sive Vistla, Guthalus, Albis*, which agrees with the present Vistula—Oder—Elbe order. Pliny's and Solinus' Guthalus is the Oder.

Twenty or thirty years after Pliny another Roman writer described Germania and the Germanic peoples. He was Cornelius Tacitus (ca. 54/56-after 116 A.D.), whose *Annals* (written ca. 116 A.D.) contain the description of Maroboduus' rise and fall, and the valuable date of 19 A.D. which proves that by this time the Goths lived in the Oder-Vistula region. His work entitled *De origine et situ Germanorum*, better known by its short title *Germania*, was written in 98 A.D. It is an ethnological

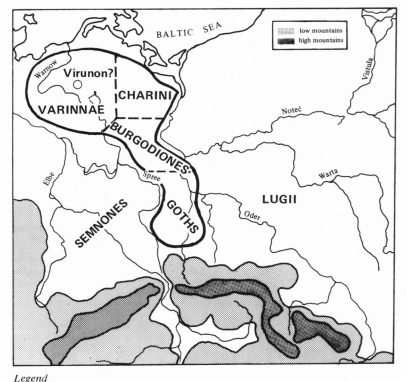

Legend
▬▬▬▬ territorial extent of the Vandilian tribes.

Map 13. Location of the Goths according to Pliny.

and geographical treatise about the land and its people, a small gold mine of the early Germanic past. "Thanks to it"—writes J. G. C. Anderson in the introduction to his edition of the *Germania*—"we know more of the Germans of the first century A.D. than of any other people outside the Roman Empire and, indeed, of many within it."[84]

Like Pliny, Tacitus used the works of earlier writers, to which he added some new information. The time of the military expeditions deep into Germania was long past, but trade relations had improved and provided new knowledge. In most cases the information came from merchants; travelers, slaves, and foreigners staying at Rome may have contributed some of it. The material was of mixed value; it consisted of reliable accounts, as well as of hearsay and fantastic stories.

In the *Germania*, the Goths are called Gotones (variant: Gothones), and Tacitus says of them that "beyond the Lugii are the Gotones, ruled by kings somewhat stricter than the other tribes of the Germani, but not completely limited in freedom. Next to them, right at the Ocean, are the Rugii and Lemovii. Characteristic for all these tribes are round shields, short swords, and obedience to their kings."[85] Tacitus' account of the Goths is the most descriptive of all reports by ancient writers discussed in this study. In a somewhat vague manner it describes the country of the Goths as situated north of the Lugii, and not reaching to the Baltic coast, which was occupied by the Rugii and Lemovii. It shows some familiarity with the way of life of other Germanic peoples also. A different form of tribal government among the Goths is mentioned, and it is described as less liberal than that of other Germanic tribes. This was true also of the Rugii and Lemovii. The type of weapons used by these three tribes is noted as different from that of other Germani.

The statement about the weapons is correct to some extent, but it also indicates that the reporter was not a military expert on Germanic armament. The basic weapons of the Germanic footmen were the spear, or lance, and the shield. Only a few Germani carried long or short swords. Anderson points out that the shields of the footmen were generally oblong; either rectangular, hexagonal, and occasionally oval. These are the forms that appear on the Roman monuments of the first century A.D. The horsemen carried larger or smaller oval shields. On the Antonine column in Rome, the prevalent form was round or oval. Anderson also mentions that the short sword was not limited to the Goths, Rugii, and Lemovii, its use having been ascertained east as well as west of the Elbe.[86]

This brief description of the weapons used by the Germanic tribes shows that neither the short sword nor the round shield were characteristic of the three above-mentioned tribes. It is also unlikely that this was the basic armament of their footmen. The Goths, as well as the other two tribes, used the spear and a large shield, which could not have been round. Tacitus' informant, in this case, must have been a merchant who may not have met Gothic, Rugian, or Lemovian armies. Probably all he saw were armed horsemen guarding the trade routes. This would also imply that he had no general knowledge of Germania, and that his observations were restricted to the stretch of country that he actually visited. This merchant most probably had made a business trip to or toward the Baltic coast, and had reached the country of the Goths. His information about the Rugii and Lemovii could have been either based upon direct observation, or supplied by local people. Once he was in the country of the Goths, he must have passed Lugia. This was a huge territory, and several trade routes traversed it toward the Baltic coast. He had the choice of three routes: the first would have led him through the Moravian Gate and down along the Vistula; the second was the ancient amber route through Kłodzko, Wrocław, and Kalisz; the third went from Wrocław down the Oder. The Goths lived north of the Lugii, i.e., either near the Lower Vistula, north of Kalisz, or near the Middle Oder. If of these three locations, two can be eliminated, the location of the Rugii and Lemovii can be established.

The etymology of the names *Rugii* and *Lemovii* (variant: *Lemonii*) is not known. Much tried to explain the name *Rugii* as 'rye eaters' and *Lemovii* as 'barkers.' He also discovered a similarity between the name *Rugii* and Ptolemy's *Rutikleioi*, which he corrected to *Rugikleioi* by substituting a gamma for the Greek capital letter tau. Schmidt accepts this correction, thinking that the name *Rugikleioi* is a contraction of *Rugii* and *Lemovii*. Steche objects to the identification of the Rutikleioi with the Rugii; in his opinion, the Rutikleioi were a western branch of the Goths, and probably the same people as the Gepids.[87]

The Rugii are mentioned in later sources. Jordanes speaks of the Ulmerugi as one of the tribes conquered by the Goths after their landing at the mouth of the Vistula. His account has been accepted by modern historians and archaeologists. The name *Ulmerugi* was interpreted as *Holm-rugi*, the 'Island-Rugi,' and their abodes were placed in Pomerania, near the Vistula. Their original home was located in Scandinavia whence they migrated to found a kingdom in the Danube region in the fifth century.[88] Jordanes may not be the best authority for locating the Ulmerugi or any other tribe with a similar name living near the Baltic shore during the first century of our era, but there is Ptolemy, who has some direct or indirect information on the Rugii. He mentions the tribe Rutikleioi, between the Oder and the Vistula, whose name was emendated by some scholars to Rugikleioi, and a settlement called Rugion near the Oder; in his words: "then the Seidinoi toward the Iadua river and after them the Rutikleioi toward the Vistula river," and "Rugion 42°30',55°40'."[89]

Ptolemy's *poleis* are not cities in the strict sense of the word but notable settlements. Many of them may have been trading posts or centers of tribal societies. They were visited by Roman and Greek merchants. The names of these places recorded by Ptolemy were not always identical with the forms used by the local population and some of them appear to be artificial creations made up by foreign merchants.

This is the case of Rugion, whose name means the 'main' or 'one of the well known settlements in the country of the Rugii.' Unfortunately, it seems that no name recorded in the area under discussion is free from problems of interpretation, and Rugion is no exception. Since the Rugii were mentioned as a tribe by Tacitus, were not recorded by Ptolemy, and appeared again in the writings of later historians, it was argued that Ptolemy was wrong, since he erroneously recorded a place named Rugion, instead of a tribe called Rugii. This seems to be the prevailing opinion in the literature on the subject, although a few historians consider the form Rugion a genuine place name.[90] Actually it matters little whether Rugion is a true place name or a corrupt tribal name. If the interpretation of this name indicates that the place was a city or settlement of the Rugii, the simple fact behind the story is that the Rugii lived there where Rugion lay. If Rugion can be located, the location of the Rugii should no longer be considered doubtful.

Müller's commentary to the *Geography* suggests that Rugion is identical with the present Darłowo (Rügenwalde), province of Koszalin, at the river Wieprza (Wipper), or with Resko (Regenwalde), province of Szczecin, at the river Rega (Regen).[91] Steche, for whom the Viadua meant either the Wieprza (Wipper), or Słupia (Stolpe), also thought of Darłowo (Rügenwalde) as the location of Rugion.[92] I have demonstrated (pp. 56-64) that both Viadua and Suebos designate the Oder. Ptolemy's longitude for the estuary of this river is the same as that of Rugion. His coordinates for Rugion can be safely corrected from 42°30′ to 39°30′ and from 55°40′ to 53°40′. Transposed on a modern map, this corresponds to a point situated about 75 kilometers south of the estuary of the Oder, i.e., a short distance south of Szczecin (Stettin). Rugion was, most likely, a trading place on the route along the Oder. If Ptolemy's Rugikleioi are identical with Tacitus' Rugii, the tribe must have occupied the region around the estuary of the Oder, and a large portion of the tribal territory must have lain east of the river.

The territory of the Lemovii, who apparently also lived close to the trade route, should consequently be placed west of the Oder. This tribe is not known from any other ancient source. Linguists have attempted to connect their name with the Germanic *Glomman,* mentioned in later times in the seventh-century Anglo-Saxon poem *Widsith,* and the Slavic *Glomacze, Glomaci,* recorded in several medieval texts of the ninth to the eleventh centuries.[93] The linguistic evidence, however, is not strong enough to contribute useful information for the location of the Lemovii in Tacitus' time.

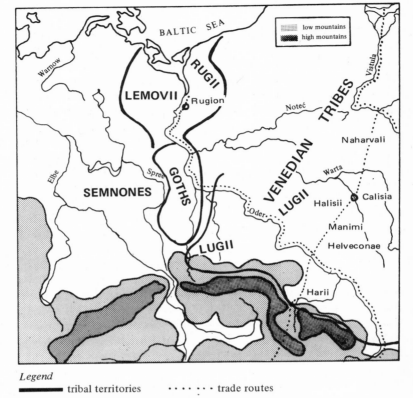

Legend
━━━━━━━ tribal territories   · · · · · · · trade routes
Map 14. Location of the Goths according to Tacitus.

With the abodes of the Rugii and Lemovii firmly established on the Baltic shore and at the estuary of the Oder, the location of the Goths in Tacitus' time can be exactly described. They lived south of the Rugii and Lemovii, in the Oder valley. Tacitus' words "beyond the Lugii" do not refer to the part of Lugia north of Kalisz or at the Lower Vistula, but mean north of modern Silesia. The Goths occupied the territory they had held in Strabo's and Pliny's times. They might have expanded northward, occupying part of the former Burgundian territory, sometime after 77 A.D. The situation along their western border remained unchanged; the Semnones continued to be their neighbors. The Lugian tribes, their eastern and southern neighbors, probably made some territorial gains by occupying further portions of the country between the Oder and the Sudeten (see map 14).

Tacitus has repeatedly been quoted to substantiate the assumption that the Goths were a superior people, excelling other tribes in political and military leadership. He has been criticized time and again for not being accurate enough, and has even been accused of being entirely mistaken concerning the location of the Goths, because he did not place them in a location that agreed with certain modern theories. There is not a word in his description expressing the concept that the Goths of the first century A.D. were a great nation, unless one has preconceived ideas of their greatness. A great nation would have occupied a correspondingly large territory, and this fact could not have escaped the attention of the merchant traders, who had an excellent concept of space, evident in the way they recorded distances from place to place and from one country to another. This factor of space and remarks concerning the importance or size of some individual peoples are encountered in the *Germania* several times, and there is no reason why Tacitus should not have so described the Goths, too, had he possessed such information. A few examples will suffice to illustrate.

Tacitus speaks of the Semnones as the most important tribe of the Suebi, saying that "they inhabit a hundred pagi (settlements or districts) and consider themselves the head of the Suebi because of the great mass of people they consist of."[94] The name of the Lugii is widely known and spreads over many tribes *(civitates)*. It is sufficient to mention the most powerful ones: the Harii, Helvecones, Manimi, Helisii, Naharvali. "The fame and strength of the Marcomanni is eminent. They even won their dwelling-places by valor, having driven out the Boii some time ago."[95] In contrast to the large tribes or peoples there were the Langobardi, "known for their small numbers: although surrounded by many and powerful peoples, they protect themselves by fights and running risks [of war] and not by submissiveness." There were several small tribes: the Marsigni, Cotini, Osi, and the Buri who "inhabit little of the plains and live mainly in the wooded upland and on the tops [and ridges] of mountains."[96] The Goths are mentioned only as living between the Lugii, Rugii, and Lemovii. Had they occupied an area as large as some prehistorians outline, the ancient explorers would surely have noted it. Tacitus' text does not prove that the Gothic territory was as large as that of the Lugii, Marcomanni, or Semnones.

A large territory and population are only two aspects of the alleged greatness of the Goths. They might have excelled other Germanic tribes in organization, or some other quality, though limited in space or number. Yet, there is no proof in Tacitus' text for such an assumption either. The style of armament the Goths, Rugii, and Lemovii possessed, as described by Tacitus' informant, differs from that of other Germanic tribes, but that does not make them superior in military art and power. The fact that their form of government, as well as that of the Rugii and Lemovii, was stricter than that of the remaining Germanic tribes, is no indication that it was on a higher level, or characteristic of great kingdoms and large nations. It does not make the system equal or superior to Maroboduus' state organization. It might have been dictated by necessities of defense and survival. The Goths lived between two major groups of peoples: the Semnones in the west, and the Lugii or other Slavic peoples who advanced from the south and east. Tension and mutual fear prevailed along the border between the Germanic and Slavic peoples. The Goths found themselves in a situation similar to that of the Langobardi: the very existence of the tribe depended on an efficient defense system. A strict form of government was a necessity in the face of the dangerous and unstable conditions in the area.

Strabo and Tacitus placed the Goths in the region of the Middle Oder. Pliny's account does not contradict their testimony. The tribe remained in this region for approximately a whole century. There might have been minor changes in the extent of their tribal territory; the Goths may have expanded, but they did not come close to the Baltic coast. If, as prehistorians claim, certain cultures in Pomerania are the product of Germanic peoples, it is nevertheless certain that these cultures are not the product of the Goths. A great Gothic kingdom did not exist in Pomerania in the first century of our era.

After Tacitus' death there were a few geographers who explored foreign countries and undertook the ambitious task of mapping and describing the entire known world. Among them was Marinus of Tyre, who wrote at the beginning of the second century A.D. (about 110 A.D.?)) and contributed fresh information on the Oder-Vistula region. Unfortunately his work has not survived until our times and is known only from quotations, corrections, and interpretations of his data in Ptolemy's writings. Ptolemy, whose full name was Claudius Ptolemaeus, and who lived between about 100 and 178 A.D., worked and wrote at or near Alexandria. His *Outline of Geography* was written between 140 and 151 A.D. and has been discussed in many works.[1] One can approach Ptolemy's work in a broad context, as one of the pillars of our civilization, and acknowledge its historical value, as George Sarton did, when he said: "During fourteen centuries, at least, the Almagest was the standard book, or call it the Bible of astronomy, while the Geography was the Bible of geography. The name Ptolemy meant geography to geographers and astronomy to astronomers."[2] One can also approach Ptolemy's work critically, minutely sifting individual passages and sentences for misjudgments, deficiencies, or errors, and this was done quite frequently. It is certainly easier to criticize him and belittle his work than to test his data and evaluate them properly.

Ptolemy's *Outline of Geography* is not a descriptive geography of the ancient world. It is a treatise on mathematical geography and cartography containing practical instructions for drawing general and sectional maps of the world. It consists of eight books, but the greater part of the text (from Book II to Book VII, 5) records names and coordinates of significant places, such as capes, estuaries, mountains, towns, etc. There is a brief description of the borders of each geographical area, and a list of the peoples that inhabited it. The data pertaining to the Oder-Vistula region are contained in Book II, Chapter 11 *(Great Germania)* and in Book III, Chapter 5 *(European Sarmatia)*. These chapters have repeatedly been classed among the more deficient parts of the the work, which is a hasty judgment. It is true that they both contain inaccurate and confused locations, because for none of these areas did Ptolemy have reference points that were fixed or verified by astronomical measurements. He had to rely on data computed from peripli, itineraries, and similar reports from the sea and land trade. Some of the inaccuracies can be attributed to early interpretations; however, not much can be done about these until a new, critical text of the *Geography* becomes available.

Ptolemy's representation of the Oder-Vistula region is affected by two major distortions: first, the cartographic shape of the country common to all medieval and modern Ptolemaic maps, and secondly, a basic error in computation which resulted in the displacement of fixed points that should have been in ancient times in the same location in which they are today. Actually, the graphic misrepresentation stems from the error in computation and is not limited to the Oder-Vistula region alone. All maps, drawn according to Ptolemy's instructions and data, show a distorted picture of Europe visible along the entire coast of the continent. Britain and Ireland are twisted, Jutland is toppling to the right. Scandinavia, not yet recognized as part of the continent, appears as a group of small islands. The region between the Danube and the Baltic coast looks much larger than on modern maps. One gets the impression that the Ptolemaic map was drawn on an elastic sheet which was then stretched at the upper right corner in a northeast direction.

Since this deformation is not a matter of drawing techniques, but the result of a miscalculation of coordinates, we can avoid a discussion of the famous question of whether or not Ptolemy had appended an atlas to his original work. I shall not use reproductions of extant medieval and early modern maps to confirm locations reported by Ptolemy. Whenever I apply the term "Ptolemaic map" in this study, it refers to any map drawn according to Ptolemy's specifications.

This distortion has puzzled scholars for quite some time, and it was only in the studies of Otto Cuntz, Paul Schnabel, and Emanuel Šimek that several questions have been answered. Continuing the work of these scholars, Steche came out with a reasonable explanation of the mystery. His observations are restricted to Germania only, but they can be applied to the entire area between the Danube and the Baltic Sea, including European Sarmatia. Steche was able to trace several itineraries and peripli. The data from the sea and land trade used by Ptolemy contained fair information on the distances from place to place or from harbor to harbor. They were, however, not accurate enough for the geographical location of a given place. Ptolemy was well aware of the fact that winding roads, mountains, heavy seas, detours, and delays of any kind were bound to result in some inaccuracy. He was compelled to make certain adjustments and needed a general framework into which he could fit his data. He used the works of earlier geographers and relied especially on Marinus of Tyre, who also worked with reliable data, but became the victim of confused geographical terminology. The story is briefly as follows: On the west coast of Spain there are two promontories which caused some perplexity in ancient times. These are the Promontorium Magnum and the Promontorium Sacrum. It has been thought by some writers that the Promontorium Magnum is today's Cape Finisterre at the northwest corner of Spain, and the Promontorium Sacrum, also known by the name Promontorium Olisippense, the modern Cape Rocca, near Lisbon in Portugal. Other geographers have called Cape Rocca Promontorium Magnum and used the name Promontorium Sacrum for today's Cape Saint Vincent, on the southeastern shore of Spain. In other words, there are two sets of points: either Cape Finisterre or Cape Rocca could have been known as the Promontorium Magnum, and either Cape Rocca or Cape Saint Vincent could have been known as the Promontorium Sacrum. The distance between the capes Finisterre and Rocca is about 420 kilometers, or 260 statute miles, that between the capes Rocca and Saint Vincent about 220 kilometers, or 137 miles. Confusion as to the location of the two capes could lead to serious mistakes, affecting the length of the coastline in a south-north direction. Under certain circumstances it could also mean a distortion of the west-east direction.

As Steche has proved, Marinus confused the terms and made errors in both directions. Describing the western and northern shores of Europe, he apparently used two sailing guides. The first one covered the route from the Strait of Gibraltar to the middle of Portugal; the second one, the route from Lisbon to Danzig. Each sailing guide mentioned the Promontorium Sacrum in a different location. To Marinus, this promontory meant Cape Saint Vincent, which he mistakenly placed in the geographical latitude of Cape Rocca, while he proceeded to compute all distances as if they were measured from Cape Saint Vincent. North of Cape Rocca, the coast shifts slightly to the east. Interpreting a dubious sentence in Pliny's text, Marinus believed that from the westernmost point of Spain the coast turns rapidly and continues far to the east. He

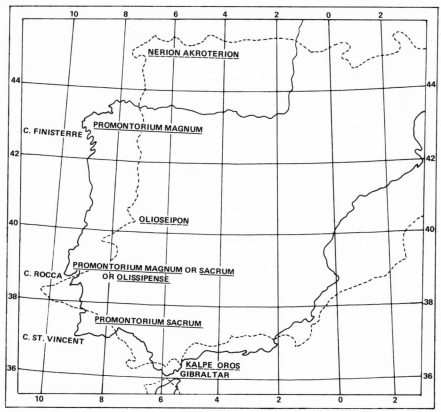

Legend

- - - - - - - - the coast of Spain according to a modern map
————————— the coast of Spain according to Ptolemy

MODERN NAMES   ANCIENT NAMES   PTOLEMY'S NAMES

Coordinates assumed: one Ptolemaic degree (latitude or longitude) equals one modern degree; location of Gibraltar (ca. 5°20' west of Greenwich) equals Kalpe Oros (7°30' west of the Fortunate Islands)

Map 15. The coast of Spain according to Ptolemy superimposed upon a modern map of the same area.

identified this point with the Promontorium Sacrum (i.e., Cape Rocca in this case), and miscalculated or overestimated the distance between that promontory and the point at which the coast resumes its general northern direction. Due to these misjudgments, Marinus' figures were about two degrees off in latitude and two in longitude. Every place

north of Cape Rocca is located on his map two degrees farther to the
north and east than on our modern maps. This error in computation is
carried systematically throughout the entire coastline of Europe. Ptolemy took Marinus' figures for granted and used them for his own
computations. As a result, most of the territory of Ptolemy's Europe in
the north and east is much larger than it is in reality.[3] (See map 15.)

Steche did not investigate in full detail all the consequences of Marinus' error for the representation of the coast of Spain and Gaul. His
study is confined to the territory of Germania, and was concerned only
with the locations east of the estuary of the Rhine. His conclusions are
in agreement with earlier studies on Ptolemy that furnish sufficient
proof of the dependence of Ptolemy's *Geography* on Marinus.[4]

Due to Marinus' error the territory of Ptolemy's Germania is enlarged by a belt of about two degrees in width. This applies also, of
course, to the country east of the Vistula, that is to European Sarmatia.
At first glance, this distortion seems to be a great handicap, but it does
not make Marinus' or Ptolemy's reports useless. Once the source of the
basic error is known, most of the secondary and minor errors can be
corrected. This error of computation has no influence on the validity of
the data contained in the peripli. Steche stresses this point, saying that
the distances recorded by the ancient Romans were surprisingly precise.
He is amazed how accurately they measured the long distance from
Lisbon to Danzig.[5]

To illustrate how Marinus' error affected the cartographic representation of Germania and European Sarmatia, Steche suggests that one
should imagine both a grid map and a map of Middle Europe, drawn to
the same scale. The latter map should be torn into two pieces. The tear
should run from the Zuider Zee, north of the source of the Ems, then
south of the sources of the Werra and Elbe toward the source of the
Vistula, and should continue in a southeast direction. The southern part
of the map should be placed beneath the grid map so that its locations
agree with those of modern maps. The northern portion should be
fitted into the grid map two degrees farther to the north, and two to
the east. On a map put together thus, there is a wide belt of non-
existent territory across Germany, Czechoslovakia, and Poland (map
16). It is into the whole expanse represented by the two parts of the
original map, together with the belt between them, that Ptolemy tried
to fit his data. The difference between the so-called Ptolemaic maps and
reality should now be apparent, and should account for many minor
errors, such as the shifting of the Upper Danube to the south, and the
misplacement of the source of the Vistula.[6]

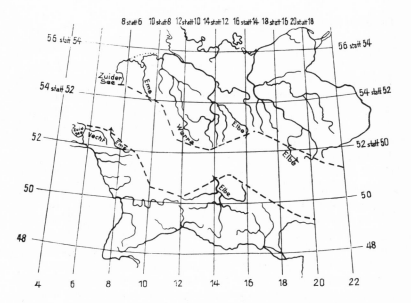

Map 16. A comparison between Ptolemy's map and a modern one according to Steche.

Had Ptolemy used only Marinus' report, or similar data from the ancient sea trade, it would not be difficult to correct them. The two degrees in both directions could be deducted to bring Ptolemy's data into agreement with modern maps. Any additional inaccuracies of measurement could be adjusted, since the points of interest of the ancient sailors were limited. They would refer to harbors, estuaries of rivers, islands, etc. All peripli would follow the same direction, from west to east or vice versa, describing the routes from Spain and Gaul. Ptolemy, however, could not restrict himself only to data obtained from the sea trade. Itineraries from the land trade were richer in content; they described the interior of the country, its physiographic features, and the ecological conditions of the inhabitants. Itineraries of trade routes were Ptolemy's main sources of information. Yet, they were more difficult to evaluate since they described roads going in various directions.

In the Oder-Vistula region, the trade routes went from the Upper Danube and from the Pontus toward the Baltic Sea. A Roman itinerary setting out from the trade centers at the Danube differed from a Greek itinerary starting with the cities at the Pontus. The merchants more than likely used a vocabulary similar to that of Tacitus or Ptolemy. It probably included words such as 'below, above, to the right,' etc., to describe the points of the compass. In a Roman road report, the words 'beyond the Carpathians' meant the country east of the mountains; the same words in a Greek itinerary meant west of them. Both Greek and Roman itineraries run in an approximate south-north direction both coming and going, with some deviations to the east or west. They describe places which should be located in the two real geographical zones, in the vicinity of the Danube and the Baltic shore, as well as places to be located in the non-existent belt created by Marinus' inaccurate computation.

The information obtained from the land trade was less dependable than the data found in sailing charts. Yet Ptolemy could not discover Marinus' error and correct it since he did not have enough knowledge at his disposal. The Vistula can serve as a typical example. He had a fairly correct location on its source and an erroneous location of its estuary. The route through the Moravian Gate went along the entire length of the river. Let us suppose that Ptolemy possessed an itinerary of this route. The total distance mentioned in that itinerary should be equal to the length of the river, i.e., 1,092 kilometers, but 40 kilometers should be deducted from the total length, this being the distance from the source to the point where the river emerges from the mountains and turns to the east. This leaves a length of 1,052 kilometers. The air route from the source to the mouth of the river is 520 kilometers long. The distance from the southwestern to the northeastern corner of an area of two degrees in latitude and two in longitude is 250 kilometers. Adding these 250 kilometers which represent the maximum of Marinus' error to the 520 kilometers we obtain a total of 770 kilometers. This is approximately 282 kilometers less than the eventual total distance of the itinerary. These 282 kilometers should be attributed to the bends and turns of the river. Thus, after adding the huge extra distance introduced by Marinus' error, both the river and the itinerary would be longer than the air route between the two points of the river known to Ptolemy. He could have become suspicious of Marinus' figures only if the course of the Vistula had been a straight line.

Neither did the location of the mountains in the Oder-Vistula region help Ptolemy. The massifs of the Sudeten and the Carpathians were never recognized by the ancient merchants as a continuous range of mountains. They recorded only the narrow strips which they crossed, and used local names or terms applying to separate parts. As a result, there are in Ptolemy's text several names for the Sudeten and Carpathians. The parts so named are located on Ptolemaic maps separately, in inaccurate and confused locations. In a straight south-north direction, Ptolemy was constantly up to 220 kilometers short whenever he compared the data from the land trade with Marinus' figures. These 220 kilometers in latitude constitute a space large enough to contain a country twice as large as Bohemia. It is a distance long enough to confuse the latitude of the source of the Vistula with that of the estuary of the Bug.

From the Roman itineraries describing the country between the Danube and the Baltic Sea Ptolemy derived an accurate location for Aquincum (present-day Budapest) and a fair knowledge of the course of the Upper Danube. The places in the interior of the described country must have looked mysterious to him, since their location would always lead him, as he thought, to wrong results. The Alexandrian scholar did what seemed sensible under the circumstances: he adjusted the locations of such places by increasing the distances between them. In this way the total distances of the itineraries would in the end agree with Marinus' figures. He had good reason for doing this. The merchants' reports were fairly accurate and suited the purposes of trade, but they were not geodetic surveys fit for geographical projection. Winding roads or delays of any kind could cause inaccurate distances. What is more, if a place was not recorded on a chart due to a copyist's omission, all the following measurements were affected.

Several studies on the *Geography* or Germania contain the assertion that Ptolemy adjusted all distances reported in Germania. After analyzing several locations, however, Steche came to the conclusion that he changed only some of them. Though Ptolemy was inclined to make changes in locations everywhere in order to comply with Marinus' final figures, the *Geography* is a basic historical source, if it is used with caution; if used thus, it is an extremely rich source of information.

The Goths appear in the *Geography* twice. They are mentioned once in the description of Germania among the tribes of Scandinavia, and a second time in European Sarmatia as a tribe living at the Lower Vistula.

In contrast to the Oder-Vistula region, which is rich in information, the ancients had little knowledge about Scandinavia. Pliny reports that the Hilleviones, who occupied 500 *pagi*, lived there; Tacitus maintains that the Suiones, known for their fleets, dwelt in that country. Ptolemy records six tribes on that 'island': the Chaideinoi, Phauonai, Phiraisoi, Goutai, Daukiones, and Leuonoi.[7] It is fruitless to draw final conclusions from these three reports that would establish a relationship between these tribes and peoples. Probably all three authors were correct. At any rate, there is no reason to doubt their words. They relate observations made in several parts of the country and generalized information collected outside of Scandinavia. Pliny's Hilleviones and Tacitus' Suiones could have been either individual tribes or local groups consisting of several tribes. Ptolemy's information refers to individual tribes. His description, which differs greatly from that of Pliny and Tacitus, indicates that he had fresh information about Scandinavia (dated after 98 A.D.). The most plausible source would be a periplus, and this would imply that all six tribes lived at, or close to, the seashore. Steche, however, supposes that Ptolemy did not use sailing charts in this case, because the location of Scandinavia is too inaccurate and confused.[8]

The Goths are located in the southern part of Sweden, which was also occupied by the Daukiones and Leuonoi.[9] Regardless of the source of Ptolemy's information, the report is not contradicted by archaeological evidence which locates the original homeland of the Goths near the Göta River. Early modern scholars, such as Kaspar Zeuss and many after him, believed that the Scandinavian Goths and those on the Lower Vistula were two different peoples. This belief was based upon linguistic evaluation, as the transmitted form of the name of the Scandinavian Goths is *Goutai* or *Gautai,* whereas the Goths on the Lower Vistula were called *Gythones.* There is no doubt now that they were one and the same tribe (see the discussion on pp. 14-15). Ptolemy's account of the Goths in both countries indicates that in his time the entire tribe had not yet emigrated from the original homeland. In this respect the Gothic migration is similar to that of the Cimbri and Teutones, who in Tacitus' time were still living in Jutland.

There is little disagreement about locating the Goths in Scandinavia, but the vortices of controversy appear again when an attempt is made to locate them in the Vistula region. This issue cannot be solved unless a firm stand is taken as to the correctness of the sources; one cannot trust Ptolemy, while accepting at the same time an ethnographic or prehistoric interpretation which insists that the Goths lived in places other than those indicated by Ptolemy. This applies also to the question of the territory occupied by the Venedian tribes. Either the Venedi lived on the Baltic coast, and the Goths south of them, or the Goths occupied the shore, and Ptolemy is entirely wrong in placing them south of the Venedi. The first alternative seems more likely and would perhaps have seemed so to many other people if the Venedi had not been considered to have been Slavs.

Ptolemy begins his ethnographic catalog of European Sarmatia with a list of its major peoples. "There live in Sarmatia very big peoples: the Venedai along the entire Venedian Gulf, and above Dakia the Peukinoi and Basternai (or Bastarnai), and along the entire Maiotis coast the Iazyges and Rhoxolanoi, and more to the interior of the country the Hamaxobioi and the Alaunoi Skythai."[10] In other words, the Venedi appear to be the inhabitants of the western part of Sarmatia, from the Baltic Sea southward. The country north of the Roman province Dacia was occupied by the Peucini-Bastarnae. Along the coast of the Sea of Azov there were the Iazyges and Roxolani. The interior of the country was occupied by the Scythian Alani and the Sarmatians, proper nomadic tribes well known from other sources. Ptolemy calls them the *Hamaxobioi,* meaning 'wagon-dwellers,' derived from Greek *hamaxa* 'the cart' and *bionai* 'to live,' an appellation apparently given them by merchants.

Of immediate interest are only the Venedi, who were neighbors of the Goths. Tacitus speaks of them as of peoples roaming over the entire forest and mountain area between the Peucini and Fenni. They appear again in Ptolemy's text as a numerous people. As such, they must have occupied an adequately large portion of land. To date it is not known how wide the Venedian territory really was; this subject is still disputed among scholars. Ptolemy, however, adds some new information that allows for the determination of their frontiers, namely, that the Venedi lived along the entire Venedian Gulf. This gulf or bay could have been situated only at the Baltic Sea. In another place, Ptolemy speaks of "Venedian Mountains," which implies that the Venedi lived not only at the Baltic Sea, but also in the mountains. Several more or less credible solutions have been suggested for the location of both gulf and mountains.

The question of the ethnic origin of the Venedi is very old. Tacitus was the first to try to solve it. Limited to a choice between Germanic and Sarmatian peoples, he classified them as Germanic. The prevailing view expressed in the literature on the subject is that the Venedi, who occupied the lands east of Germania, are the Slavs of ancient times; this view has been adopted by me as the basis for geographical investigation of certain parts of the Venedian territory. For the sake of accuracy, however, it should be mentioned that Piotr Nikolaievich Tret'iakov's archaeological studies point to a different conclusion. According to him, the term Venedi is tantamount to the name of all eastern neighbors of the Germani; the Slavs were thus only a part of the Venedi. [12] In theory, Tret'iakov's definition could have some bearing on the ex-

planation of certain local conditions, since among the non-Slavic eastern neighbors of the Germani there were a few Celtic and Baltic tribes
in the southwestern or northern parts of the Oder-Vistula region. In
practice, however, it makes no difference in our discussion whether all
of the Venedi or only some of them were Slavs.

The name Venedi, Venethi, and other variants is not restricted to the
Oder-Vistula region. It also appears in Celtic and Illyrian tribal names in
Brittany, in Northern Italy, in the northern part of Macedonia, and
other places. It is derived from the Indo-European *ven 'to like, to be
friendly' or 'the friendly people, the clan' (German die Befreundeten,
die Versippten). The later Germanic form is *weni 'friend,' Irish *venia
'kindred, clan, tribe.' It appears in tribal names such as *winidos and
*vinithos, which meant a friendly or neighboring people. This root
survived in Germanic languages for a long time under the forms Winida,
Venda, Vinda, Winden, Veonodland, to denote the Slavs, their individual tribes, or their territory. Even today, the German name for the
Polabian Serbs is Wenden. At the same time, the name is absent and
unknown in the Slavic languages. No Slavic tribe or ethnic unit ever
called itself by the name Venedi or any related form. It is only a
Germanic collective name for some Slavic groups.[13]

From the above linguistic summary two conclusions, acceptable to
all, may be drawn. They are strictly geographical and should help to
locate Ptolemy's Venedi. The first conclusion is that the Venedi must
not be placed in the same category as the individual tribes or, as Ptolemy calls them the "smaller peoples," though some of these tribes or
"smaller peoples" in the area may have belonged to the Venedian
group. The second conclusion is that wherever the form Venedi appears
as part of a geographical name, it indicates that the place was inhabited
by Venedi, or that Venedian groups lived in its proximity. At the same
time, it reveals that some Germanic tribes lived nearby in order to give
it that name. However, there may be exceptions to the second inferred
rule. A place name containing a form derived from the name of the
Venedi could have been used by traveling merchants, for whom a local
name might have been difficult to remember or to pronounce. They
might have taken a characteristic ethnographic term and applied it to a
place. The Venedian mountains could have been a sharp dividing line
between Germanic and Slavic tribes; they might also have been a mountain range situated somewhere in a region predominantly inhabited by
Slavic peoples. Greek or Roman merchants could have named these
mountains just as they used the appellations 'the river of the Suebi' or

'the river of the Goths' instead of the local names of the Oder. These two propositions, insignificant as they may appear, are of utmost value in an attempt to outline the territory of Ptolemy's Venedi. According to his text the Goths were their immediate neighbors and lived at the Vistula. This indicates that the Goths lived at the border between Germania and Sarmatia.

From the passage of the *Geography* quoted earlier, it appears that the Venedi lived "along the entire Venedian Gulf." In the general description of European Sarmatia Ptolemy says that it "borders in the north upon the Sarmatian Ocean along the Venedian Gulf and the land which is partially unknown, along the following line: beyond the estuary of the Vistula which has a location of 45°,56°, there is the estuary of the Chronos River at 50°,56°, . . . in the west, the Vistula River and the land between its source and the Sarmatian Mountains, which have been described already."[14]

No question has ever been raised regarding the Sarmatian Ocean, which can only be the Baltic Sea, but there are different opinions about the location of the Venedian Gulf. Ptolemy describes the northern frontier of Sarmatia in a west-east direction. This is logical since the ancient navigators approached this portion of the world only from the west. The Venedian Gulf thus appears to have been situated in the northwestern part of Sarmatia. Such a location points to the Gulf of Danzig, which is embraced by the shore east and west of the estuary of the Vistula. In the belief of the ancients the Vistula was the dividing line between Germania and Sarmatia. According to Ptolemy the Venedi lived along the entire Venedian Gulf, which means that they lived east and west of the Vistula or, in other words, partly in Germania and partly in Sarmatia. At least, it appeared so to the ancient navigators, and there is no reason to doubt the correctness of their observations.

Some modern historians believe that the country west of the Vistula, called in ancient times Germania, was inhabited entirely by Germanic tribes; no Venedi, therefore, could have lived west of the river. Consequently, these scholars have suggested other places for the location of the Venedian Gulf farther away from the Vistula. The Vistula Lagoon (Zalew wiślański, Frisches Haff) is a favorite suggestion for the location of the gulf. The Courland Lagoon (Zalew kuroński, Kurisches Haff) and the Gulf of Riga have also been considered as possible locations. All these places seem doubtful or impossible solutions. They lead to the paradoxical conclusion that the Venedian Gulf was situated in a place where peoples other than the Venedi lived. Most of the shoreline along the Vistula Lagoon would have been inhabited by Balts, and only the southwestern corner would have been occupied by Slavs. Entering the lagoon the ancient navigators would have met predominantly Baltic peoples; the name "Venedian Gulf" in a Baltic country would make little sense. The Courland Lagoon was entirely inhabited by Balts, and the Gulf of Riga by Baltic and Finno-Ugric tribes. In Ptolemy's account, the location of the Venedian Gulf causes more confusion the farther it is removed from the Vistula. Archaeological evidence indicates that Slavic prehistoric cultures did not extend farther east than to the Pasłęka. Hence, one must go back to the Gulf of Danzig as the only possible location for Ptolemy's Venedian Gulf. It has also been suggested that the name Venedian Gulf refers to the Baltic Sea, or to a certain part of it. This solution is not very fortunate either, since it conflicts with the name "Sarmatian Ocean," the term used by Ptolemy for the Baltic Sea.

Prehistoric maps of the northern Oder-Vistula region do not prove that the Vistula was a dividing line between two different archaeological cultures since the same cultural forms were found on both sides of the river. A change in forms occurs only near the Pasłęka. If Germanic peoples lived along the Baltic coast west of the Vistula, they must have lived also along the coast between the Vistula and the Pasłeka. The country east of the Pasłęka belonged to the archaeological West Baltic culture, and was inhabited by Baltic tribes. In other words, there is no space left for placing the Venedi between the Germanic and the Baltic tribes. However, since the Venedi were the western neighbors of the Balts, they must be placed west of the Pasłeka and consequently also west of the Vistula. It follows that the Germanic tribes of the Baltic maritime region lived farther from the Vistula. When Ptolemy speaks of a "Venedian Gulf," he repeats observations made by ancient navigators, experienced sailors who knew their nautical terminology. For them a gulf was a portion of the sea enclosed by land, whose existence was indicated by sea currents. Sailing eastward, they could not have been unaware of the Gulf of Danzig, situated between the Hel and Sambia peninsulas. The westerly winds created sea currents which pointed from Hel directly to the environs of the present city of Gdynia.[15] It is this gulf that was the first gulf in the Sarmatian Ocean; named by sailors the "Venedian Gulf," it coincides with the present Gulf of Danzig.[16]

The Venedian Mountains pose a different problem. According to Ptolemy, they were situated 47°30′ east of the Fortunate Islands at the latitude of 55°.[17] By deducting the maximum of Marinus' error, this location should be corrected to 45°30′ and 53°. These figures correspond with a location of 19°24' east of Greenwich (counting 30 Ptolemaic minutes east of the estuary of the Vistula), and the present-day fifty-third parallel. If Ptolemy's distance from the Vistula to the Venedian Mountains was not affected by Marinus' error, the location of the mountains would be 21° east of Greenwich (counting 2°30' Ptolemaic degrees east of the estuary of the Vistula) and 53° latitude. On Ptolemaic maps the Venedian Mountains are drawn as a small mountain range along the fifty-fifth (i.e., our fifty-third) parallel. The entire Venedian territory is squeezed into a small strip of land between the Venedian Mountains on the south, the Baltic coast on the north, the Vistula on the west, and the Rudon on the east.[18] These representations do not agree with reality. Ptolemy's figures refer to the Mazovian Lowland, and the orographic structure of the country has not changed since. If in that area there are no mountain ranges today, there could not have been any in Ptolemy's times either. On the other hand, it should be emphasized that Ptolemy did not invent the name in Alexandria. The conclusion is obvious; the Venedian Mountains lay somewhere else, and Ptolemy apparently misinterpreted data from one itinerary and applied them to locations found in another source.

The entire Mazovian Lake district is a lowland with some hilly parts in the south. The hypsometric structure shows a markedly lower elevation (under 150 meters) in the west than in the east. Between Lubawa and Nidzica it exceeds 200 meters, with peaks of up to 312 meters (Góra Dylewska, formerly Kernsdorfer Höhe). In the central part, the elevation is between 180 and 200 meters. In the eastern part, the Szeskie Hills (Seester Höhe), the highest point is 309 meters above sea level. In the Dylewskie Hills, the Dylewska Góra is the only hill higher than 300 meters. The neighboring hills have a height ranging between 213 and 233 meters.[19]   In simple terms this is a hilly country which cannot be called mountainous. Whether the ancient merchants called them hills or mountains is difficult to say. They came from Rome or from the Pontus. They had crossed the Sudeten or traveled along the Carpathians and had seen hundreds of hills of the type of the Mazovian Hills. Why should they suddenly have been impressed by these hills and have called them mountains?

Since no real mountains could be discovered in the place indicated by Ptolemy, the entire chain of the Mazovian Hills or parts of it were suggested as possible or tentative locations for the Venedian Mountains. According to Tymieniecki, the search for these mountains near the Baltic coast is a "geographical surprise." There have been attempts to explain this "surprise" by considering the possibility that to the ancient navigators sailing along the coast, these hills might have looked much higher than they really were.[20] This optical illusion appears to be a highly unrealistic solution. The Mazovian Hills are not visible from the coast, they lie inland, at a distance of about 100 to 160 kilometers from the shore. It would have required from four to six days of overland travel to reach the tops of these hills. The country between the coast and the alleged Venedian Mountains was inhabited by Venedi. A sailor or merchant coming from the coast could not pick up a Germanic name for these mountains. The name Venedian was justified for the Gulf of Danzig, since it reflected a change in population. Coming into the area from the west, however, the sailors traveled for several weeks along a coast where they constantly met Germanic speakers. Approximately near the Hel Peninsula they encountered people who spoke a different language. The Germanic traders called them Venedi. It was, therefore, natural to name the Gulf of Danzig the Venedian Gulf. But once the foreign sailors set foot on Venedian soil, they would not have heard the name Venedi any longer, because it was not used by the local population. The name Venedian Mountains did not get into Ptolemy's source material via the sea trade; it was acquired from an itinerary. Any traveler coming from the north or east would have picked a Slavic or Baltic name, provided that the Venedian Mountains were situated in the province of Olsztyn. Since the name is of Germanic origin, it was contained in an itinerary that described a route passing through Germanic territory, and in this case, the Venedian mountains did not lie in the province of Olsztyn.

Scholars studying the early history of the Slavic peoples have been puzzled by the graphic representation of the Venedian Mountains on Ptolemaic maps. They did not want to accept Ptolemy's computation and the size of the Venedian territory as shown on these maps, and have argued that since Ptolemy had described the Venedi as a numerous people, they could not have lived in the narrow stretch of land between the Baltic Sea, the Mazovian Hills, the Vistula, and the Pasłęka, because the land east of the Pasłęka was Baltic. This would amount to an area of 70 kilometers in width and 100 kilometers in length. Hence, they reached the conclusion that Ptolemy must have made an error, and tended to locate these mountains in other places. Niederle was the first to raise this issue. He called them "the Slavic Mountains," which were identical with the Carpathians, despite the fact that in another place in Ptolemy's work, the Carpathians are listed by their proper name.

Niederle explains that Ptolemy took the information from two sources, recording the same mountain range by two different names.[21] This interpretation has been accepted by Dvornik and Tymieniecki.[22] Another explanation was offered by Lehr-Spławiński, who doubted the validity of identifying the Venedian Mountains with the Carpathians. He emphasized that both mountain ranges are listed in Ptolemy's text separately and close to each other. It should not be necessary to suspect duplication of names in the text, he says, it looks rather as if the names designated two different mountains in close proximity. Hence he suggested the Świetokrzyskie Mountains, in the province of Kielce.[23] This view was endorsed by Jan Czekanowski, who reproduces in his works a map by Jażdżewski. Jażdżewski, however, proposes it only as a possible solution.[24]

All critical speculations as to the area occupied by the Venedi contain an erroneous concept, namely the assumption that the Venedi lived only between the Venedian Gulf and the Venedian Mountains, and that by fixing these two places the territory occupied by the Venedi can be established. Nowhere in his text did Ptolemy make such a statement.

The text contains four separate statements. 1. The Venedi are a prominent or large people of European Sarmatia; 2. They live near the Vistula and north of the Goths; 3. There exists a Venedian gulf; 4. There exists a mountain range called the Venedian Mountains. These statements contain different pieces of information. One should not draw the premature conclusion that the entire Venedian group was confined solely to the space between the Baltic coast and the territory occupied by the Goths, and that consequently the Venedian Mountains were the border between the Venedi and the Goths. This is the impression one may gain from Ptolemaic maps.

When Ptolemy records the Venedi (III, 5, 19) as one of the six (or seven) major ethnic groups of European Sarmatia, his only spatial reference is that they lived "along the entire Venedian Gulf," by which he indicates a general location in the northwestern part of European Sarmatia. The territory occupied by Venedian tribes, indeed, was large; historical sources supported by archaeological evidence prove that it embraced most of the Oder-Vistula region. The Venedian Mountains could have existed only in a mountainous part of this large territory. Mountainous regions exist only in the southwestern or southern part but not in the northern section of the Oder-Vistula region. The etymology of the name Venedi indicates that these mountains lay presumably but not necessarily in a border area between Slavic and Germanic tribes.

The theory of the Mazovian Hills, therefore, can be safely excluded from further discussions for these reasons, and for the simple fact that they lay in a country inhabited by Baltic, and not by Germanic or Slavic tribes.

On the other hand, when Ptolemy describes the Venedi as the northern neighbors of the Goths and Galindi (III, 5, 20), his words "below the Venedai" do not refer to the entire Venedian ethnic group, but only to those Venedian units that lived on the Baltic coast and the Lower Vistula. The Gothic and Burgundian territory was an enclave in Venedian lands and could have been surrounded by many Venedian tribes of whom Ptolemy mentions only those living north of the Goths.

Discussion of the Venedian question is essential, since it reveals the two different concepts of the Venedi present in Ptolemy's text, i.e., the Venedi as a large ethnic group, and Venedian units dispersed over the entire Venedian territory. This clear distinction is the key to the successful location of the Goths.

The Goths of European Sarmatia are counted among the "smaller peoples." Ptolemy lists these peoples in columns starting with those living along the Vistula. The columns are arranged in a west-east direction, and within each column the peoples are listed in a north-south order.

The Goths appear in the first column, which says that "Sarmatia is inhabited by the [following] smaller peoples; at the Vistula river below the Venedai there are the Gythones, then the Finnoi, then the Bulanes (or Sulones), below them there are the Frugundiones, then the Varenoi (or Abarinoi) at the source of the Vistula river. Below them there are the Ombrones, then the Anartofraktoi, then the Burgiones, then the Arsietai, then the Sabokoi, then the Piengitai, and the Biessoi at the Karpates mountains[25] (see map 17).

As mentioned earlier, Ptolemy's term "below" indicates a general southern location meaning south, southeast, or southwest. He places the Goths at the Vistula, south of the Venedi. It is not necessary to emphasize that he has the territory east of the Vistula in mind, since he is describing the peoples of European Sarmatia. Together with the Goths, he also lists the Finns and Sulones, not using the word "below" however. Therefore, the Goths, Finns, and Sulones did not live south of each other, but in a different order from north to south. The Finns are listed here by mistake, since their abodes were situated farther to the northeast. This leaves only the Goths and the Sulones as the southern neighbors of the Venedi living on the Baltic coast. Since the Goths

Map 17. Trade routes in the Oder-Vistula region during the first and second centuries A.D. and Ptolemy's first column of peoples inhabiting European Sarmatia.

occupied the territory along the east bank of the river, the Sulones could have lived either east of the Goths, which would not be at the Vistula anymore, or west of the Goths, i.e., beyond the river, in Germania. Of these two possible locations of the Sulones, the country east of the Goths has to be excluded, since this space was taken by the Galindi. Therefore, the location of the Sulones has to be set as west of the Goths, that is, in Germania.

South of the Goths there were the Frugundiones, whose location shall be discussed with that of the Burgundians (see p. 127ff). Somewhere near the source of the Vistula there were the Varenoi (Avarini). In describing their location, Ptolemy reaches the Carpathian Mountains.

He speaks of the Ombrones as living south of the Varenoi (Avarini), i.e., in modern Slovakia or Hungary, areas that were outside the territory of Sarmatia. Ptolemy uses the word "below" for the last time to describe the respective locations of the Varenoi and Ombrones. The subsequent name of the Anartofraktoi looks like a Latin-Greek compound and may be related to the Anartoi, or Anartes, living in Dacia.[26] All the succeeding tribes of this column, i.e., the Burgiones, Arsietai, Sabokoi, Piengitai, and Biessoi, would then be inhabitants of Dacia, the Karpates Mountain being the southwestern slopes of the Carpathians.

Not much imagination is necessary to discover that there is something wrong in the order within the column. Its first part fits into a description of the western part of European Sarmatia, along the Vistula. The second part looks as if Ptolemy had gone across the Sarmatian border and continued listing the inhabitants of Sarmatia in Dacia. It is easy to discover Ptolemy's error, and it is not difficult to correct it, following a close look at the network of reconstructed ancient trade routes along the Vistula.

There was one route coming from Carnuntum through the Moravian Gate that followed the course of the Vistula, almost from its source. The ancient amber route went through Kłodzko and Kalisz toward the Lower Vistula. Two routes were coming from the Pontus; one joined the route along the Vistula at the estuary of the San, the other at the estuary of the Bug. All itineraries describing these routes mention the Vistula and the Baltic Sea. Each of them was compiled in a different manner, and each reported different observations; this alone could have furnished a serious source of confusion. The various parts of the river are covered separately. The country between the Moravian Gate and the estuary of the San is described by one itinerary only. Two itineraries deal with the distance between the San and the Bug. Three itineraries speak of the portion between the Bug and Bydgoszcz. The distance between Bydgoszcz and the Baltic coast is covered by four itineraries.

Despite the abundance of trade routes and the possible existence of several itineraries, Ptolemy's knowledge about the Vistula was fragmentary. He records only two points, the source and the estuary of the river, the latter in an adjusted location. All information obtained from itineraries had to be applied to the course of an unknown river, and the distances reported along this unknown river had to be adjusted to comply with Marinus' computation.

Ptolemy used at least two Roman itineraries describing the routes along the Vistula. Since he mentions the source of the river and some peoples in its vicinity, he must have been familiar with a report on the route from the Moravian Gate to the Upper Vistula which went along the river. The recording of Kalisz shows that he used a description of the ancient amber route. In addition to the Roman material, he also had an itinerary describing the route from the Pontus to the Bug and Narew. This itinerary mentions the Vistula too. However, the point at which this route reached the Vistula was the estuary of the Bug, and not the source of the Vistula. There is a distance of more than two degrees in latitude between these two points, a distance Ptolemy was suspicious of. He had a valid location for the Vistula (i.e., its source), and the Greek itinerary did not specify the point at which it reached the river (i.e., at the estuary of the Narew). Therefore, Ptolemy did not see any need for adjusting the distances reported in the Greek itinerary. These two points, i.e., the Vistula at its source and at the estuary of the Bug, became one point in his calculations. As a consequence of this, peoples listed as living along the Narew, the Bug, and toward the south-eastern slopes of the Carpathians are listed as living between the source of the Vistula and the southwestern slopes of the Carpathians.

All that needs to be done to correct Ptolemy's error is to split the first column into two sections. The first should contain the names of the peoples living along the Vistula, and the second, the names of those which Ptolemy inadvertently placed in Dacia. The second section should not be continued in a southward direction from the source of the Vistula, but should be placed parallel to the beginning of the first section, perhaps somewhere at the Lower Bug or Lower Narew. Thus all the tribes of the first column can be placed in Sarmatia instead of in Sarmatia and in Dacia. The second section of the list should contain the names of tribes living along the Bug toward the eastern slopes of the Carpathians. They should be placed tentatively in the eastern part of the country, between the Vistula and the Bug, in order not to interfere with the geographical location of peoples listed in Ptolemy's second column. However, a proper point must be found at which to divide the column and this has to be as close as possible to the source of the Vistula, since only Roman merchants coming through the Moravian Gate would pass this region.

Ptolemy places the Varenoi near the source of the Vistula, and says that south of them there were the Ombrones. This surely must be information supplied by Roman merchants, because only they would have known the tribes living near the source of the river and those who lived farther south. It is doubtful who supplied the information on the location of the Anartofraktoi. If they are identical with the Anartes, known to Caesar, the Roman merchants could have supplied the information on that tribe too, though the name may have reached Ptolemy through intermediary channels. The next tribe, however, the Burgiones, do not fit into a Roman itinerary, since their alleged location deep in Dacia was too far from the environs of the Upper Vistula. There is some disagreement among scholars about this tribe. The majority agrees that the name is of Germanic origin. Etymologically it is considered similar to or identical with that of the Burgundians. A relationship was also discovered between the name of the Burgundians and that of the Frugundiones.[27] In ancient writings these three names apply to human groups that appear in various places, vaguely or inaccurately described. Modern historical criticism and prehistoric evidence have not succeeded in bringing these groups together in one area. Some evaluations of linguistic evidence thus went in one direction, and the location of the groups in another. The names Burgundians - Frugundiones - Burgiones can be three variants of one and the same name or one variant each of three different names. Our investigation shall eventually lead to the conclusion that all three names refer to one and the same tribe.

The Burgundian question has been mentioned before (pp. 84-85) and only its main aspects will be highlighted here. In Pliny's, and perhaps also in Strabo's time, the Burgundians lived west of the Middle Oder. After 77 A.D. they moved to the Lower Vistula. Ptolemy's Burgundians (Buguntai) of Germania lived on the west side of the Lower Vistula; his Burgundians (Frugundiones) of European Sarmatia lived on the east side of this river. These two territories lay in the same general area. The Burgiones, the first people listed in the second section of Ptolemy's first column, should be placed near the estuary of the Bug. This puts the Burgiones in exactly the same area where the Buguntai-Frugundiones have already been located. The final conclusion is that the Buguntai-Frugundiones-Burgiones are one and the same people, known as Burgundians. Their abodes lay partly in Germania and partly in Sarmatia, with the Vistula and the Narew flowing through their lands. Their territory has been tentatively equated with the present-day districts of Inowrocław, Włocławek, and Płock.

The identification of the Burgiones with the Burgundians in their location at the Lower Vistula justifies the division of the first column into two sections and brings about a few changes on Ptolemy's map. All the peoples listed in the second section of the first column can now safely be placed between the Vistula, the Bug, and the region south of these two rivers without interfering with the second column (see figures 11 and 12).

It is interesting to note that in the first section of the first column

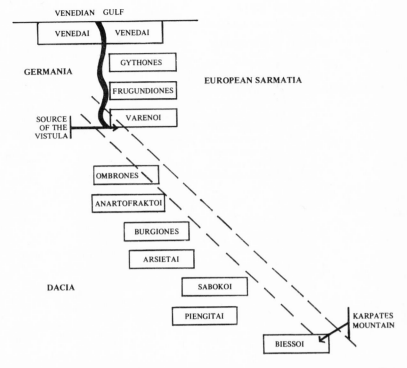

Figure 11. Schematic location of the "smaller peoples" of European Sarmatia listed in the first column (Ptolemy, III, 5, 20).

Ptolemy uses the word "below" several times for clearly southern directions, while he applies the term "then" to undefined locations. The Goths, Frugundiones, and Ombrones are described in a precise north-south order. The Varenoi are reported in a well-defined locality, i.e., at the source of the Vistula. The word "then" puts the Finns in a wrong, the Sulones in an uncertain, and the Anartofraktoi in a correct place, but this correct place was outside of Sarmatia. In the second section Ptolemy does not use the term "below" at all, and introduces all locations with the word "then." He must have had good reason for changing the terminology; there are two possible circumstances that might have prompted him to do so. The first is that the Roman report of the route along the Vistula, used for compiling the first section, contained more precisely described data than the Greek report of the route along the Bug, which supplied information for the second section. The second

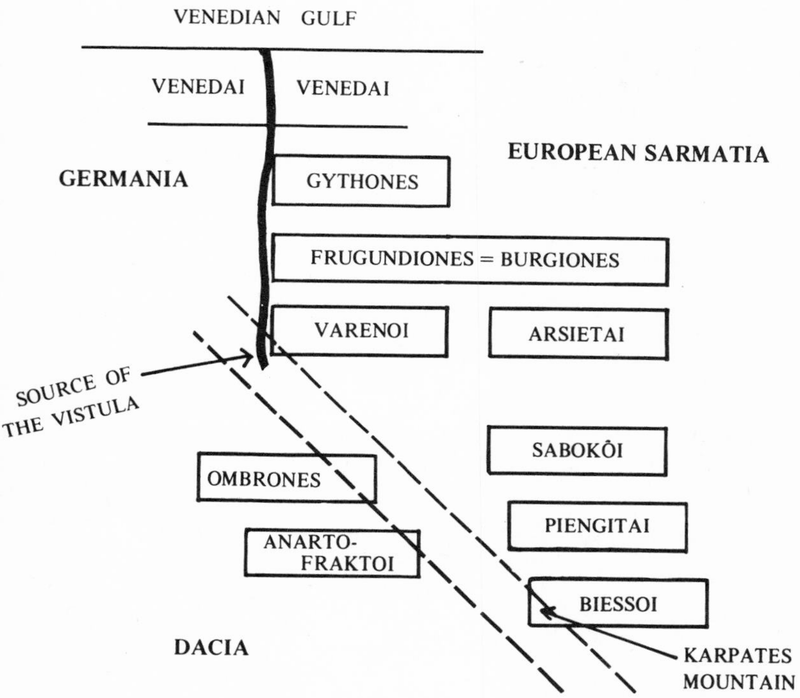

Figure 12. Schematic location of the "smaller peoples" of European Sarmatia listed in the first column (Ptolemy, III, 5, 20) after the identification Frugundiones = Burgiones.

possibility is that both itineraries were similar in content and style, but that Ptolemy became confused in the process of compiling his data. He was convinced that he was continuing a list of peoples who lived along the western border of Sarmatia, i.e., south of the source of the Vistula. Actually, he took his information from an itinerary describing the route along the Bug. This route went from the southeastern slopes of the Carpathians in a north-northwest direction. North of Brest, the Bug, and also the trade route, turned slowly toward the west, in a direction continued by the course of the Narew and part of the Vistula. All points situated north of Brest were reported as distances toward the west. Between Brest and Bydgoszcz there is a longitudinal distance of more than five degrees in modern measurement, or almost seven in Ptolemy's, i.e., a distance longer than that between the estuaries of the Vistula and the Oder, or between the source of the Vistula and a point west of the Elbe. A deviation to the west of such immense extent must have looked suspect to Ptolemy. Yet, scrupulous as he was, he did not want to omit names of peoples who, according to the merchants' reports, lived in that area. Since he thought that the directions were wrong while the distances appeared to be correct, he had no choice but to record the location of the peoples involved with less precision by using the term "then" instead of north and west or east and south.

The tract of land and routes between the estuary of the Bug and Bydgoszcz were bound to create confusion in the minds of ancient scholars who had to work without maps. Trade routes from the southwest, south, and east entered the area and left it somewhere north of Bydgoszcz, forking in two directions, to the Gulf of Danzig and the Gulf of Riga.

Diagrams drawn in accordance with the text of the itineraries reveal the following sequences along the various routes (see figure 13):

1. Kalisia–Lower Vistula–Venedi–Finns (Gulf of Riga)
2. Kalisia–Lower Vistula–Goths–Venedi (Gulf of Danzig)
3. Frugundiones–Goths–Venedi (Gulf of Danzig)
4. Frugundiones–Goths–Finns (Gulf of Riga)
5. Arsietai–Burgiones–Sulones–Finns (Gulf of Riga)
6. Arsietai–Burgiones–Sulones–Venedi (Gulf of Danzig).

Under these circumstances, Ptolemy's ethnographic catalog could misplace the locations of several peoples recorded in the itineraries; in fact this is exactly what happened to the Finns and Sulones.

Ptolemy's Finnoi are identical with Tacitus' Fenni (Finns), the inhabitants of northeast Sarmatia. The name was a collective appellation for the Ugro-Finnic peoples of northeastern Europe, who occupied the land stretching from the Ural Mountains to the Baltic Sea, including also the Gulf of Riga.[28] This gulf was the terminal point of a trade route coming from the Lower Vistula. Neither the gulf, nor the Finns would have been omitted from an itinerary describing this route. Ptolemy's location of the Finns in a wrong place is actually a minor error, although it involves a long distance. The itinerary apparently mentioned some Venedian tribes living between the route and the Baltic coast (i.e., north of the route), and then the Finns at the terminal point. Ptolemy already knew that the Goths lived south of the Venedi, and therefore placed the Finns south of the Goths, in a location closer to the Vistula than to the Gulf of Riga.

The location of the Sulones is disputable, because it is difficult to

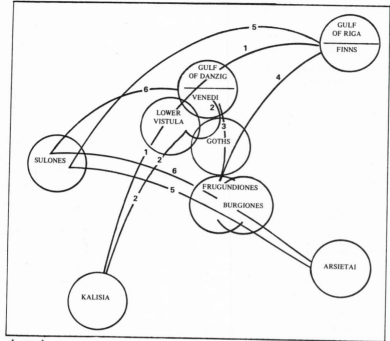

Legend

1 Kalisia–Lower Vistula–Venedi–Finns (Gulf of Riga)
2 Kalisia–Lower Vistula–Goths–Venedi (Gulf of Danzig)
3 Frugundiones–Goths–Venedi (Gulf of Danzig)
4 Frugundiones–Goths–Finns (Gulf of Riga)
5 Arsietai–Burgiones–Sulones–Finns (Gulf of Riga)
6 Arsietai–Burgiones–Sulones–Venedi (Gulf of Danzig)

Figure 13. Possible deviations caused by interpreting directions recorded in itineraries.

figure out from which itinerary Ptolemy took his information on that tribe. In manuscripts the name appears as Sulones, Sulanes, Bulanes.[29] The reading Sulones seems to be generally preferred, though it has been mentioned that the original form of Bulanes was Sulanes. Since the tribe is not known from any other source, there have been several attempts to emendate the spelling to forms resembling the names of other peoples. One of them aimed at the discovery of a possible relationship between the Bulanes and the Borani. The name Sulones was corrected to Sudones, and in the latter form, identified with that of the Sudinoi, one of the distant neighbors of the Goths. The equation of their names would eliminate the existence of one of these two tribes. It is a questionable solution. Tymieniecki rejects a correction from Bulanes to Pulanes, a form which allegedly survived in the medieval tribal name Polanie. Steche speaks against the identification of the Sulones with the Suiones.[30] As in other similar cases, the attention of scholars has been focused on the name and ethnic origin of the tribe. In the emendated form Suiones they were considered a Germanic tribe, but several historians, such as Niederle, Plezia, and Tymieniecki, have suggested a possible Slavic origin.[31]

On Ptolemaic maps the Sulones are usually placed near the Middle Vistula, south of the Goths and Finns. Tymieniecki located them halfway between the Baltic coast and the Carpathians, in the country west of the Vistula, south of the Frugundiones, with their territory extending probably as far as beyond the Sudeten. His maps place the center of the tribe on the Middle Warta.[32] According to Ptolemy's text, the Sulones must have lived in the vicinity of the Vistula, either near the estuary of the Bug, or near Bydgoszcz. Earlier in this study their abodes were tentatively set west of the Goths, since there is not enough space for them between the Goths and the peoples of Ptolemy's second column. This tentative location seems to be the proper solution to the problem. Apparently Ptolemy took their location from an itinerary of the route along the Bug which must have mentioned the Burgiones west of the Arsietai. In the country of the Burgiones, the route crossed the Vistula, and west of that river the itinerary must have mentioned the Sulones, still in the direction Arsietai–Burgiones–Sulones. It is also possible that this itinerary mentioned both Sulones and Goths north of the Burgiones. In any case, the Sulones were inhabitants of Germania, and either the western or southwestern neighbors of the Goths. There is, however, a remote possibility that the Sulones appeared in a description of the route from the Lower Vistula to the Gulf of Riga. Ptolemy's order Goths–Finns–Sulones changed to Goths–Sulones–Finns would place the Sulones between the Goths and the Gulf of Riga. In this case, a connection could be established between the names Sulones and Sudini. As mentioned from the beginning, this is only a remote possibility, and, therefore, the location of the Sulones in Germania was considered the better solution.

This ends the discussion of Ptolemy's first column. The following four major conclusions may be drawn: 1. Ptolemy used two different listings and combined both in one straight column running from north to south, instead of placing them parallel to each other; 2. Some Venedian tribes occupied the region around the estuary of the Vistula;

3. The Buguntai–Frugundiones–Burgiones are one and the same people, generally known by the name Burgundians, and they occupied the land around the estuary of the Bug; 4. The Goths occupied a territory situated east of the Lower Vistula, south of the Venedi, north of the Burgundians, and had the Sulones as their western or southwestern neighbors.

Ptolemy's second column is a list of peoples living east of those mentioned in the first column. It reads: "there are further to the east of the mentioned [peoples] and still below the Venedai, the Galindai (or Galidanoi) and the Sudenoi (or Sudinoi) and the Stauanoi as far as to the Alaunoi, below them the Igylliones, then the Koistobokoi and Transmontanoi toward the Peukines Mountains."[33] The expected order is a general north-south direction, but the word "below" is sparingly used in this column. The location "south of" refers only to the Galindi and Igulliones; all other locations are expressed by the indefinite directions "then" or "and."

The structure of this column is similar to that of the first one. The column consists of two parts put together, but this time the two sections are clearly visible. The Igulliones cannot be placed south of the Alani, who were one of the Sarmatian tribes that in Ptolemy's time lived north of the Caucasus region, most likely between the rivers Don and Donets.[34] Placing the Igulliones south of the Alani makes them inhabitants of the Caucasus region. Consequently, the Koistobokoi and Transmontanoi should be placed between the Caucasus and the Peukines Mountains (i.e., the southern tips of the Carpathians). This creates an erratic pattern extending from the Lower Vistula to the Caucasus in a southeast direction and switching to the west, from the Caucasus to the Carpathians.

Ptolemy's text, therefore, has to be interpreted in a different manner. At the beginning of the column he lists the Galindi and then the Sudini, the Stavani, and the Alani in an approximate southeast direction. Later on he goes back to the beginning of the column and describes the Igulliones, Koistobokoi, and Transmontanoi in an approximate southern direction toward the Carpathians. Thus the Alani are at the end of the first section, the Igulliones at the beginning of the second, and the southern part of the Carpathians at its end. The passage in the text "below them the Igulliones" refers to the Galindi, and not to the Alani (figure 14).

Of the peoples listed in the second column, only the locations of the Galindi and Igulliones as possible immediate neighbors of the Goths shall be discussed. However, the Sudini should be mentioned briefly,

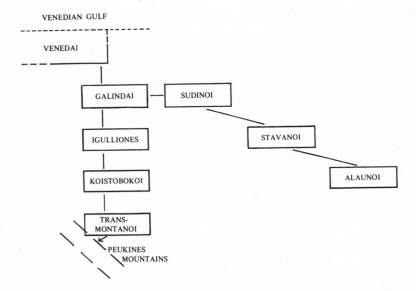

Figure 14. Schematic location of the "smaller peoples" of European Sarmatia listed in the second column (Ptolemy, III, 5, 21).

since the territories of the Galindi and Sudini are frequently discussed at the same time. The name Galindi appears in manuscripts as *Galindai* and *Galidanoi,* but the form Galindi (Galindai) is generally preferred.[35] Their ethnic origin has been viewed in various ways by scholars who have considered them either a Germanic, a Slavic or a Baltic tribe. According to Gustaf Kossinna they were Germanic, probably related to the Goths.[36] Franciszek Bujak maintains that the identification of the Galindi as Balts is doubtful; the Sudini, however, should be related to the later Sudawi-Jadźwingi.[37] Franke is undecided on the ethnic origin of the Sudini.[38] Kiessling believes that both the Galindi and the Sudini were "originally Slavic tribes" living in the interior of the present province of Olsztyn, in the country south of the Gulf of Danzig and the Courland Lagoon.[39] Rudnicki has tried to prove that the Galindi were Slavs. He derives their name from the Proto-Slavic roots *go-*ledi;* the prefix *go* as appearing in names such as *Go-plo, Go-lubie,* the root **ledi* appearing in later Slavic names as *Ledizi (Lendizi), *Leda (Lenda: Landa)* and several other forms.[40]

The majority of scholars believes that both the Galindi and the Sudini were of Baltic origin.[41] This belief is based chiefly on etymological analysis of the tribal names and on some archaeological evidence. There is a striking similarity between the names Galindi and Sudini, and Galindite and Sudowite, which are the names of two Prussian tribes recorded in the fourteenth century among the inhabitants of the present-day province of Olsztyn. The territories of the Galindite and Sudowite have been copiously described. To justify the equation Galindi-Galindite and Sudini-Sudowite, it was stressed that the situation along the former Venedian-Baltic frontier was more stable than along the Venedian-Germanic one, and the general ethnographic picture more stable. Major cultural or ethnic changes were not supposed to have taken place in this area, which witnessed only minor migratory moves. Apparently this lack of unrest was a characteristic feature of the stationary habit of the Balts.

No one needs to question the similarity or identity of the names Galindi and Galindite, and the Baltic origin of this people. However, one should not expect that the territorial extent of the medieval Galindite, described variously by scholars anyway, can be transferred without any change to a map of Ptolemy's time. After all, more than a thousand years elapsed between the recording of the Galindi and the Galindite. As a matter of fact, it is not even necessary to be influenced by the size and location of the territory of the medieval Galindite. Ptolemy's recording and its analysis, the assumption that the Galindi may have been a Baltic tribe, and the demarcation line between two archaeological cultures give enough information to permit the tentative location of their tribal territory.

Ptolemy's recording falls in the prehistoric Early Roman period (1-200 A.D.). At that time the eastern border of the Venedian, Pit-Grave or East-Germanic culture—whichever term is preferred—went from the Baltic coast southward along the Pasłęka. From the source of that river it turned southeast and then continued in a general eastern direction, parallel to and north of the Narew. Ptolemy placed Venedian tribes along the Gulf of Danzig. He listed the "smaller peoples" of European Sarmatia in several columns arranged in a general north-south order. The first column contains the names of tribes living at the western border of European Sarmatia. This appears from the location of the Goths "at the Vistula river below the Venedai." This location does not conflict with the correction we have proposed for his listing, which divides the first column into two parallel sections. Ptolemy's first column starts with the Goths living south of the Venedi, east of the Vistula, and north of the Burgundians, who occupied the country around the estuary of the Bug. The Pasłęka was the eastern border of the prehistoric Venedian culture; consequently, one would expect peoples other than Venedian east of that river. The hypothetical Gothic-Venedian border—tentatively set at the line Grudziądz-Pasłeka—was not longer than about 120 kilometers, a relatively short distance indicating a small territory.

Ptolemy's second column starts with the Galindi living "further to the east" of the peoples mentioned in the first column, "and still below the Venedai." This is a very accurate description of a southeast location. The territory south of the Venedi at the Lower Vistula was occupied by the Goths; the Galindi, therefore, lived east of them. Since the territory of the Goths was rather small, and there was hardly enough space for two peoples in the area between the Lower Vistula and the Pasłęka, the Galindi must be placed east of the Pasłęka. The Galindi, it follows, lived outside of the territory occupied by the Venedian culture, and should be classified as a Baltic tribe. This concluded fact, in turn, permits the definition of their tribal territory. Its western and southern limits were the upper Pasłęka, the area around the source of that river, and then a line somewhere north of and parallel to the Narew.

It is with genuine pleasure that one notes again the amazing accuracy of the observations found in ancient sources. As with many other cases, the vicinity of a trade route was responsible for the reliability of the information, correctly evaluated and computed by Ptolemy. A trade route heading toward the Gulf of Riga branched off at the Vistula near Bydgoszcz and traversed or bypassed the territories occupied by the Goths and Galindi. Merchants taking this road had on their right hand the country of the Goths and Galindi, and on their left the region occupied by Venedian tribes. This route must have been near the northern border of the Gothic and Galindian territory. Correctly interpreting information obtained from itineraries, Ptolemy located the Venedi, Goths, and Galindi with fair accuracy, though not quite precisely enough. The territory of the Galindi as described by Ptolemy is in agreement with the findings of some prehistorians, e.g., with those of Jósef Kostrzewski, who visualizes them as the ancient occupants of the present-day districts of Szczytno and Mrągowo (Ortelsburg and Sensburg).[42]

Next on Ptolemy's list are the Igulliones. By the phrase "below them the Igylliones" Ptolemy must have meant that the Igulliones lived "below" or south of the Galindi, and not south of any other peoples.

R. G. Latham, however, interprets Ptolemy's words differently, placing the Igulliones between the Stavani and Koistobokoi. In his words, "this would place the Igulliones in the southern part of Lithuania, or in the parts of *Grodno, Podolia,* and *Volhynia,* in the country of the *Jazwingi* of the thirteenth century,—there or thereabouts." He quotes Kaspar Zeuss, who adopts the reading *Ityngiones* instead of *Igylliones* and identifies it with the name *Jazwingi.*[43] The Jazwingi (Russian *Iatviagi,* Polish *Jaćwięgi, Jaćwingowie, Jadźwingowie*) were the same people as the Sudovians (Sudowite). In the thirteenth century they did not reach as far as Podolia or Volhynia, but were confined to a territory between the Niemen and the Narew. It is doubtful whether they ever reached the Narew, since several scholars claim that the Baltic population never extended beyond the Biebrza.[44]

Tymieniecki compares the name *Igulliones* (of unknown origin) to Polish place names of the type *Igołomia,* and sets the abode of the tribe broadly south of the Galindi, Sudini, and Stavani, placing the center east of the Vistula, close to the estuary of the Narew. It is the large territory of Mazowia that—as he explains—was in later times always occupied by Slavs; therefore it can hardly be expected that the situation was different in the Roman period. The Balts, he claims, never penetrated the area from the north, neither did the Germani from the west, the Thracians from the south, nor the Sarmatians from the east.[45] There is actually no reason to cast doubt upon the Slavic origin of the Igulliones, since their dwelling-places lay within the limits of the Venedian culture; no proof has ever been furnished that they could have been a Germanic tribe. However, Ptolemy's text, as interpreted in this study, indicates that two Germanic tribes, namely the Goths and the Burgundians, had crossed the Vistula from the west and settled in the western part of European Sarmatia. The tribal center of the Igulliones, therefore, lay farther to the east than Tymieniecki supposes.

Taken literally, Ptolemy's text places the Igulliones south of the Galindi, in the unoccupied space between the country around the source of the Pasłęka and the Narew. It is possible that their territory extended beyond the Narew, but it is impossible to determine how far it reached to the south. The Igulliones, like the Goths and many other tribes of the same category, were among the "smaller peoples" of European Sarmatia, which implies that their country could not have been very extensive. To the west it bordered on the countries of the Goths and Burgundians, and the demarcation line of the Venedian culture was their approximate northern border. With the settling of the

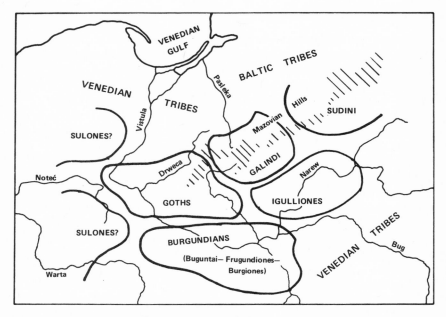

Map 18. Location of the Goths according to Ptolemy.

western and northern borders of the Igulliones, the circle around the Goths is closing, making it possible to define the area of the Gothic tribal territory.

In Ptolemy's time, they were one of the "smaller peoples" of European Sarmatia, which suggests that they did not occupy a large amount of land. The bulk of their abodes lay on the eastern side of the Lower Vistula valley, in the bend of the river between Włocławek and Grudziądz. Jażdżewski's map, which was described earlier, shows traces of Germanic cultures in this area that could be ascribed to the Goths (see figures 12 and 13). The country north of an imaginary straight line running between the source of the Pasłęka and the Vistula was inhabited by some of the Venedian tribes. Other Venedian tribes, the Sulones among them, were neighbors of the Goths in the west. It is possible that the Goths also occupied a stretch of land along the western bank of the Vistula. South of them was the country occupied by the Burgundians. The Igulliones were their neighbors in the east, and the Galindi probably in the northeast corner (map 18). The maximal extent of the Gothic territory should be visualized as an area enclosed by the following circle: Lubawa, Chełmno, Bydgoszcz, Włocławek, Ciechanów, Mława, and back to Lubawa.

Ptolemy is the last ancient author to record the Goths in the Oder-Vistula region. When they reappear in history, they are established at the Black Sea near the estuaries of the Danube. The exact time of their departure from the Lower Vistula is not known. The year 214 A.D. is usually mentioned as the first record of their presence in Dacia. Objections have been raised against this date, since it is based solely on an anecdote in the life of Caracalla.[46] The first Gothic settlers must have reached the Black Sea many years before 214 A.D. After about 230 A.D. they were strong enough to harass the frontiers of the Roman Empire at the Danube; the first major armed conflict between the Goths and the Romans is recorded in 238-39.[47]

Historians set the beginning of the Gothic migrations shortly after 150 A.D., pointing out that the Marcomannic wars (166-180 A.D.) were caused by the pressure of better organized barbarian tribes from the north, and implying that the Goths were of their number. This. supposition is not supported by any evidence or justification unless it was a fruitless attempt to settle in Pannonia. The idea of settling near the Black Sea must have existed during the Marcomannic wars or shortly before; the Black Sea was easier to reach via the trade routes along the Vistula or Bug to the Dniester, than through Pannonia. Due to the absence of recorded information the migration of the Goths can be dated only as some time after 150 and before 238 A.D. The first settlers probably started to move southward during the last decades of the second century, and the transfer of the entire population was completed before 230 A.D.

The general unrest in the Oder-Vistula region, the scarcity of arable land, and economic conditions may have been the factors that caused their emigration from the Lower Vistula. The Marcomannic wars undoubtedly worsened trade relations between the Roman Empire and the Baltic coast. This, in itself, was not the decisive factor for leaving the country, since the Gothic tribal society was agricultural-pastoral and did not depend on foreign trade. The general situation in the area, however, was very unstable; Slavic and Germanic tribes moved in all directions. The Goths were surrounded by relatively powerful tribes; expansion and acquisition of arable land by force was not possible. Large-scale deforestation was beyond the capability of primitive tribal organizations. The Goths, as many other tribes in the same situation, were compelled to leave their country and try their luck somewhere else. They chose to move toward the Black Sea.

The natural passages to the Black Sea were the Vistula and the Bug. A trade route went along the Vistula and the San, another along the

Bug, and both led to the Dniester; either or both could have been used by the Goths. Since their migration was a slow and long-lasting process, it is natural to suppose that they preferred to move along well-known trade routes, rather than to adventure on unknown paths.

Many efforts have been made to retrace the migration of the Goths. With the exception of Jordanes' tale — perhaps another of Cassiodorus' inventions — which relates that they went through Oium,[48] a mysterious place situated somewhere in "Scythia," there is no historical record or convincing archaeological evidence as to which route they used. Several possibilities have been taken into consideration, including as eastern a route as that along the Dvina and the Dnieper, and as western a way as that along the Elbe and the Danube.[49] Since there is no trace of the itinerary of the Goths toward the Black Sea, there can be no proof as to which way they went. They left the Lower Vistula and arrived at the Black Sea; only this much is known. Most likely, the path of their migration led along one or both of the trade routes along the Vistula and the Bug.

My final conclusion on the Goths in the Lower Vistula valley is that they arrived there sometime after 98 A.D. and started to leave during the last two or three decades before the end of the second century of our era. Sometime before 230 A.D., their territory was taken over by neighboring tribes, who thus accelerated their departure. The stay of the Goths at the Lower Vistula lasted for a period of about seventy to at most one hundred years.

 Investigations conducted in this study have re-vealed that the traditional view of the prehis-toric and protohistoric past of the Goths rests on weak foundations. In the past many argu-ments leading toward a final conclusion have suffered from undue gen-eralization, biased interpretation, and disagreement with historical evi-dence recorded during the first two centuries of the Christian era. This final conclusion, therefore, cannot be valid.

The original homeland of the Goths has been placed in Väster-götland and identified with the spatial extent of a prehistoric culture existing in that area. This culture expanded gradually, covering even-tually most of Southern Sweden, a space not occupied by the Goths alone but shared by several Germanic tribes. At the present stage of research it cannot be ascertained how much of this territory was ac-tually inhabited by the Goths at the time of their migration from Sweden. It has been assumed that the minimal extent of their tribal territory was the region of the Göta River. Consequently, they had access to the sea at the Kattegat only, which means that their voyage to the Oder-Vistula region started from the environs of Göteborg. To reach the south coast of the Baltic Sea the Goths had either to cross the open sea or to sail in the waters of the Swedish coast and the Danish Archipelago to Jutland or Mecklenburg.

A voyage across the open sea from the southern tip of Sweden to the estuary of the Vistula or the Oder was an impossibility, due to the low technological development of the ancient Germanic watercraft. A mass transfer of population from Sweden to the southern Baltic coast through the Danish Islands was hardly feasible, since it involved mili-tary control of the Danish Archipelago. It was concluded that the emi-gration from Sweden was a peaceful move carried out over decades by small human groups. The revised sea route leads along the west coast of Sweden, through the Danish Islands, to Mecklenburg, along the Baltic coast toward the estuary of the Oder, and into the interior of the country on or along this river.

The Gothic emigration started approximately at the middle of the first century B.C. and was completed at the beginning of our era, after a large part of the tribe had settled in the region of the Middle Oder, while the other part remained in Sweden and was still living there in the second century. The Goths of the Oder region became subject to Maroboduus' rule shortly after 1 A.D., and this relationship continued for about twenty years. Their stay in the Oder region is confirmed by a historical analysis of the texts of Strabo, Pliny, and Tacitus. Ptolemy mentions the Goths in another place, namely on the Lower Vistula, among the "smaller peoples" of European Sarmatia. Analysis of his data revealed that this tribal territory lay between the estuary of the Narew and the space along the Gulf of Danzig which was occupied by some Venedian tribes. There are no traces of Goths living in the Oder region in the second century. It was concluded, therefore, that shortly after 98 A.D. the Goths had moved from the Middle Oder to the Lower Vistula, where they remained for about seventy years. Sometime after 150 A.D. they started to drift slowly toward the Black Sea using the trade routes along the Vistula and the Bug.

The migrations of the Goths into and within the Oder-Vistula region were not acts of a political or military nature. The political leadership attributed to them is an invention of modern historians. The idea is not found in the works of ancient writers, who, rather, considered the Goths an average-sized or a small tribe. Their migrations—as those of other contemporary Germanic tribes—were determined for reasons of an economic nature. Lack of arable land and pastures may have been the cause of their departure from Sweden; the impossibility or inability to enlarge the territory of the newly acquired lands in the Oder-Vistula region was responsible for their moving from the Oder to the Vistula, and from the Vistula to the Black Sea.

This revised image of the protohistoric past of the Goths emerges from an analysis of the historical sources of the first two centuries of the Christian era, which are incomplete but trustworthy contemporary reports. The works of the ancient geographers and historians present a geographical image less colorful and glorious than the traditional national view, but more true to fact. The traditional view is merely a theory invented in the first half of our century and promoted chiefly by archaeologists, whose assertions were never proven by archaeological methodology. On the contrary, recent archaeological studies have pointed out that there is absolutely no connection between the prehistoric cultures of Scandinavia and of the Black Sea region. Criteria used for identification of forms found around the estuary of the Vistula and for comparison with those of Sweden did not prove the continuation of a Gothic Scandinavian culture in Pomerania. This theory is corroborated only by an untrustworthy or, at least, a very doubtful source from the sixth century. Moreover, Jordanes' story or Cassiodorus' tale is contradicted by the historians and geographers of the first two centuries of our era. A powerful Gothic kingdom never existed in Pomerania—nor did the Goths ever live on the Baltic coast as a large, organized, human group.

NOTES

Notes to chapter 1

1. Hanno Helbling, *Goten und Wandalen; Wandlung der historischen Realität* (Zurich: Fretz & Wasmuth, 1954).

2. Helbling, *Goten und Wandalen,* pp. 27-29.

3. Jordanes, *Getica* IV, 24 (English translation by Charles C. Mierow).

4. Ibidem, IV, 27; XVII, 94, 96.

5. "Die Ubereinstimmung der gotischen Kulturen in Västergötland und an der Weichsel ist nicht sehr gross." Eric Oxenstierna, *Die Urheimat der Goten* (Leipzig: Barth, 1948), p. 190.

✓ 6. Kazimierz Tymieniecki, *Ziemie polskie w starożytności; ludy i kultury najdawniejsze* (Poznań: Poznańskie Towarzystwo Przyjaciół Nauk, 1951), pp. 511-22, 609-12, 669, 782-84; *Pisma wybrane* (Warsaw: PWN, 1956), pp. 437-52.

7. Curt Weibull, *Die Auswanderung der Goten aus Schweden* (Göteborg: Elanders Boktryckeri Aktiebolag, 1958).

8. Jerzy Kmieciński, *Zagadnienie tzw. kultury gocko-gepidzkiej na Pomorzu Wschodnim w okresie wczesnorzymskim* (Lódż: Zakład Narodowy im. Ossolińskich we Wrocławiu, 1962).

✓ 9. Oxenstierna, *The World of the Norsemen* (Translated by Janet Sondheimer. Cleveland and New York: World Publishing, 1967), pp. 29-30, and *The Norsemen* (Translated and edited by Catherine Hutter. Greenwich, Conn.: New York Graphic Society, 1965), p. 24.

10. Βούτωνας in Strabo VII, 1, 3 (c. 290), corrected to Γούτωνας by Gustav Kramer.

11. Pliny IV, 99 and 100.

12. Tacitus, *Germania,* p. 43.

13. Γοῦται (variants: Γαῦται, Οῦτοι, Δοῦται) in Ptolemy (Müller) II, 11, 34.

14. Γύθωνες in Ptolemy III, 5, 20.
15. Γαύται in Procopius, *Bellum Gothicum* II, 15.
16. Kaspar Zeuss, *Die Deutschen und die Nachbarstämme* (Munich: I. J. Lentner, 1837), vol. 1, p. 134.
17. Torsten Evert Karsten, *Die Germanen; eine Einführung in die Geschichte ihrer Sprache und Kultur* (Berlin and Leipzig: De Gruyter, 1928), pp. 75, 86.
18. Rudolf Much, articles "Gauten" and "Goten" in Johannes Hoops, *Reallexikon der germanischen Altertumskunde,* 4 vols. (Strasbourg: Trübner, 1913-1919), vol. 2, pp. 126-27, 306.

Notes to chapter 2

1. Caesar, *Bellum Gallicum* IV, 4; VI, 25.
2. Strabo VII, 2, 4 (c. 294).
3. E. H. Bunbury, *A History of Ancient Geography among the Greeks and Romans; From the Earliest Ages till the Fall of the Roman Empire* (With a new introduction by W. H. Stahl, 2nd ed., New York: Dover Publications, 1959), vol. 2, p. 177; Rudolf Hanslik, "M. Vipsanius Agrippa" in *Paulys Realencyclopädie der classischen Altertumswissenschaft* (Newly revised by Wissowa, Kroll, Mittelhaus. 24 vols. and 12 suppl. in progress, Stuttgart: Metzler *et al.,* 1894-1970), II. Reihe, 17. Halbbd. (1961), col. 1270-71.
4. Tymieniecki, *Ziemie polskie,* p. 549.
5. "Germania . . . ab oriente Sarmaticarum confinio gentium . . . obducta est," and "Sarmatia . . . ab his quae secuntur Vistula amne discreta," Mela, *De chorographia* III, 25 and 33.
6. "Amnes clari in Oceanum defluunt Guthalus, Visculus sive Vistla, Albis, Visurgis, Amisis, Rhenus, Mosa;" "Agrippa totum . . . ad flumen Vistlam a desertis Sarmatiae prodidit;" "Quidam haec habitari ad Vistlam usque fluvium a Sarmatis, Venedis, Sciris, Hirris tradunt." Pliny IV, 100, 81, and 97.
7. Bunbury, *A History of Ancient Geography,* vol. 2, pp. 371-78; H. F. Tozer, *A History of Ancient Geography* (2nd ed., with additional notes by M. Cary. New York: Biblo and Tannen, 1964), p. 264; J. Oliver Thomson, *History of Ancient Geography* (Cambridge: University Press, 1948), p. 227.
8. Pliny IV, 99 and 91.
9. καὶ ἡ μετὰ τὰ ὄρη ἐπὶ τὴν εἰρημένην κεφαλὴν τοῦ Οὐιστούλα

ποταμοῦ, καὶ ἔτι αὐτὸς ὁ ποταμὸς ἕως θαλάσσης Ptolemy II, 11, 6: ἀπὸ δε δυσμῶν τῷ τε Οὐιστούλᾳ ποταμῷ καὶ τῇ μεταξὺ τῆς κεφαλῆς αὐτοῦ καὶ τῶν Σαρματικῶν ὀρέων *Ibid.* III, 5, 5.

10. "Germania omnis a Gallis Raetibusque et Pannoniis Rheno et Danuvio fluminibus, a Sarmatis Dacisque mutuo metu aut montibus separatur: cetera Oceanus ambit, latos sinus et insularum immensa spatia complectens, nuper cognitis quibusdam gentibus ac regibus, quos bellum aperuit." Tacitus, *Germania* 1.

11. "Peucinorum Venethorumque et Fennorum nationes Germanis an Sarmatis adscribam dubito. quamquam Peucini, quos quidam Bastarnas vocant, sermone cultu sede ac domiciliis ut Germani agunt. sordes omnium ac torpor procerum: conubiis mixtis nonnihil in Sarmatarum habitum foedantur. Venethi multum ex moribus traxerunt; nam quidquid inter Peucinos Fennosque silvarum ac montium erigitur latrociniis pererrant. hi tamen inter Germanos potius referuntur, quia et domos figunt et scuta gestant et pedum usu et pernicitate gaudent: quae omnia diversa Sarmatis sunt in plaustro equoque viventibus." Tacitus, *Germania* 46.

12. Brief summaries in English of the various theories on the origin and early expansion of the Slavs, and the earliest Germanic-Slavic relations, may be found in Francis Dvornik, *The Slavs; their Early History and Civilization* (Boston: American Academy of Arts and Sciences, 1956), pp. 3-14, and Roman Smal-Stocki, *Slavs and Teutons; the Oldest Germanic-Slavic Relations* (Milwaukee: Bruce Publishing, 1950), pp. 18-23.

13. Wolfgang La Baume, "Teutons, Slavs and Prussians in Eastern Germany," in Paul Pagel ed., *The German East* (Berlin: Lemmer, 1954), p. 9; the map is at p. 11.

14. Konrad Jażdżewski, *Atlas to the Prehistory of the Slavs* (Łódź: Łódzkie Towarzystwo Naukowe, 1948-1949), vol. 1, maps 8 and 9.

15. Jan Filip, "Gepidae," and "Goten," in Jan Filip, ed., *Enzyklopädisches Handbuch zur Ur- and Frühgeschichte Europas. Manuel Encyclopédique de préhistoire et protohistoire européennes.* 2 vols. (Stuttgart, Berlin, Cologne, Mainz: Kohlhammer, 1966-1969(, pp. 396-97, 426; Ludwig Schmidt, *Geschichte der deutschen Stämme bis zum Ausgange der Völkerwanderung* (Berlin: Weidmann, 1904-1918), vol. 1, p. 306.

16. Kmieciński, *Zagadnienie tzw. kultury gocko-gepidzkiej,* pp. 186-191 (English summary).

17. Filip, "Burgunden," in Filip, *Enzyklopädisches Handbuch,* p. 187.

Notes to chapter 3

1. Caesar, *Bellum Gallicum* I, 2-29.

2. Johannes Bühler, *Deutsche Geschichte* (6 vols. Revised and enlarged. Berlin: De Gruyter, 1950-1960), vol. 1, pp. 54-60; Ihm, "Cimbri," in *Paulys Realencyclopädie,* vol. 3 (1899), col. 2247-53; Kurt Pastenaci, *Die Kriegskunst der Germanen* (Karlsbad and Leipzig: Adam Kraft Verlag, 1943), pp. 68-116.

3. "Ambrones. Völkerschaft unbestimmter Herkunft ... Das gemeinsame Auftreten der A. mit Cimbern und Teutonen wird als Hinweis für ihre Herkunft aus den n. germanischen Gebieten gewertet." H. Cüppers, "Ambrones," in *Der Kleine Pauly: Lexikon der Antike* (Prepared and edited by Konrat Ziegler and Walther Sontheimer. Stuttgart: Alfred Druckenmüller, 1964- in progress: vols. 1-4, 1964-1972), vol. 1, p. 295.

4. Some authors believe that the Toygeni were not an individual tribe. Apparently the name Toygeni is a corrupt form of Teutones; cf. Wolfgang Aly, *Strabon von Amaseia: Untersuchungen über Text, Aufbau und Quellen der Geographika* (Bonn: Habelt, 1957), pp. 300-309.

5. Bühler, *Deutsche Geschichte,* vol. 1, pp. 58-60.

6. Strabo VII, 1, 3 (c. 291).

7. Plutarch, *Marius* XI, 4, in *Plutarch's Lives.* With an English translation by Bernadotte Perrin, 11 vols. (Cambridge: Harvard University Press; London: Heinemann, 1914-1926).

8. A. Gieysztor, "Medieval Poland," in *History of Poland* (Editor in Chief: Stefan Kiniewicz. Warsaw: PWN, 1968), p. 36.

9. Caesar, *Bellum Gallicum* I, 12-13.

10. Plutarch, *Marius* XVIII, 1.

Notes to chapter 4

1. Ole Klindt-Jensen, *Denmark before the Vikings* (Translated from the Danish by Eva and David Wilson. London: Thames and Hudson, 1957), pp. 86-87 and plate 49; Haakon Shetelig and Hjalmar Falk,

Scandinavian Archaeology (Translated by E. V. Gordon. Oxford: Clarendon Press, 1937), pp. 186, 347, 353; Oxenstierna, *The World of the Norsemen*, p. 28.

2. J. G. D. Clark, *Prehistoric Europe; the Economic Basis* (Stanford: Stanford University Press, 1966), p. 289.

3. Klindt-Jensen, *Denmark before the Vikings*, p. 87.

4. Shetelig and Falk, *Scandinavian Archaeology*, p. 353; W. Vogel, "Schiff (und seine Teile)," in Hoops, *Reallexikon*, vol. 4, p. 99; Tacitus, *Germania* (Much), p. 394.

5. Clark, *Prehistoric Europe*, p. 290; Klindt-Jensen, *Denmark before the Vikings*, pp. 112-13 and plate 72; Shetelig and Falk, *Scandinavian Archaeology*, p. 355.

6. Romola Anderson and R. C. Anderson, *The Sailing Ship; Six Thousand Years of History* (New Ed. New York: Bonanza Books, 1963), pp. 63-68; Oxenstierna, *The World of the Norsemen*, p. 64; Stuart Piggott, *Ancient Europe: From the Beginning of Agriculture to Classical Antiquity* (Chicago: Aldine, 1965), p. 250; Schmidt, *Geschichte der deutschen Stämme*, vol. 1, p. 41; W. Vogel, "Schiff (und seine Teile)," in Hoops, *Reallexikon*, vol. 4, p. 99 and plate 11; Ernst Wahle, "Ur– und Frühgeschichte im mitteleuropäischen Raum," in Bruno Gebhardt, *Handbuch der deutschen Geschichte* (Eighth edition, completely revised, Stuttgart: Union Deutsche Verlagsgesellschaft, (1954-1959), vol. 1, p. 42.

7. "Jedenfalls scheint der hervorragende Bau auf eine nicht geringe Seetüchtigkeit und lange nautische Entwicklung hinzuweisen." Vogel, "Schiff (und seine Teile)," in Hoops, *Reallexikon*, vol. 4, p. 100.

8. Klindt-Jensen, *Denmark before the Vikings*, p. 113.

9. Shetelig and Falk, *Scandinavian Archaeology*, p. 347.

10. Tacitus, *Annales* II, 6-24.

11. Tacitus, *Annales* (Jackson) II, 6.

12. A part of the legions had been sent back by land. Tacitus, *Annales* II, 22.

13. Tacitus, *Annales* II, 23-24.

14. Tacitus, *Annales* XI, 18.

15. "Germaniae praedones singulis arboribus cavatis navigant, quarum quaedam et XXX homines ferunt," Pliny XVI, 76.

16. Tacitus, *Historiae* V, 23 (Jackson's translation).

17. "Suionum hinc civitates, ipso in Oceano, praeter viros armaque classibus valent. forma navium eo differt quod utrimque prora paratam semper adpulsui frontem agit. nec velis ministrant nec remos in ordinem

lateribus adiungunt: solutum, ut in quibusdam fluminum, et mutabile, ut res poscit, hinc vel illinc remigium." Tacitus, *Germania* 44.

18. "Einzelne Völker haben sich schon früh zur See ausgezeichnet, so namentlich die skandinavischen Germanen, deren bedeutende Schiffsmacht schon Tac. Germ. 44 hervorhebt"; "Auf einer höheren Stufe standen zu derselben Zeit die Schiffe der Suionen, der Bewohner Schwedens: nach Tacitus (Germ. 44) waren dieselben vorn und hinten gleich gebaut, zum sofortigen Vorwärts- und Rückwärtsfahren ohne Umwenden eingerichtet, mit losen Ruderbänken versehen." Schmidt, *Geschichte der deutschen Stämme*, vol. 1, pp. 40-41.

19. "*Viros armaque* bezieht sich auf die Landmacht im Gegensatz zu *classibus*, der Seemacht, obwohl auch die Schiffe der Bemannung mit Bewaffneten bedürfen." Tacitus, *Germania* (Much), p. 392.

20. Tacitus, *Germania* (Anderson), p. 204.

21. Tacitus, *Germania* 44.

22. Tacitus, *Germania* (Anderson), p. 205.

23. "*Nec remos in ordinem lateribus adiungunt/* Es wären also nicht feste Widerlager für die Ruder, Dollen, angebracht. Diese Beschreibung ebenso wie die folgende *solutum . . . remigium* zeigt, dass Tac. hier an das sogenannte Paddeln denkt. Doch verkennt er den Sachverhalt, da solches bei grossen, seetüchtigen Schiffen mit hoher Bordwand—und um solche handelt es sich hier zweifellos—nicht zur Anwendung kommen konnte." Later on, speaking about propulsion by paddles, he says: "Derartiges kannte Tac. offenbar durch Augenschein und übertrug es irrtümlich auf die swionischen Schiffe." Tacitus, *Germania* (Much), pp. 394-95.

24. "The apparatus of rowing is unfixed, and shifted from side to side." *The Complete Works of Tacitus* (Translated from the Latin by Alfred John Church and William Jackson Brodribb. New York: Modern Library, 1942), p. 730; "They row . . . sometimes on one side sometimes on the other." *The Works of Tacitus* (The Oxford Translation. 2 vols. Revised, with notes. London: G. Bell, 1910-1911), vol. 2, p. 337.

25. Tacitus, *Germania* (Anderson), p. 205.

Notes to chapter 5

1. Edward Gibbon, *The History of the Decline and Fall of the Roman Empire* (6 vols. New York: Euclid Press, 1890), vol. 1, pp. 522-23.

2. Henry Bradley, *The Goths; From the Earliest Times to the End*

of the Gothic Dominion in Spain (5th ed. London: Fisher Unwin, 1888), pp. 7-8.

3. "An die Odermündung zu denken liegt deshalb nahe, weil diese der skandinavischen Südspitze am nächsten ist und eine auswandernde grössere Volksmenge sicher einen kürzeren Seeweg dem längeren vorgezogen hat." Schmidt, *Geschichte der deutschen Stämme,* vol. 1, p. 51.

4. "Die gotischen Stammessagen lassen keinen Zweifel darüber, dass Skandinavien das Ursprungsland der Goten ist. Von hier sind sie über die Ostsee nach dem gegenüberliegenden Festland an der Weichselmündung gekommen, von wo sie später zu ihrem Siegeszug durch halb Europa aufbrachen." Christoph Obermüller, *Die deutschen Stämme; Stammesgeschichte als Namensgeschichte und Reichsgeschichte* (Second printing, slightly revised. Bielefeld: Velhagen & Klasing, 1941), p. 34; his map is reproduced on p. 3.

5. Mikołaj Rudnicki, "Zagadnienie pobytu drużyn germańskich na ziemiach polskich w czasie do VI w. w świetle imiennictwa," *Przegląd Zachodni,* 7, no. 5/6 (1951), pp. 164-65.

6. Oxenstierna's map is reproduced on p. 13. This map was copied with small alterations by Smal-Stocki.

7. S. Gutenbrunner, "Namenkundliche Zeugnisse zur germanischen Urgeschichte," in *Germanen und Indogermanen; Volkstum, Sprache, Heimat, Kultur. Festschrift Für Herman Hirt* (Edited by Helmuth Arntz. 2 vols. Heidelberg: Winter, 1936), vol. 2, p. 460; Tadeusz Lehr-Spławiński, *O pochodzeniu i praojczyźnie Słowian* (Poznań: Instytut Zachodni, 1946), pp. 68, 139, 178, 210; "Odra," art. 1 by the editorial staff, art. 2 by Andrzej Wędzki in Polska Akademia Nauk. Komitet Słowianoznawstwa. *Słownik starożytności słowiańskich; encyklopedyczny zarys kultury Słowian od czasów najdawniejszych* (Edited by Władysław Kowalenko, Gerard Labuda and Tadeusz Lehr-Spławiński. Wrocław: PWN, 1961- in progress; vols. 1-4, 1961-1970), vol. 3, pp. 458-59; Rudnicki, "Nazwa Odry i jej dopływów," in Andrzej Grodek, ed., *Monografia Odry* (Poznań: Instytut Zachodni, 1948), pp. 68-69; Ernst Schwarz, *Die Ortsnamen der Sudetenländer als Geschichtsquelle* (Munich: R. Lerche, 1961), p. 26; Theodor Steche, *Altgermanien im Erdkundebuch des Klaudius Ptolemäus* (Leipzig: Kabitzsch, 1937), p. 37.

8. Σουήβου Ptolemy II, 11, 4 and II, 11, 13. Müller's and Cuntz's text have Συήβου (at II, 11, 2 and II, 11, 7 in their arrangement). Οὐιάδου Ptolemy II, 11, 4 and Ἰαδούα ibid. II, 11, 14. In Müller's

text Οὐιαδούα (at II, 11, 2 and II, 11, 7); in Cuntz's text Οὐιάδου (at II, 11, 2) andΟὐιαδούα at II, 11, 7). The variants of the name *Suebos* recorded by Müller or Cuntz are: Σουίβου , Σουίκου, Σουήβου, Συίβου, Σιήβου, Σουήβρου ; for *Viadua:* Οὐιλδου, Οὐαδούα, Ἰαδουα, Οὐάδου and the Latin forms *Iaduam, Iadum, Viadum.*

9. Ptolemy's map of Jutland is discussed by I. A. Richmond, "Ptolemy's Map of Denmark: a Study in Conflicting Evidence," *Scottish Geographical Magazine,* vol. 39 (1923), pp. 99-102. However, he did not compare the Ptolemaic locations of the estuaries between the Albis and the Vistula with modern coordinates, and did not notice, therefore, Ptolemy's elongated distance between the Albis and the Chalusos.

10. Bronisław Biliński, "Drogi świata starożytnego ku zachodnim ziemiom polskim i problem Odry u Ptolemeusza," *Eos,* vol. 41, no. 1/2 (1940-1946), pp. 179-96; Gutenbrunner, "Namenkundliche Zeugnisse zur germanischen Urgeschichte," in *Germanen und Indogermanen,* vol. 2, p. 460; Lehr-Spławiński, *O pochodzeniu i praojczyźnie Słowian,* pp. 81, 192; Schwarz, *Die Ortsnamen der Sudentenländer,* p. 26; Steche, *Altgermanien im Erdkundebuch des Ptolemäus,* pp. 36-37.

Notes to chapter 6

1. Bunbury, *History of Ancient Geography,* vol. 2, p. 213.
2. Strabo VII, 2, 4 (c. 294).
3. "Natione magis quam ratione barbarus," Gaius Velleius Paterculus II, 108.
4. Tacitus, *Annales* II, 62.
5. "The exiled Marcomannic nobleman Catualda," G. Ekholm, "The Peoples of Northern Europe," *The Cambridge Ancient History* (12 vols. Cambridge: University Press, 1923-1939), vol. 11, p. 57; "Der Markomanne Catualda," Schönfeld, "Goti," in *Paulys Realencyclopädie,* Suppl. vol. 3 (1918), col. 798; "Catualda, vornehmer Gotone . . .." Stein, "Catualda," in *Paulys Realencyclopädie,* vol. 3 (1899), col. 1795; "Należący do szlachty gockiej Catualda," Tymieniecki, *Ziemie polskie,* p. 669.
6. Tacitus, *Annales* II, 62.
7. Strabo VII, 1, 3 (c. 290). The manuscripts read Βούτωνας variant: Βούτονας corrected to Γούτωνας in Kramer's edition of the *Geography.* Newer editions have either the form Βούτωνας orΓούτωνας. A different emendation is suggested by Aly.
8. Schmidt, *Geschichte der deutschen Stämme,* vol. 1, p. 52.

9. "Ein weiterer Fall, wo abenfalls Poseidonios als Vermittler in Betracht kommt, sind die Guiones bei Plin. XXXVII, 35, während IV, 99 der Name Gutones erhalten ist, an deren Stelle Strabon VII, 1, 3, Βούτωνες überliefert. Man schreibt dort seit Kramer Γούτωνες was die Eigenart der Strabonüberlieferung nicht ohne weiteres gestattet. Da aber dort gleichzeitig die Burgunder fehlen, wird man nicht etwa Βουργωνδίωνες schreiben, sondern Βου(ρ)γουνδίωνες καὶ Γούϳτωνες ergänzen. Dieser Fehler wäre also erst in den Strabonhandschriften eingetreten." Aly, *Strabon von Amaseia*, pp. 455-56.

10. Strabo VII, 1, 3 (c. 290).

11. Tacitus, *Germania* 42-43.

12. Λουγίους τε, μέγα ἔθνος, καὶ Ζούμους καὶ Βούτωνας καὶ Μουγίλωνας καὶ Σιβίνους καὶ τῶν Σουήβων αὐτῶν μέγα ἔθνος Σέμνωνας. Strabo VII, 1, 3 (c. 290).

13. Tacitus, *Germania* 43.

14. Ptolemy II, 11, 18 and II, 11, 20.

15. "Lugiowie," art. 2 by Andrzej Kunisz in Polska Akademia Nauk, *Słownik starożytności słowiańskich,* vol. 3, p. 103.

16. Steche, *Altgermanien im Erdkundebuch des Ptolemäus,* p. 98.

17. Ekholm, "The Peoples of Northern Europe," *The Cambridge Ancient History,* vol. 11, p. 60; F. Miltner, "Vandalen," in *Paulys Realencyclopädie,* 2. Reihe, 15. Halbbd, (1955), col. 298-300; Much, "Germani," in *Paulys Realencyclopädie,* Suppl. vol. 3 (1918), col. 551-54; Schmidt, *Geschichte der deutschen Stämme,* vol. 1, pp. 354-56; Schönfeld, "Lugii," in *Paulys Realencyclopädie,* vol. 13 (1927), col. 1715-18.

18. Tymieniecki, *Ziemie polskie,* pp. 631-33; Henryk Łowmiański, *Początki Polski; z dziejów Słowian w I. tysiacleciu n. e.* (4 vols. Warsaw: PWN, 1963-1970), vol. 1, pp. 191-95;

19. Schmidt, *Geschichte der deutschen Stämme,* vol. 1, p. 355.

20. Hans Krahe, "Germanisch und Illyrisch," in *Germanen und Indogermanen,* vol. 2, p. 572; Łowmiański, *Początki Polski,* vol. 1, p. 196; vol. 2, p. 22.

21. Tacitus, *Germania* (Much), p. 378; Max Vasmer, "Lugii und Mugilones," in *Sybaris; Festschrift Hans Krahe zum 60. Geburtstag am 7. Februar 1958* (Wiesbaden: Harrassowitz, 1958), p. 190; "Lugiowie," art. 2 by Andrzej Kunisz in Polska Akademia Nauk, *Słownik starożytności słowiańskich,* vol. 3, p. 104.

22. Tacitus, *Germania* (Much), p. 378.

23. Schönfeld, "Lugii," in *Paulys Realencyclopädie,* vol. 13 (1927), col. 1716-17.

24. Vasmer, "Lugii und Mugilones," p. 190.

25. L. Schmitz, "Ly'gii, Lu'gii or Li'gii," in William Smith, ed., *A Dictionary of Greek and Roman Geography* (2 vols. London: J. Murray, 1873; New York: AMS Press, 1966), vol. 2, p. 230.

26. For a summary and bibliography see Tymieniecki, *Ziemie polskie*, pp. 631-33.

27. Lehr-Spławiński, *O pochodzeniu i praojczyźnie Słowian*, pp. 141-42, 222-23; and "Lugiowie," art.1 in Polska Akademia Nauk, *Slownik starożytności słowiańskich*, vol. 3, p. 103. Major objections against the Slavic etymology were raised by Vasmer, "Lugii und Mugilones," pp. 190-93, and Helmut Preidel, *Die Anfänge der slawischen Besiedlung Böhmens und Mährens* (Vol. 1. Gräfelfing bei München: Gans, 1954), p. 29.

28. Tymieniecki, *Ziemie polskie*, pp. 633-43 and 800-806 (French summary).

29. Gieysztor, "Slavic antiquity," in *History of Poland*, pp. 33 and 34.

30. Tacitus, *Germania* 43.

31. Tacitus, *Germania* (Robinson), pp. 135, 243, 319.

32. Bronisław Biliński, "Dwa świadectwa antyczne: Kalisia Ptolemeusza (Geographia, II, 11, 13) i Halisii Tacyta (Germania 43,2)," in *Osiemnaście wieków Kalisza: studia i materiały do dziejów miasta Kalisza i regionu kaliskiego*, (3 vols. Kalisz: Wydawnictwo Posnańskie, 1960-1962), vol. 2, pp. 7-40.

33. "Calisia (Kalisia)," and "Kalisz," in Filip, *Enzyklopädisches Handbuch*, pp. 196, 569; "Kalisz," art. 1 by Stanislaw Urbańczyk and "Helizjowie," by Andrzej Kunisz in Polska Akademia Nauk, *Słownik starożytności słowiańskich*, vol. 2, pp. 353, 198.

34. "Denn den Laut Z enthielt vor der hochdeutschen Lautverschiebung keine germanische Sprache." Steche, *Altgermanien im Erdkundebuch des Ptolemäus*, p. 98.

35. "Die Ζοῦμοι sind jedenfalls keine Slaven." Vasmer, "Lugii und Mugilones," p. 193.

36. Λούγιοι οἳ Δοῦνοι (ῆ Λογγιδιοῦνοι) Ptolemy II, 11, 18.

37. In Greek capitals the forms *Zumoi* and *Dunoi* look fairly similar: ΖΟΥΜΟΙ and ΔΟΥΝΟΙ.

38. "Do kurhanów i małych pagórkow stosowali nasi prasłowiańscy przodkowie rodzimą nazwę *mogyla (doslownie: 'wynioslość o tepym szczycie')." Kazimierz Moszyński, *Pierwotny zasiąg języka prasłowiańskiego* (Wrocław-Cracow: Zakład Narodowy im. Ossolińskich, 1957), p. 158.

39. Jerzy Nalepa, "Mugilones," in Polska Akademia Nauk, *Słownik starożytności słowiańskich*, vol. 3, p. 327.

40. Vasmer, "Lugii und Mugilones," pp. 193-94.

41. "Strabonovi Μουχίλωνεςslov. Mogilanum (od sl. mogyla), jmenovaným Detmarem v X. stoleti *pagus Mogelini, Mogilina urbs* poblize Misne." Lubor Niederle, *Rukovět' slovanských starožitností (K vydáni připravil akademik* Jan Eisner. Prague: Naklad. Ceskoslovenské Akademie Ved, 1953), p. 104.

42. "Najprawdopodobniej słowiańską jest nazwa ... zapisana u Strabona: Μουχίλωνες (= Mugilones), która tak dalece przypomina twór słowiański odpowiadajacy pol. *Mogilanie*, że trudno wątpić o jej słow. pochodzeniu. Trudności fonetyczne, które się niekiedy przeciw temu objaśnieniu podnosi, sa istotnie iluzoryczne." Lehr-Spławiński, *O pochodzeniu i praojczyźnie Słowian*, p. 142; cf. also p. 223.

43. Jażdżewski, *Atlas*, vol. 2, p. 66; Tymieniecki, *Ziemie polskie*, pp. 635, 637, 692, 796.

44. Schönfeld, "Sibini," in *Paulys Realencyclopädie, 2. Reihe*, vol. 2 (1923), col. 2071.

45.ΣΙΒΙΝΟΙand ΣΙΛΙΓΓΟΙ.

46. Πάλιν ὑπὸ μὲν τοὺς Σέμνονας οἰκοῦσι Σιλίγγαι. Ptolemy II, 11, 18.

47. Steche, *Altgermanien im Erdkundebuch des Ptolemäus*, p. 92.

48. Tymieniecki, *Ziemie polskie*, pp. 686-88.

49. "... the Semnones round the Havel and Spree ... " Ekholm, "The Peoples of Northern Europe," *The Cambridge Ancient History*, vol. 11, p. 54; "Semnen ... in der heutigen Mark Brandenburg zwischen Oder und Elbe." Steche, *Altgermanien im Erdkundebuch des Ptolemäus*, p. 91; "auf der anderen Seite der Elbe." Tacitus, *Germania* (Much), p. 337; "Semnonen wohnten kurz nach Christi Geburt im Gebiet der Havel und Spree und reichten im Norden bis nach Mecklenburg hinein." Tacitus, *Germania* (Mauersberger), p. 137; "Semnonen ... wohnten östlich der mittleren Elbe bis gegen die Oder, im Spree— und Havelland, etwa in der heutigen Provinz Brandenburg, früher auch in der Altmark." Tacitus, *Germania* (Schweizer-Sidler), p. 98; "Semnones ... their territory lay between the middle Elbe and the Oder, in Brandenburg and Lausitz." Tacitus, *Germania* (Anderson), p. 181; "Semnonowie znajdują się bliżej Markomanów (w Czechach)." Tymieniecki, *Ziemie polskie*, p. 641; "Semnonowie, lud swewski (germański), osiedli nad środkową Łabą." *Ibid.*, p. 643; "Lud Semnonów nad średnią Łabą." *Ibid.*, p. 687; "Silingowie ... (bliżej Magdeburga?) W takim

razie Semnonowie siedzieli nad Hobolą i jej ujściem do Łaby lub jeszcze dalej na południe." *Ibid.*, p. 688.

50. Velleius Paterculus II, 106.

51. Bunbury, *A History of Ancient Geography*, vol. 2, pp. 372-442; Thomson, *A History of Ancient Geography*, pp. 227-28; Tozer, *History of Ancient Geography*, pp. 263-74.

52. "Ein vorzüglicher Kenner germanischer Verhältnisse war der ältere Plinius." Schmidt, *Geschichte der deutschen Stämme*, vol. 1, p. 8.

53. "Germanorum genera quinque: Vandili . . . Inguaeones . . . Istuaeones . . . Hermiones . . . quinta pars Peucini, Basternae." Pliny IV, 99-100.

54. "Scatinavia . . . Hillevionum gente quingentis incolente pagis." Pliny IV, 96; "Rhenum autem accolentes Germaniae gentium in eadem provincia Nemetes, Triboci, Vangiones, in ubis colonia Agrippinensis, Guberni, Batavi et quos in insulis diximus Rheni." *Ibid.*, IV, 106.

55. Karsten, *Die Germanen*, pp. 232-35.

56. "Bastarnen, ein durch schriftliche Quellen im 3. Jh. v. u. Z. im nordwestlichen Schwarzmeergebiet belegter Volksstamm. Seine Herkunft u. ethnische Zugehörigkeit sind nicht völlig geklärt; scheinbar handelt es sich um ein gemischtes Volk." "Bastarnen," in Filip, *Enzyklopädisches Handbuch*, pp. 94-95.

57. "Germanen im strengen Sinne sind sie aber damals längst nicht mehr gewesen, da sie schon zur Zeit des Tacitus mit anderen Völkerschaften stark vermischt waren, doch haben sie mancherlei Sitten aus ihrer früheren Zeit beibehalten." Bühler, *Deutsche Geschichte*, vol. 1, pp. 50-51.

58. Tymieniecki, *Ziemie polskie*, pp. 577, 601-3, 659-63.

59. "Vandili quorum pars Burgodiones, Varinnae, Charini, Gutones." Pliny IV, 99; Mayhoff's edition has the following variants of the above-listed names: *Vandili, Uindili, Uindilici, Uindelici, Uandilici, Uiandilici, Uandalici; Burgodiones, Burgondiones, Burgudiones, Burgundiones; Varinnae, Uarinnae, Uari////, Uarine, Uarinne, Uarini; Charini, Charinni, Carini; Gutones, Gu////nes, Gniones, Guttones.*

60. "Plures deo ortos pluresque gentis appellationes, Marsos Gambrivios Suebos Vandilios adfirmant, eaque vera et antiqua nomina." Tacitus, *Germania* 2.

61. "Plin. N. H. IV, 99. Hier gilt also Vandili als Gesamtname für die ostgermanischen Völker." Schönfeld, "Goti," in *Paulys Realencyclopädie*, Suppl. vol. 3 (1903), col. 798; Steche, *Altgermanien im Erdkundebuch des Ptolemäus*, p. 98.

62. Karsten, *Die Germanen,* pp. 232-35; Schmidt, *Geschichte der deutschen Stämme,* vol. 1, pp. 30-31.

63. "Burgundiowie," art. 1 by Lehr-Spławiński; art. 2 by Jerzy Linderski in Polska Akademia Nauk, *Słownik starożytności słowiańskich,* vol. 1, pp. 204-5; Cüppers, "Burgundiones," in *Der Kleine Pauly,* vol. 1, p. 973; Filip, "Burgunden," in Filip, *Enzyklopädisches Handbuch,* p. 187; Ihm, "Burgundiones," in *Paulys Realencyclopädie,* vol. 3 (1899), col. 1063-65; Gustaf Kossinna, *Ursprung und Verbreitung der Germanen in vor- und frühgeschichtlicher Zeit* (3., unveränderte Aufl. Leipzig: Kabitzsch, 1936), p. 5; Józef Kostrzewski, "Slady archeologiczne pobytu drużyn germańskich w Polsce w pierwszej połowie I stulecia naszej ery," *Przegląd Zachodni,* 7, no. 5/6 (1951), pp. 104-5, and *Wielkopolska w pradziejach* (Zmien. 3. wyd. Warsaw: Zakład im. Ossolińskich, 1955), pp. 188-204, 213-35; Schmidt, *Geschichte der deutschen Stämme,* vol. 1, pp. 367-426; Schmitz, "Burgundio'nes, Burgundii," in Smith, *A Dictionary of Greek and Roman Geography,* vol. 1, p. 458; Tymieniecki, *Ziemie polskie,* pp. 685-86.

64. Tacitus, *Germania* 43.

65. Ptolemy II, 11, 15; II, 11, 18; II, 11, 20.

66. Tymieniecki, *Ziemie polskie,* p. 688 and map 18.

67. Tacitus, *Germania* 40.

68. Tacitus, *Germania* (Anderson), p. 186.

69. *Ibid.*

70. Οὐιρουνοι Ptolemy II, 11, 17, and Οὐίρουνον, μ ⸱, ῡε. *ibid.,* II, 11, 27.

71. Αὔαρποι Ptolemy II, 11, 17, and Φαροδεινοί *ibid,* II, 11, 13. "Die Namen Οὐίρουνοι und Αὔαρποι " die Ptolemaios 2, 11, 19 nördlich von den Semnonen ansetzt, sind aus Οὐάρινοι, Οὐάρινοι verderbt." Tacitus, *Germania* (Much), p. 348; "Var'ini, a German tribe . . . are probably the same as the Pharodini . . . The Viruni . . . seem to have been a branch of the Varini," and "it is highly possible also, that the Varni (Οὐάρνοι) of Procopius . . . are the people as the Varini." Schmitz, "Var'ini," in Smith, *Dictionary of Greek and Roman Geography,* vol. 2, p. 1259; "Manche Forscher glauben Ptolemäus *Wiruner* u. *Awarper* seien zwei Verderbnisse des Namens Warnen (OYAPNOI) . . . Gleichsetzung ist recht gewagt." Steche, *Altgermanien im Erdkundebuch de Klaudius Ptolemäus,* p. 104.

72. Σαξόνων δὲ καὶ Σουήβων... Οὐιρουνοι Ptolemy II, 11, 17. For the location of the Saxons see *ibid.* II, 11, 11, and for that of the Suebi-Semnones, *ibid.* II, 11, 15.

73. "Die taciteischen Harii dürften mit den plinianischen Chari (n) i zusammenfallen." Schmidt, *Geschichte der deutschen Stämme,* vol. 1, p. 475; "The Harii are probably identical with Pliny's Charini, a subdivision of the Vandili." Tacitus, *Germania* (Anderson), p. 199; "Harii, germ. Stamm . . . Wahrscheinlich mit den Plin. nat. 4,99 aufgeführten *Charini* ident." Cüppers, "Harii," in *Der Kleine Pauly,* vol. 2, p. 939.

74. Much, "Harii," in Hoops, *Reallexikon,* vol. 2, p. 450, and Tacitus, *Germania* (Much), p. 385; Ihm, "Charini," in *Paulys Realencyclopädie,* vol. 3 (1899), col. 2143; A. Kunisz, "Hariowie, Harii," in Polska Akademia Nauk, *Słownik starożytności słowiańskich,* vol. 2, p. 196; Rappaport, "Harii," in *Paulys Realencyclopädie,* vol. 7 (1912), col. 2365.

75. Pliny (Mayhoff) IV, 99.

76. *Ibid.* IV, 100.

77. Diehl, "C. Iulius Solinus," in *Paulys Realencyclopädie,* vol. 10 (1918), col. 823-38.

78. "Amnes clari in Oceanum defluunt Guthalus, Visculus sive Vistla, Albis, Visurgis, Amisis, Rhenus, Mosa." Pliny IV, 100.

79. "De internis eius partibus Alba Guthalus Viscla amnes latissimi praecipitant in Oceanum." Solinus XX, 2-3.

80. Bunbury, *History of Ancient Geography,* vol. 2, pp. 403-4.

81. "Guthalus," art. 1 by Lehr-Spławiński, art. 2 by Henryk Kowalewicz in Polska Akademia Nauk, *Słownik starożytności słowiańskich,* vol. 2, p. 179; Kiessling, "Guthalus," in *Paulys Realencyclopädie,* vol. 7 (1912), col. 1952.

82. "Dziś jednak tożsamość *Guthalus*=Odra ma tylko historyczną wartość i prawie powszechnie uznany jest pogląd, że *Guthalus* to nie Odra, lecz Pregoła lub Niemen." Biliński, "Drogi świata starożytnego ku zachodnim ziemiom polskim," p. 179.

83. "Guthalus," art. 1 by Lehr-Spławiński in Polska Akademia Nauk, *Słownik starożytności słowiańskich,* vol. 2, p. 179.

84. Tacitus, *Germania* (Anderson), p. XXVII.

85. "Trans Lugios Gotones regnantur, paulo iam adductius quam ceterae Germanorum gentes, nondum tamen supra libertatem. Protinus deinde ab Oceano Rugii et Lemovii; omnium harum gentium insigne rotunda scuta, breves gladii et erga reges obsequium." Tacitus, *Germania* 43.

86. Tacitus, *Germania* (Anderson), pp. 61-63. Some of Anderson's data are taken from Martin Jahn, *Die Bewaffnung der Germanen in der älteren Eisenzeit, etwa von 700 v. Chr. bis 200 n. Chr.* (Würzburg: Kabitzsch, 1916), which was not available to me.

87. Tacitus, *Germania* (Much), pp. 388-89; Schmidt, *Geschichte der deutschen Stämme,* vol. 1, p. 327; Steche, *Altgermanien im Erdkundebuch des Ptolemäus,* p. 102.

88. Jordanes, *Getica* IV, 25-26; Rappaport, "Rugi," in *Paulys Realencyclopädie,* 2. Reihe, vol. 1 (1920), col. 1213-23; Schmidt, *Geschichte der deutschen Stämme,* vol. 1, pp. 325-33; Tacitus, *Germania* (Anderson), p. 203; Tacitus, *Germania* (Much), pp. 388-89.

89. Εἶτα Σειδινοὶ μέχρι τοῦ Ἰαδούα ποταμοῦ, καὶ μετ' αὐτοὺς Ῥουτίκλειοι μέχρι τοῦ Οὐίστούλα ποταμοῦ. Ῥούγιον - μβ ∠, νε γό Ptolemy II, 11, 14, and II, 11, 27.

90. Biliński, "Drogi świata starożytnego ku zachodnim ziemiom polskim," p. 185; Rappaport, "Rugium," in *Paulys Realencyclopädie,* 2. Reihe, vol. 1 (1920), col. 1223; Schmidt, *Geschichte der deutschen Stämme,* vol. 1, p. 327; Steche, *Altgermanien im Erdkundebuch des Ptolemäus,* pp. 127, 147.

91. Ptolemy (Müller), p. 267.

92. Steche, *Altgermanien im Erdkundebuch des Ptolemäus,* pp. 36-38, 127, 147.

93. Tacitus, *Germania* (Much), pp. 389-90; Łowmiański, *Początki Polski,* vol. 1, pp. 237-39; "Głomacze," art. 2 by Jerzy Nalepa in *Polska Akademia Nauk, Słownik starożytności słowiańskich,* vol. 2, p. 111.

94. "Centum pagis habitant, magnoque corpore efficitur ut se Sueborum caput credant." Tacitus, *Germania* 39.

95. "Ex quibus latissime patet Lugiorum nomen in plures civitates diffusum. valentissimas nominasse sufficiet, Harios, Helveconas, Manimos, Helisios, Naharvalos." "Praecipua Marcomanorum gloria viresque, atque ipsa etiam sedes pulsis olim Boiis virtute parta." Tacitus, *Germania* 43 and 42.

96. "Contra Langobardos paucitas nobilitat: plurimis ac valentissimis nationibus cincti non per obsequium sed proeliis et periclitando tuti sunt." "Omnesque hi populi pauca campestrium ceterum saltus et vertices montium [iugumque] insederunt." Tacitus, *Germania* 40 and 43.

Notes to chapter 7

1. An extensive annotated bibliography on the *Geography* has been compiled by William Harris Stahl, *Ptolemy's Geography: A Select Bibliography* (New York: New York Public Library, 1953). Major discussions of the *Geography* can be found in: Bunbury, *History of Ancient Geography,* vol. 2, pp. 546-644; Gisinger, "Geographie,"

Pauly's Realencyclopädie, Suppl. vol. 4 (1924), col. 654-70; Erich Polaschek, "Ptolemy's Geography in a New Light," *Imago Mundi,* 14 (1959), pp. 17-37, and "Ptolemaios als Geograph," *Pauly's Realencyclopädie,* Suppl. vol. 10 (1965), col. 680-83; Thomson, *History of Ancient Geography,* pp. 335-47; Tozer, *History of Ancient Geography,* pp. 340-53.

2. George Sarton, "Ptolemy and His Time," in *Ancient Science and Modern Civilization* (Lincoln: University of Nebraska Press, 1954), p. 50.

3. Steche, *Altgermanien im Erdkundebuch des Ptolemäus,* pp. 32-34.

4. *Ibid.,* p. 33.

5. "Für sich genommen, ist diese lange Strecke überraschend richtig dargestellt; man muss staunen, wie genau die Entfernungsmessungen der alten Römer gewesen sind und wie gut sich die Einzelfehler gegenseitig aufgehoben haben." *Ibid.,* p. 34.

6. *Ibid.,* pp. 44-45.

7. Pliny IV, 96; Tacitus, *Germania* 44; Ptolemy II, 11, 35.

8. Steche, *Altgermanien im Erdkundebuch des Ptolemäus,* p. 108.

9. τὰ δὲ μεσημβρινὰ Γοῦται καὶ Δαυκίωνες τὰ δὲ μέσα Λευῶνοι. Ptolemy II, 11, 35.

10. Κατέχει δὲ τὴν Σαρματίαν ἔθνη μέγιστα οἵ τε Οὐενέδαι παρ' ὅλον ὃν Ουενεδικὸν κόλπον· καὶ ὑπὲρ τὴν Δακίαν Πευκῖνοί τε καὶ Βαστέρναι (ἢ Βαστάρναι)· καὶ παρ' ὅλην τὴν πλευρὰν τῆς Μαιώτιδος Ἰάζυγες καὶ Ῥωξολανοί, καὶ ἐνδοτέρω τούτων δέ τε Ἁμαξόβιοι καὶ ἀ Ἀλαῦνοι Σκύθαι. Ptolemy III, 5, 19.

11. Tymieniecki, *Ziemie polskie,* p. 605.

12. Petr Nikolaevich Tret'iakov, *Vostochnoslavianskie plemena* (Moscow: Izd-vo AN SSSR, 1948), pp. 52-57; *Finno-ugry balty i slaviane na Dnepre i Volge* (Moscow: Nauka, 1966), p. 196; *U istokov drevnerusskoi narodnosti* (Leningrad: Nauka, 1970), pp. 16-17.

13. From the abundant literature on the subject we quote a few selected titles: Paul Diels, *Die slavischen Völker* (Mit einer Literaturübersicht von Alexander Adamczyk. Wiesbaden: Harrassowitz, 1963), p. 19; Dvornik, *The Slavs,* pp. 13-14; Lehr-Spławiński, *O pochodzeniu i praojczyźnie Słowian,* pp. 16-18; Much, "Wenden," in Hoops, *Reallexikon,* vol. 4, pp. 508-9; Niederle, *Rukovet',* p. 39; Polaschek, "Venedai," in *Pauly's Realencyclopädie,* 2. Reihe, 15. Halbbd. (1955), col. 698-99; Reinhold Trautmann, *Die slavischen Völker und Sprachen; eine*

Einführung in die Slavistik (Göttingen: Vandenhoeck & Ruprecht, 1947), p. 22.

14. Ἡ ἐν Εὐρώπῃ Σαρματία περιορίζεται ἀπὸ μὲν ἄρκτων τῷ τε Σαρματικῷ ὠκεανῷ κατὰ τὸν Οὐενεδικὸν κόλπον καὶ μέρει τῆς ἀγνώσου γῆς, κατὰ περιγραφὴν τοιαύτην · μετὰ τὰς τοῦ Οὐιστούλα ποταμοῦ ἐκβολάς· αἳ ἐπέχουσι μοίρας –με, νς, χρόνου ποταμοῦ ἐκβολαί–ν, νς ... ἀπὸ δὲ δυσμῶν τῷ τε Οὐιστούλα ποταμῷ καὶ τῇ μεταξὺ τῆς κεφαλῆς αὐτοῦ καὶ τῶν Σαρματικῶν ὀρέων γραμμῇ καὶ αὐτοῖς τοῖς ὄρεσιν, ὧν ἡ θέας εἴρηται-Ptolemy III, 5, 1-2 and 5. The Venedian Gulf is also mentioned in a later periplus, *Marciani Heracleensis ex Pontu, Periplus Mari Exteri II, 39, 40,* in Karl Müller, *Geographi graeci minores* (Paris: F. Didot, 1855-1861), vol. 1, pp. 515-62, and table XXIX. Marcianus of Heraclea probably flourished at the beginning of the fifth century, but nothing is known with any certainty concerning the period in which he wrote. His work is based on Ptolemy's *Geography.* Cf. Bunbury, *History of Ancient Geography,* vol. 2, pp. 660-61.

15. A description and map of the present sea currents in the Gulf of Danzig can be found in Stanisław Lencewicz and Jerzy Kondracki, *Geografia fizyczna Polski* (Warsaw: PWN, 1959), pp. 19-21.

16. A few selected quotations will suffice to show the diversity of opinion in the interpretation and location of the Venedian Gulf: "... toteż nie tylko Zatoka Gdańska nazywa sie slusznie u Ptolemeusza *Venedikos Kolpos,* ale i Bałtyk południowy był istotnie Morzem Wenedyjskim." Franciszek Bujak, *Wenedowie na wschodnich wybrzezach Baltyku* (Danzig: Instytut Bałtycki, 1948), p. 37; "To the great bay thus formed by the Northern Ocean east of the Vistula he [i.e., Ptolemy] gives the name of the Venedic Gulf." Bunbury, *History of Ancient Geography,* vol. 2, p. 591; "... Uenedikós kólpos ("venedischer Meerbusen"), man denkt an eine der grossen Ostseebuchten, die Danziger oder die Rigaer." Diels, *Die slavischen Völker,* p. 19; "The Baltic he also calls the Sea of the Slavs (Οὐενεδικὸς κόλπος)." Dvornik, *The Slavs,* pp. 13-14, and "Ptolemy spoke of the 'Baltic sea of the Venedi'," *The Making of Central and Eastern Europe* (London: Polish Research Centre, 1949), p. 14; "Venedicus Sinus ... a bay of the Sarmatian Ocean, or Baltic, ... in all probability the Gulf of Riga." T. H. Dyer, "Venedicus Sinus," in Smith, *Dictionary of Greek and Roman Geography,* vol. 2, p. 1270; "No wonder, therefore that this part of the Baltic Sea (it is not known whether it merely involved the Bay of Gdańsk or some larger portions of the Baltic coast) where they were settled was called 'Venedian Bay' (Ouenedikòs kólpos-Sinus Vene-

dicus)." Jażdżewski, *Atlas,* vol. 2, p. 64, and "the 'Venedian Bay,' probably the counterpart of the present Gulf of Gdańsk (Danzig)," *Poland* (New York: Praeger, 1965), p. 144; "Venedy lokalizuiutsia po beregu Venedskogo zaliva, t. e. Baltiiskogo moria." O.V. Kudriavtsev, *Issledovaniia po istorii balkano-dunaiskikh oblastei v period Rimskoi imperii i stat'i po obshchim problemam drevnei istorii* (Moscow: Izd-vo AN SSSR, 1957), p. 35; ". . . nazwę zatoki Weneckiej (gr. Οὐενεδικὸς κόλπος), która odpowiada oczywiście zatoce Gdańskiej." Lehr-Spławiński, *O pochodzeniu i praojczyźnie Słowian,* p. 101; "Biorąc pod uwagę sztuczne rozgraniczenie Oceanu Germańskiego i Sarmackiego, jako mórz przyleglych do krajów tak nazwanych, należy wnosić, że i Zatoka Wenecka nie przeszła do *Geografii* z terenu, lecz została utworzona przez aleksandryjskich erudytów, jako umowne określenie wód, nad którymi mieszkali Weneci," and " 'Zatoka Wenecka', jako jedynej zatoki na morzach północnych dowodzi, że Ptolemeusz powziął nader wysokie wyobrażenie o Wenetach, jako ludzie wyjątkowo potężnym i zajmującym rozległe wybrzeże morskie, Lowmiański, *Początki Polski,* vol. 1, pp. 173-74; "Neubildungen sind auch Γερμανικὸς ὠκεανός des Ptolemaios 2, 11, 1 für die Ostsee bis zur Weichsel und Σαρματικὸς ὠκεανός mit dem Οὐενεδικὸς κόλπος (3, 5, 1)für dasselbe Meer weiter im Osten." Tacitus, *Germania* (Much), pp. 402-3; "Venedy-Slovany . . . rozšiřeny za Vislou mezi mořem Baltickým (záliv Venedský)." Niederle, *Rukovět',* p. 39; "Ptolemeusz, który Zatokę Gdańską nazywa Zatoką Wenedzką." Ludwik Piotrowicz, "Goci i Gepidowie nad dolną Wisła i ich wędrówka ku Morzu Czarnemu i Dacji," *Przegląd Zachodni,* 7, no. 5/6 (1951), p. 65; "Wzdłuż zatoki Wenedyjskiej," explained in footnote 2 "Zatoka Gdańska." Marian Plezia, *Greckie i łacińskie źródła do najstarszych dziejów Słowian: Część I (do VIII. wieku)* (Poznań-Cracow: Polskie Towarzystwo Ludoznawcze, 1952), p. 38; "Ob freilich die ptolemäischen Bezeichnungen Οὐενεδικὸς κόλπος . . . auf die Danziger Bucht . . . zu beziehen sind, ist fraglich. Bei älteren, östlicheren Wohnsitzen der V. verdienen der Meerbusen von Riga . . . Aufmerksamkeit." Polaschek, "Venedai," in *Paulys Realencyclopädie,* 2. Reihe, 15 Halbbd. (1955), col. 699; ". . . zatoki wenedzkiej, przez którą należy rozumieć cały południowy Bałtyk, a nie zatokę Gdańską, ponieważ mapa Ptolemeusza wcale nie zna Zatoki Gdańskiej." Rudnicki, "Plemiona prasłowiańskie w dorzeczu górnej Noteci, średniej Warty i dolnej Wisły," *Slavianskaia filologiia; sbornik statei* (Moscow: Izd-vo AN SSSR, 1958), vol. 1, pp. 150-51; "Aber der Wenedische Meerbusen muss doch irgendwo an der Ostsee gelegen haben, diesen kann man nicht nach Süden verschieben; man kann auch nicht den Namen einfach wegleugnen und Ptolemäus kann ihn nicht in der Stadt Alexandria erfunden haben." Steche, *Altgermanien im Erdkundebuch des Ptolemäus,* p. 121; ". . . 'po Venedskomu zalivu,' t.e. po Baltiiskomu moriu." Tret'iakov, *Vostochnoslavianskie plemena,* p. 41, cf. also *Finno-ugry, balty i slaviane,* p. 196, and *U istokov drevnerusskoi narodnosti,* p. 16; ". . . zatoka Wenedyjska, przez którą skłonni jesteśmy rozumieć Bałtyk, a przynajmniej jego część południową." Tymieniecki, *Ziemie polskie,* p. 559.

17. τὰ Οὐενεδικὰ ὄρη ...μ̃ζ̃ι, ν̃ε Ptolemy III, 5, 15.

18. Heinrich Kiepert, *Formae orbis antiqui* (Berlin: Reimer, 1893-1914), map 35; Kossinna, *Ursprung der Germanen,* map 1; Plezia, *Greckie i łacińskie źródła,* map 3.

19. Lencewicz and Kondracki, *Geografia fizyczna Polski,* pp. 228-29.

20. Dyer, "Venedici montes," in Smith, *Dictionary of Greek and Roman Geography,* vol. 2, p. 1270; Łowmiański, *Początki Polski,* vol. 1, pp. 171-72; Plezia, *Greckie i łacińskie źródła,* p. 41; Polaschek, "Venedai," in *Paulys Realencyclopädie,* 2. Reihe, 15 Halbbd. (1955), col. 699; Steche, *Altgermanien im Erdkundebuch des Ptolemäus,* pp. 112, 121; Tymieniecki, *Ziemie polskie,* p. 557.

21. Niederle, *Starożytności słowiańskie,* vol. 1, pp. 210-11, quoted after Tymieniecki, *Ziemie polskie,* p. 558. The Venedian mountains as the Carpathians are also briefly mentioned as "Karpaty (Venedské hory)" in Niederle, *Rukovět',* p. 39.

22. Dvornik, *The Slavs,* p. 13; Tymieniecki, *Ziemie polskie,* pp. 557, 593, 600, 639, 641, 787.

23. Lehr-Spławiński, *O pochodzeniu i praojczyźnie Słowian,* pp. 16, 101.

24. Jan Czekanowski, *Polska-Słowiańszczyzna; perspektywy antropologiczne* (Warsaw Wydawnictwo S. Arcta, 1948), map 1, and *"Wstęp do historii Słowian; perspektywy antropologiczne, etnograficzne i językowe* (2 wyd. Poznań: Instytut Zachodni, 1957), map 8. ". . . and the mountains extending north of the Carpathians and south of the Baltic Sea, i.e., most probably the Świętokrzyskie Mountains (Łysogóry Mountains) bear the name of 'Venedian Mountains' (Ouenediká Ore)." Jaźdźewski, *Atlas,* vol. 2, p. 64; ". . . the 'Venedian Mountains' (the last designating either the Świętokrzyskie Mountains or the northern slopes of the Carpathians)." Jaźdźewski, *Poland,* p. 144.

25. Ἐλάσσονα δὲ ἔθνη νέμεται τὴν Σαρματίαν, παρὰ μὲν τὸν

Οὐιστούλαν ποταμὸν ὑπὸ τοὺς Οὐενέδας Γύθωνες, εἶτα Φίννοι, εἶτα
Βούλανες (ἢ Σούλωνες)· ὑφ᾽ οὓς Φρουγουνδίωνες, εἶτα Αὔαρηνοὶ (ἢ
Ἀβαρινοὶ) παρὰ τὴν κεφαλὴν τοῦ Οὐιστούλα ποταμοῦ· ὑφ᾽ οὓς
Ὄμβρωνες, εἶτα Ἀναρτοφράκτα εἶτα Βουργίωνες, εἶτα
Ἀρσιῆται, εἶτα Σαβῶκοι ἢ Σαβόκαι, εἶτα Πιεγγῖται καὶ Βίεσσοι
παρὰ τὸν Καρπάτην ὄρος. Ptolemy III, 5, 20.

26. The Anartoi are recorded by Ptolemy in III, 8, 5; the Anartes by
Caesar, *Bellum Gallicum* VI, 25. A. Jankowski, "Anartofraktowie," in
Polska Akademia Nauk, *Słownik starożytności słowiańskich*, vol. 1, p.
23; "Anartowie," art. 1 by Lehr-Spławiński, art. 2 by Jankowski, *ibid.*,
vol. 1, p. 23.

27. "Burgundowie," art. 1 by Lehr-Spławiński, art. 2 by Linderski in
Polska Akademia Nauk, *Slownik starożytności słowiańskich*, vol. 1, pp.
204-5; Filip, "Burgunden," in Filip, *Enzyklopädisches Handbuch*, p.
187; Ihm, "Burgiones," in *Paulys Realencyclopädie*, vol. 3, col. 1063,
and "Burgundiones," *ibid.*, col. 1063-65; Jankowski, "Burgionowie," in
Polska Akademia Nauk, *Słownik starożytności słowiańskich*, vol. 1, p.
204, Kowalewicz, "Frugundiones," *ibid.*, vol. 2, p. 73; Schmidt, *Geschichte der deutschen Stämme*, vol. 1, p. 368; Schmitz, "Burgundio'nes, Burgundii," in Smith, *Dictionary of Greek and Roman Geography*, vol. 1, p. 458; Steche, *Altgermanien im Erdkundebuch des
Ptolemäus*, pp. 113, 116; Tymieniecki, *Ziemie polskie*, pp. 614, 617,
642-43, 689.

28. Cüppers, "Fenni," in *Der Kleine Pauly*, vol. 2, p. 534; "Fin-
owie," art. 1 by Lehr-Spławiński, art. 2 by Jan Reychman in Polska
Akademia Nauk, *Słownik starożytności słowiańskich*, vol. 2, pp. 56-57;
Ihm, "Fenni (Finni)," in *Paulys Realencyclópädie*, vol. 6 (1909), col.
2186.

29. Σούλωνες, Σούλανες, Βούλανες Ptolemy (Müller) III, 5, 8.

30. Tymieniecki, *Ziemie polskie*, p. 613; Steche, *Altgermanien im
Erdkundebuch des Ptolemäus*, p. 117.

31. Niederle, *Rukovět'*, p. 134; Plezia, *Greckie i łacińskie źródła*, p.
37; Tymieniecki, *Ziemie polskie*, p. 617.

32. Tymieniecki, *Ziemie polskie*, p. 614 and map 18. The same map
can be found in his "Położenie Słowian wśród ludów Europy albo tzw.
pierwsze millenium. Zmiany w sytuacji międzynarodowej przed powstaniem państwa polskiego," *Początki Państwa Polskiego; Księga Tysiąclecia* (2 vols. Poznań: PWN, 1962), vol. 1, p. 25.

33. Τῶν δὲ εἰρημένων εἰσὶν ἀνατολικώτεροι, ὑπὸ μὲν τοὺς
Οὐενέδας πάλιν Γαλίνδαι (ἢ Γαλιδανοί) καὶ Σουδηνοὶ (ἢ
Σουδινοὶ), καὶ Σταυανοί μέχρι τῶν Ἀλαύνων· ὑφ᾽ οὓς Ἰγυλλίωνες

εἶτα Κοιστοβῶκοι, καὶ Τρανσμονζανοί μέχρι τῶν Πευκίνων ὀρέων.
Ptolemy III, 5, 21.

34. "Alanowie," art. 1 by Lehr-Spławiński, art. 2 by Tadeusz
Lewicki in Polska Akademia Nauk, *Słownik starożytności słowiańskich,*
vol. 1, pp. 10-11; Christo M. Danoff, "Alani Ἀλανοί." in *Der Kleine
Pauly,* vol. 1, p. 230; Tomaschek, "Alani," in *Paulys Realencyclopädie,*
vol. 1 (1894), col. 1282; Tymieniecki, *Ziemie polskie,* p. 619.

35. Γαλίνδαι, Γάλινδαι, Γαλιδανοί Ptolemy (Müller) III, 5, 9.

36. "Der germanische Stamm der Galinden, die vielleicht den Goten
nah verwandt waren." Kossinna, *Das Weichselland, ein uralter Heimatboden der Germanen* (3rd rev. ed. Leipzig: Kabitzsch, 1940), p. 38.

37. Bujak, *Wenedowie na wschodnich wybrzeżach Bałtyku,* p. 38.

38. Franke, "Sudinoi," in *Paulys Realencyclopädie,* 2. Reihe, vol. 4
(1931), col. 563-64.

39. "Daraus ergibt sich, dass die G. und Sudinoi als ursprünglich
slavische Stämme im Hinterland der Danziger Bucht und des Kurischen
Haffs, also in Ostpreussen zu suchen sind." Kiessling, "Galindai," in
Paulys Realencyclopädie, 13. Halbbd. (1910), col. 606.

40. Rudnicki, "Plemiona prasłowiańskie w dorzeczu górnej Noteci,"
pp. 144-57.

41. "Bałtowie," art. 1 by Lehr-Spławiński, art. 2 by Jażdżewski in
Polska Akademia Nauk, *Słownik starożytności słowiańskich,* vol. 1, pp.
73-77; Czekanowski, *Wstęp do historii Słowian,* pp. 130-31; "Galin-
der," in Filip, *Enzyklopädisches Handbuch,* vol. 1, p. 385 (containing a
printing error: *Szczecin* instead of *Szczytno*); "Galindia," art. 1 by
Lehr-Spławiński, art. 2 by Marzena Pollakówna in Polska Akademia
Nauk, *Słownik starożytności słowiańskich,* vol. 2, pp. 78-79; Marija
Gimbutas, *The Balts* (New York: Praeger, 1968), pp. 22, 28; "Jaćwieź,"
art. 1 by Lehr-Spławiński, art. 2 by Gieysztor, art. 3 by Jerzy Antoniewicz and Aleksander Kamiński, art. 4 by Gieysztor, in Polska Akademia Nauk, *Słownik starożytności słowiańskich,* vol. 2, pp. 305-8; Jaż-
dzewski, *Atlas,* vol. 2,, pp. 64-65, and *Poland,* pp. 144, 151, 159; Kostrzewski, *Pradzieje Polski* (Poznań: Ksiegarnia Akademicka, 1949), p.
217; Lehr-Spławiński, *O pochodzeniu i praojczyźnie Słowian,* pp. 16,
66, 96, 112; Niederle, *Rukověť',* p. 144; Steche, *Altgermanien im Erdkundebuch des Ptolemäus,* p. 117; Tymieniecki, *Ziemie polskie,* pp.
611-12, 614, 618-19, 622, 794.

42. Kostrzewski, *Pradzieje Polski,* p. 217.

43. R. G. Latham, "Igullio'nes," in Smith, *Dictionary of Greek and
Latin Geography,* vol. 2, p. 30.

44. Cf. note 41.

45. Tymieniecki, *Ziemie polskie,* pp. 621-22 and map 18; also "Polożenie Słowian wśród ludów Europy," p. 25.

46. Schönfeld, "Goti," in *Paulys Realencyclopädie,* Suppl. vol. 3 (1918), col. 800; Stein, "Geticus," *ibid.,* vol. 7 (1912), col. 1336; "M. Aurelius Antoninus (Caracalla)," *ibid.,* vol. 2 (1896), col. 2448.

47. A. Lippold, "Goti," in *Der Kleine Pauly,* vol. 2, p. 858.

48. Jordanes, *Getica* IV, 27. The various locations of Oium are discussed in E. Ch. Skrzhinskaia's edition of the *Getica,* pp. 195-96.

49. The route along the Dvina and the Dnieper was suggested by Carl Schuchhardt, *Vorgeschichte von Deutschland* (5th rev. ed. Munich and Berlin: Oldenbourg, 1943), p. 300. Tymieniecki's suggested route along the Elbe and the Danube was the consequence of his locating the Goths near the Middle Elbe; cf. Tymieniecki, *Ziemie polskie,* p. 517. Further discussions can be found in: Piotrowicz, "Goci i Gepidowie nad dolną Wisłą," pp. 69-70; "Goci," art. 3 and map by Kmieciński, and art. 4 by Tadeusz Manteuffel, in Polska Akademia Nauk, *Słownik starożytności słowiańskich,* vol. 2, pp. 125-26.

SELECTED BIBLIOGRAPHY

Primary sources

Caesar, Gaius Julius. *C. Iuli Caesaris Belli gallici libri VII, cum A. Hirti libro octavo. In usum scholarum iterum recognovit, adiecit Galliam antiquam tabula descriptam Bernardus Dinter.* Leipzig: in aedibus B. G. Teubneri, 1899.

Caesar, Gaius Julius. *The Gallic War.* With an English translation by H. J. Edwards. Cambridge: Harvard University Press; London: Heinemann, 1952.

Isidorus, Hispalensis. *Isidore of Seville's History of the Kings of the Goths, Vandals, and Suevi.* Translated by Guido Donini and Gordon B. Ford. Leiden: Brill, 1966.

Jordanes. *The Gothic History of Jordanes.* In English version with an Introduction and a Commentary by Charles Christopher Mierow. 2nd Ed. Cambridge: Speculum Historiale; New York: Barnes & Noble, 1960.

Jordanes. *Iordan o proiskhozhdenii i deianiiakh getov—Getica—.* Vstupitel'naia stat'ia, perevod, kommentarii E. Ch. Skrzhinskoi. Moscow: Izd-vo vostochnoi literatury, 1960.

Jordanes. *Iordanis Romana et Getica.* Recensuit Theodorus Mommsen. Berlin: apud Weidmannos, 1882.

Mela, Pomponius. *Pomponii Melae De chorographia libri tres.* Recognovit Carolus Frick. Leipzig: in aedibus B. G. Teubneri, 1880.

Monumentum Ancyranum. "Res gestae divi Augusti. With an English Translation by Frederick W. Shipley." In Velleius Paterculus, C. *Compendium of Roman History.* London: Heinemann; New York: Putnam, 1924, pp. 331-431.

Plinius Secundus, Gaius. *C. Plinii Secundi Naturalis historiae libri XXXVII.* Post Ludovici Iani obitum recognovit et scripturae discrepantia adiecta edidit Carolus Mayhoff. 3 vols. Leipzig: in aedibus B. G. Teubneri, 1870-1898 (vols. 1-2, in rev. ed., 1906-1909).

Plinius Secundus, Gaius. *Natural History.* With an English Translation by H. Rackham. 10 vols. Cambridge: Harvard University Press, 1938-1963.

Plutarchus. *Plutarch's Lives.* With an English Translation by Bernadotte Perrin. 11 vols. Cambridge: Harvard University Press; London: Heinemann, 1914-1926.

Procopius, of Caesarea. *Procopius.* With an English Translation by H. B. Dewing. 7 vols. London: Heinemann; New York: Macmillan, 1914-1954.

Ptolemaeus, Claudius. *Claudii Ptolemaei Geographia.* Edidit C. F. A. Nobbe, cum introductione a Aubrey Diller. 3 vols. in one. Hildesheim: Olms, 1966.

Ptolemaeus, Claudius. *Die Geographie des Ptolemaeus; Galliae, Germania, Raetia, Noricum, Pannoniae, Illyricum, Italia.* Handschriften, Text und Untersuchung von Otto Cuntz. Berlin: Weidmannsche Buchhandlung, 1923.

Ptolemaeus, Claudius. Κλαυδίου Πτολεμαίου Γεωγραφικῆ Ὑφηγήσις. *Claudii Ptolemaei Geographia.* E codicibus recognovit, prolegomenis, annotatione, indicibus, tabulis instruxit Carolus Müllerus. 2 parts. Paris: Didot, 1883-1901.

Ptolemaeus, Claudius. *Geography of Claudius Ptolemy.* Translated into English, and edited by Edward Luther Stevenson. Based upon Greek and Latin manuscripts and important late 15th and early 16th century printed editions, including reproductions of the maps from the Ebner Manuscript, ca. 1460. New York: New York Public Library, 1932.

Pytheas of Massalia. *Pytheas von Massalia.* Collegit Hans Joachim Mette. Berlin: De Gruyter, 1952.

Solinus, Gaius Iulius. *Collectanea rerum memorabilium.* Iterum recensuit Th. Mommsen. Berlin: apud Weidmannos, 1895.

Strabo. *Geografiia v 17 knigakh.* Perevod, statia i kommentarii G. A. Stratanovskogo. Pod obshchei redaktsii S. L. Utchenko. Redaktor perevoda O. O. Kriuger. Leningrad: "Nauka," 1964.

Strabo. *Géographie.* Texte établi et traduit par François Lasserre. Paris: Societé d'Edition "Les Belles Lettres, 1966- (in progress: vols. 2-3 [books 3-6] 1966-1967).

Strabo. *The Geography of Strabo.* With an English translation by Horace Leonard Jones. 8 vols. London: Heinemann; New York: Putnam, 1917-1933.

Strabo. *Strabonis Geographica*. Recensuit, commentario critico instruxit Gustavus Kramer. 3 vols. Berlin: Libraria Frederici Nicolai, 1844-1852.

Strabo. *Strabonis Geographica*. Recognovit Augustus Meineke. 3 vols. Leipzig: Teubneri, 1876-1877.

Tacitus: Works, Annals, and Histories

Tacitus, Cornelius, *The Complete Works of Tacitus*. Translated from the Latin by Alfred John Church and William Jackson Brodribb. Edited by Moses Hadas. New York: Modern Library, 1942.

Tacitus, Cornelius. *Cornelii Taciti libri qui supersunt*. Quartum recognovit Carolus Halm. 2 vols. Leipzig: in aedibus B. G. Teubneri, 1897-1901.

Tacitus, Cornelius. *The Histories*. With an English translation by Clifford H. Moore. *The Annals*. With an English translation by John Jackson. 4 vols. London: Heinemann; New York: G. Putnam, 1925-1937.

Tacitus, Cornelius. *Sochineniia*. Otv. red. S. L. Utchenko. 2 vols. Leningrad: "Nauka," 1969.

Tacitus, Cornelius. *The Works of Tacitus; The Oxford Translation*. Revised, with notes. 2 vols. London: G. Bell, 1910-1911.

Tacitus: The Germania *(separate editions)*

Tacitus, Cornelius. *Cornelii Taciti De origine et situ Germanorum*. Edited by J. G. C. Anderson. Oxford: Clarendon Press, 1958.

Tacitus, Cornelius. *Germania*. Hrsg., übersetzt und mit Erläuterungen versehen von Eugen Fehrle. 5. überarbeitete Aufl. besorgt von Richard Hühnerkopf. Heidelberg: Carl Winter, 1959.

Tacitus, Cornelius. *Cornelii Taciti De Germania*. Edited by Henry Furneaux. Oxford: Clarendon Press, 1894.

Tacitus, Cornelius. *Dialogus, Agricola, Germania*. Translated by Maurice Hutton. London: Heinemann; New York: Putnam, 1925.

Tacitus, Cornelius. *Publius Cornelius Tacitus Germania*. Lateinisch und deutsch, übertragen und erläutert von Arno Mauersberger. Bremen: Schünemann, 1957.

Tacitus, Cornelius. *Die Germania des Tacitus*. Erläutert von Rudolf Much. 2. Aufl., durchgesehen von Richard Kienast. Heidelberg: Carl Winter, 1959.

Tacitus, Cornelius. *The Germania of Tacitus*. A critical edition by Rod-

Tacitus, Cornelius. *Tacitus' Germania.* Erläutert von Heinrich Schweizer-Sidler, erneuert von Eduard Schwyzer. 8. Aufl. Halle: Buchhandlung des Waisenhauses, 1923.

Velleius Paterculus, Gaius. C. *Vellei Paterculi ex Historiae Romanae libri duobus quae supersunt.* Edidit Carolus Halm. Leipzig: Teubner, 1909.

Velleius Paterculus, Gaius. *Compendium of Roman History. Res gestae divi Augusti.* With an English translation by Frederick W. Shipley. London: Heinemann; New York: Putnam, 1924.

Secondary sources

Books

Akademiia nauk SSSR. *Vsemirnaia istoriia.* Glavnyi redaktor: E. M. Zhukov. 10 vols. Moscow: Gosud. izd-vo polit. lit-ry, 1955-1965.

Akademiia nauk SSSR. Institut istorii. *Istoriia SSSR s drevneishikh vremen do nashikh dnei.* 12 vols. Moscow: "Nauka," 1966- (in progress, vols. 1-9, 1966-1971).

Aly, Wolfgang. *Strabon von Amaseia; Untersuchungen über Text, Aufbau und Quellen der Geographika.* Bonn: Habelt, 1957.

Anderson, Romola, and Anderson, R. C. *The Sailing Ship; Six Thousand Years of History.* New ed. New York: Bonanza Books, 1963.

Antoniewicz, Jerzy. *The Sudovians.* Translated by Halina Modrzewska. Bialystok: Scientific Society, 1962.

Antoniewicz, Włodzimierz. *Archeologja Polski; zarys czasów przedhistorycznych i wczesnodziejowych Polski.* Warsaw: Trzaska, Evert, Michalski, 1928.

Atlas of Ancient and Classical Geography. London and Toronto: Dent; New York: Dutton, 1928.

Bagrow, Leo. *History of Cartography.* Rev. and enl. by R. A. Skelton. English translation by D. L. Paisy. London: C. A. Watts, 1964.

Bibby, Geoffrey. *The Testimony of the Spade.* New York: Knopf, 1971.

Bradley, Henry. *The Goths; From the Earliest Times to the End of the Gothic Dominion in Spain.* 5th ed. London: Fisher Unwin, 1888.

Brown, Lloyd A. *The Story of Maps.* Boston: Little, Brown and Co., 1949.

Bühler, Johannes. *Deutsche Geschichte.* 6 vols. (vols. 1-3 in revised reprint, 1954). Berlin: De Gruyter, 1950-1960.

Bujak, Franciszek. *Wenedowie na wschodnich wybrzeżach Bałtyku.* Danzig: Instytut Bałtycki, 1948.

Bunbury, E. H. *A History of Ancient Geography among the Greeks and Romans; From the Earliest Ages till the Fall of the Roman Empire.* 2nd ed., with a new introduction by W. H. Stahl. 2 vols. New York: Dover Publications, 1959.

Bury, J. B. *The Invasion of Europe by the Barbarians.* New York: Russell & Russell, 1963.

The Cambridge Ancient History. 12 vols. Cambridge: University Press, 1923-1939.

The Cambridge History of Poland. Edited by W. F. Reddaway and others. 2 vols. Cambridge: University Press, 1941-1950.

The Cambridge Medieval History. 8 vols. Cambridge: University Press, 1924-1936.

Carsten, F. L. *The Origins of Prussia.* Oxford: Clarendon Press, 1954.

Casson, Lionel. *The Ancient Mariners; Seafarers and Sea Fighters of the Mediterranean in Ancient Times.* New York: Macmillan, 1959.

Charlesworth, Martin Percival. *Trade-Routes and Commerce of the Roman Empire.* Hildesheim: Olms, 1961 (Reprint of the Cambridge 1924 edition).

Childe, V. Gordon. *The Dawn of European Civilization.* 6th ed., rev. New York: Knopf, 1958.

Clark, J. G. D. *Prehistoric Europe; the Economic Basis.* Stanford: Stanford University Press, 1966.

Clark, J. G. D. *World Prehistory.* 2nd ed. Cambridge: University Press, 1969.

Coon, Carleton Stevens. *The Races of Europe.* New York: Macmillan, 1948.

Crone, Gerald Roe. *Maps and Their Makers: An Introduction into the History of Cartography.* London: Hutchinson University Library, 1953.

Cross, Samuel Hazzard. *Slavic Civilization through the Ages.* Edited, with a foreword by Leonid I. Strakhovsky. Cambridge: Harvard University Press, 1948.

Czekanowski, Jan. *Polska-Słowiańszczyzna; perspektywy antropologiczne.* Warsaw: Wydawnictwo S. Arcta, 1948.

Czekanowski, Jan. *Wstęp do historii Słowian; perspektywy antropologiczne etnograficzne i językowe.* 2.wyd., na nowo opracowane. Poznań: Instytut Zachodni, 1957.

Derzhavin, Nikolai Sevastianovich. *Slaviane v drevnosti; kul'turno-istoricheskii ocherk.* Moscow: Izd-vo A.N. SSSR, 1945.

Diels, Paul. *Die slavischen Völker*. Mit einer Literaturübersicht von Alexander Adamczyk. Wiesbaden: Harrassowitz, 1963.

Diller, Aubrey. *The Tradition of the Minor Greek Geographers*. New York: American Philological Association, 1952.

Dvornik, Francis. *The Making of Central and Eastern Europe*. London: Polish Research Centre, 1949.

Dvornik, Francis. *The Slavs in European History and Civilization*. New Brunswick: Rutgers University Press, 1962.

Dvornik, Francis. *The Slavs, Their Early History and Civilization*. Boston: American Academy of Arts and Sciences, 1956.

East, W. Gordon. *An Historical Geography of Europe*. 4th ed. London: Methuen, 1950.

Entwistle, W. J., and Morison, W. A. *Russian and the Slavonic Languages*. London: Faber and Faber, 1949.

Filip, Jan. *Pradzieje Czechosłowacji*. Z języka czeskiego przełożył Józef Kostrzewski. Poznań: Instytut Zachodni, 1951.

George, Hereford Brooke. *The Relations of Geography and History*. 5th ed., edited by O. J. R. Howarth, with an additional chapter by C. B. Fawlett. Oxford: Clarendon Press, 1930.

Gibbon, Edward. *The History of the Decline and Fall of the Roman Empire*. With notes by Dean Milman, M. Guizot and William Smith. 6 vols. New York: Euclid Press, 1890.

Gimbutas, Marija. *The Balts*. New York: Praeger, 1968.

Gimbutas, Marija. *The Slavs*. New York: Praeger, 1971.

Günther, Hans. *Rassenkunde Europas, mit besonderer Berücksichtigung der Rassengeschichte der Hauptvölker indogermanischer Sprache*. 3., wesentlich vermehrte und bearb. Aufl. Munich: Lehmann, 1929.

Hahne, Hans. *Das vorgeschichtliche Europa; Kulturen, Völker und Rassen*. 2nd ed. Bielefeld: Velhagen & Klasing, 1935.

Halecki, Oscar. *Borderlands of Western Civilization: A History of East Central Europe*. New York: Ronald Press, 1952.

Hassinger, Hugo. *Geographische Grundlagen der Geschichte*. Freiburg im Breisgau: Herder, 1931.

Heichelheim, Fritz. *An Ancient Economic History: From the Palaeolithic Age to the Migrations of the Germanic, Slavic, and Arabic Nations*. Revised and complete English ed., translated by Joyce Stevens. 3 vols. Leiden: Sijthoff, 1968-1970.

Helbling, Hanno. *Goten und Wandalen: Wandlung der historischen Realität*. Zurich: Fretz & Wachsmuth, 1954.

Hennig, Richard. *Terrae incognitae*. 2., verb. Aufl. 4 vols. Leiden: Brill, 1944-1956.

Hensel, Witold. *Die Slaven im frühen Mittelalter; ihre materielle Kultur.* Berlin: Akademie-Verlag, 1965.

Hirt, Herman Alfred. *Die Indogermanen: ihre Verbreitung, ihre Urheimat und ihre Kultur.* 2 vols. Strasbourg: Truebner, 1905-1907.

History of Poland. Editor-in-chief: Stefan Kiniewicz. Warsaw: PWN, 1968.

Istoriia iuznykh i zapadnykh slavian. Red. kollegiia: I. M. Beliavskaia *et al.* Moscow: Izd-vo Moskovskogo universiteta, 1969.

Jażdżewski, Konrad. *Atlas to the Prehistory of the Slavs.* 2 vols. Łódź: Łódzkie Towarzystwo Naukowe, 1948-1949.

Jaźdżewski, Konrad. *Poland.* Translated from the Polish by Maria Abramowicz and Robin Place. New York: Praeger, 1965.

Jones, Gwyn. *A History of the Vikings.* London: Oxford University Press, 1968.

Karsten, Torsten Evert. *Die Germanen; eine Einführung in die Geschichte ihrer Sprache und Kultur.* Berlin and Leipzig: De Gruyter, 1928.

Kiepert, Heinrich. *Formae orbis antiqui.* Berlin: Reimer, 1893-1914.

Klindt-Jensen, Ole. *Denmark before the Vikings.* Translated from the Danish by Eva and David Wilson. London: Thames & Hudson, 1957.

Kmieciński, Jerzy. *Zagadnienia t.zw. kultury gocko-gepidzkiej na Pomorzu wschodnim w okresie wczesnorzymskim.* Łódź: Zakład Narodowy im. Ossolińskich we Wrocławiu, 1962.

Kočka, Wojciech. *Zagadnienia etnogenezy ludów Europy.* Wrocław: PWN, 1958.

Kossinna, Gustaf. *Die Herkunft der Germanen; zur Methode der Siedlungsarchäologie.* Würzburg: Kabitzsch, 1911.

Kossinna, Gustaf. *Die Indogermanen; ein Abriss. I Teil, das indogermanische Urvolk.* Leipzig: Kabitzsch, 1921.

Kossinna, Gustaf. *Ursprung und Verbreitung der Germanen in vor- und frühgeschichtlicher Zeit.* 3rd printing. Leipzig: Kabitzsch, 1936.

Kossinna, Gustaf. *Das Weichselland, ein uralter Heimatboden der Germanen.* 3. verb. Aufl. Leipzig: Kabitzsch, 1940.

Kostrzewski, Józef. *Pradzieje Polski.* Poznań: Księgarnia Akademicka, 1949.

Kostrzewski, Józef. *Wielkopolska w pradziejach.* Zmienione 3. wyd. *Wielkopolski w czasach przedhistorycznych.* Warsaw: Zakład im. Ossolińskich, 1955.

Krahe, Hans. *Indogermanische Sprachwissenschaft.* 2nd ed. Berlin: De Gruyter, 1948.

Krahe, Hans. *Sprache und Vorzeit; europäische Vorgeschichte nach dem Zeugnis der Sprache.* Heidelberg: Quelle & Meyer, 1954.

Krahe, Hans. *Sprachverwandschaft im Alten Europa.* Heidelberg: Winter, 1951.

Kudriavtsev, O. V. *Issledovaniia po istorii balkano-dunaiskikh oblastei v period Rimskoi imperii i stat'i po obshchim problemam drevnei istorii.* Moscow: Izd-vo AN SSSR, 1957.

Kukharenko, Iurii Vladimirovich. *Arkheologiia Pol'shi.* Moscow: "Nauka," 1969.

Labuda, Gerard. *Fragmenty do dziejów Słowiańszczyzny Zachodniej, I.* Poznań: Wyd. Poznańskie, 1960.

Lehr-Spławiński, Tadeusz. *O pochodzeniu i praojczyźnie Słowian.* Poznań: Instytut Zachodni, 1946.

Lencewicz, Stanisław, and Kondracki, Jerzy. *Geografia fizyczna Polski.* Warsaw: PWN, 1959.

Łowmiański, Henryk. *Początki Polski; z dziejów Słowian w I. tysiacleciu n. e.* 4 vols. Warsaw: PWN, 1963-1970.

Mendell, Clarence W. *Tacitus, the Man and His Work.* New Haven: Yale University Press, 1957.

Miller, Konrad. *Mappaemundi; die ältesten Weltkarten.* Stuttgart: Roth, 1895-1898.

Miller, Konrad. *Die Peutingerische Tafel oder Weltkarte des Castorius.* 2nd ed. Stuttgart: Strecker & Schröder, 1929.

Miller, Mykhailo Oleksandrovych. *Archaeology in the USSR.* New York: Praeger, 1956.

Mongait, Aleksandr L'vovich. *Archaeology in the USSR.* Translated and adapted by M. W. Thompson. Baltimore: Penguin Books, 1961.

Moszyński, Kazimierz. *Pierwotny zasiąg języka prasłowiańskiego.* Wrocław-Cracow: Zakład Narodowy im. Ossolińskich, 1957.

Much, Rudolf. *Deutsche Stammeskunde.* 3. verb. Aufl. Berlin and Leipzig: De Gruyter, 1920.

Müller, Karl. *Geographi graeci minores.* E codicibus recognovit, prolegomenis annotatione, indicibus instruxit, tabulis aeri incisis illustravit Carolus Müllerus. 2 vols. Paris: Firmin-Didot, 1855-1861.

Niederle, Lubor. *Rukovĕt' slovanských starožitnosti.* K vydáni připravil akademik Jan Eisner. Prague: Naklad. Ceskoslovenské Akademie Vĕd, 1953.

Neustupný, Evzen, and Neustupný, Jiri. *Czechoslovakia before the Slavs.* New York: Praeger, 1961.

Norden, Eduard. *Die germanische Urgeschichte in Tacitus Germania.* 3. Abdruck mit Ergänzungen. Leipzig: Teubner, 1923.

Obermüller, Christoph. *Die deutschen Stämme; Stammesgeschichte als Namensgeschichte und Reichsgeschichte.* 2., fast unveränderte Aufl. Bielefeld: Velhagen & Klasing, 1941.

Owen, Francis. *The Germanic People; Their Origin, Expansion and Culture.* New York: Bookman Associates, 1960.

Oxenstierna, Eric. *The Norsemen.* Translated and edited by Catherine Hutter. Greenwich, Conn.: New York Graphic Society Publishers, 1965.

Oxenstierna, Eric. *Die Urheimat der Goten.* Leipzig: Barth, 1948.

Oxenstierna, Eric. *The World of the Norsemen.* Translated by Janet Sondheimer. Cleveland and New York: The World Pub. Co., 1967.

Pastenaci, Kurt. *Die Kriegskunst der Germanen.* Karlsbad and Leipzig: Adam Kraft Verlag, 1943.

Paszkiewicz, Henryk. *The Origin of Russia.* London: Allen and Unwin, 1954.

Petersen, Ernst. *Die frühgermanische Kultur in Ostdeutschland und Polen.* Berlin: De Gruyter, 1929.

Petersen, Ernst. *Germanen in Schlesien.* Breslau: Flemming, 1937.

Petersen, Ernst. *Der ostelbische Raum als germanisches Kraftfeld im Lichte der Bodenfunde des 6.-8. Jahrhunderts.* Leipzig: Kabitzsch, 1939.

Piggott, Stuart. *Ancient Europe: From the Beginning of Agriculture to Classical Antiquity.* Chicago: Aldine Pub. Co., 1965.

Plezia, Marian. *Greckie i łacińskie źródła do najstarszych dziejów Słowian; Część I (do VIII wieku).* Poznań-Cracow: Polskie Towarzystwo Ludoznawcze, 1952.

Preidel, Helmut. *Die Anfänge der slawischen Besiedlung Böhmens und Mährens.* Bd. I. Gräfelfing bei München: Gans, 1954.

Powell, T. G. E. *The Celts.* New York: Praeger, 1958.

Reimers, Erich. *Der Kampf um den deutschen Osten.* Leipzig: Goldmann, 1939.

Reinhardt, Kurt F. *Germany: 2,000 Years.* Milwaukee: Bruce Pub. Co., 1950.

Rice, Tamara Talbot. *The Scythians.* 2nd. ed. London: Thames and Hudson, 1958.

Sanders, A. *Osteuropa in kontinentaleuropäischer Schau: I. Teil: Osteuropa bis zum Mongoleneinbruch.* Munich: Hoheneichen Verlag, 1942.

Sarton, George. *Ancient Science and Modern Civilization.* Lincoln: University of Nebraska Press, 1954.

Schmidt, Ludwig. *Geschichte der deutschen Stämme bis zum Ausgange der Völkerwanderung*. 2 vols. Berlin: Weidmann, 1904-1913.

Schreiber, Hermann. *Teuton and Slav; the Struggle for Central Europe*. Translated from the German by James Cleugh. New York: Knopf, 1965.

Schuchhardt, Carl. *Vorgeschichte von Deutschland*. 5., durchges. Aufl. Munich and Berlin: Oldenbourg, 1943.

Schwarz, Ernst. *Die Ortsnamen der Sudetenländer als Geschichtsquelle*. 2., durchges., teilweise umgearb. und erweiterte Aufl. Munich: Lerche, 1961.

Shepherd, William R. *Historical Atlas*. 8th ed. Pikesville, Maryland: Colonial Offset Co., 1956.

Shetelig, Haakon, and Falk, Hjalmar. *Scandinavian Archaeology*. Translated by E. V. Gordon. Oxford: Clarendon Press, 1937.

Shevelov, George Y. *A prehistory of Slavic; The Historical Phonology of Common Slavic*. New York: Columbia University Press, 1965.

Spekke, Arnolds. *The Ancient Amber Routes and the Geographical Discovery of the Eastern Baltic*. Stockholm: Goppers, 1957.

Spekke, Arnolds. *Balts and Slavs; Their Early Relations*. Washington: Alpha Print Co., 1965.

Smal-Stocki, Roman. *Slavs and Teutons; the Oldest Germanic-Slavic Relations*. Milwaukee: Bruce Pub. Co., 1950.

Stahl, William Harris. *Ptolemy's Geography; A Select Bibliography*. New York: The New York Public Library, 1953.

Steche, Theodor. *Altgermanien im Erdkundebuch des Klaudius Ptolemäus*. Leipzig: Kabitzsch, 1937.

Stender-Petersen, Adolf. *Slavisch germanische Lehnwortkunde; eine Studie über die ältesten germanischen Lehnwörter im Slavischen in sprach- und kulturgeschichtlicher Beleuchtung*. Göteborg: Elanders Boktryckeri Aktiebolag, 1927.

Stjernquist, Berta. *Simris; On Cultural Connections of Scania in the Roman Iron Age*. Bonn: Habelt; Lund: CWK Gleerups, 1955.

Strantz, Kurd von. *Der Romanismus als 2,000-jähriger Fluch des Germanentums, besonders des Deutschtums*. Leipzig: Klein, 1936.

Sulimirski, Tadeusz. *Najstarsze dzieje narodu polskiego*. Wyd. 4. London: Liber Publ., 1947.

Sulimirski, Tadeusz. *The Sarmatians*. New York: Praeger, 1970.

Thompson, Edward Arthur. *The Visigoths in the Time of Ulfila*. Oxford: Clarendon Press, 1966.

Thompson, James Westfall, and Johnson, Edgar Nathaniel. *An Introduction to Medieval Europe, 300-1,500*. New York: Norton, 1937.

Thomsen, Vilhem. *The Relations between Ancient Russia and Scandinavia and the Origin of the Russian State.* New York: Burt Franklin, (1877) 1964.

Thomson, J. Oliver. *History of Ancient Geography.* Cambridge: University Press, 1948.

Tozer, H. F. *A History of Ancient Geography.* 2nd ed., with additional notes by M. Cary. New York: Biblo and Tannen, 1964.

Trautmann, Reinhold. *Die slavischen Völker und Sprachen; eine Einführung in die Slavistik.* Göttingen: Vandenhoeck & Ruprecht, 1947.

Tret'iakov, Petr Nikolaevich. *Finno-ugry, balty i slaviane na Dnepre i Volge.* Moscow: "Nauka," 1966.

Tret'iakov, Petr Nikolaevich. *U istokov drevnerusskoi narodnosti.* Leningrad: "Nauka," 1970.

Tret'iakov, Petr Nikolaevich. *Vostochnoslavianskie plemena.* Moscow: Izd-vo AN SSSR, 1948.

Tret'iakov, Petr Nikolaevich, and Mongait, Aleksandr L'vovich. *Ocherki istorii SSSR; pervobytno-obshchinnyi stroi i drevneishie gosudarstva na territorii SSSR.* Moscow: Izd-vo AN SSSR, 1956.

Turville-Petre, G. *The Heroic Age of Scandinavia.* London: Hutchinson House, 1951.

Tymieniecki, Kazimierz. *Pisma wybrane.* Warsaw: PWN, 1956.

Tymieniecki, Kazimierz. *Ziemie polskie w starożytności; ludy i kultury najdawniejsze.* Poznań: Poznańskie Towarzystwo Przyjaciól Nauk, 1951.

Ułaszyn, Henryk. *Praojczyzna Słowian.* Łódź: Zakład Naukowy im. Ossolińskich, 1959.

Vasiliev, Alexander Alexandrovich. *The Goths in the Crimea.* Cambridge: The Medieval Academy of America, 1936.

Vernadsky, George. *Ancient Russia.* New Haven: Yale University Press, 1943.

Walsh, Warren Bartlett. *Russia and the Soviet Union; A Modern History.* Ann Arbor: University of Michigan Press, 1958.

Warmington, E. H. *Greek Geography.* London: Dent; New York: Dutton, 1934.

Weibull, Curt. *Die Auswanderung der Goten aus Schweden.* Göteborg: Elanders Boktryckeri Aktiebolag, 1958.

Wheeler, Mortimer. *Rome beyond the Imperial Frontiers.* New York: Philosophical Library, 1955.

Zeuss, Kaspar. *Die Deutschen und die Nachbarstämme.* Munich: I. J. Lentner, 1837.

Articles and essays

Antoniewicz, Włodzimierz. "Zagadnienie Gotów i Gepidów na ziemiach Polski w okresie rzymskim." *Przegląd Zachodni*, 7, No. 5/6 (1951), 26-59.

Biliński, Bronisław. "Drogi świata starożytnego ku zachodnim ziemiom polskim i problem Odry u Ptolemeusza." *Eos; Organ Polskiego Towarzystwa Filologicznego*, 41, No. 1-2 (1940-1946), 157-96.

Biliński, Bronisław. "Dwa świadectwa antyczne: Kalisia Ptolemeusza (Geographia, II, 11, 13) i Halisii Tacyta (Germania, 43,2)." In *Osiemnaście wieków Kalisza: studia i materiały do dziejów miasta Kalisza i regionu kaliskiego*. 3 vols. Kalisz: Wydawnictwo Poznańskie, 1960-1962), vol. 2, pp. 7-40.

Cross, Samuel Hazzard. "Slavic origins and migrations." In Strakhovsky, Leonid I., ed. *A Handbook of Slavic Studies*. Cambridge: Harvard University Press, 1949, pp. 1-23.

Czekanowski, Jan. "Przyczynki antropologiczne do zagadnienia stosunków słowiańsko-germańskich." *Przegląd Zachodni*, 7, no. 5/6 (1951), 1-25.

Czekanowski, Jan. "Zagadnienie praojczyzny Słowian i ich różnicowania się." In Polska Akademia Nauk. Komitet Językoznawstwa. *Z polskich studiów slawistycznych*. 2 vols. Warsaw: 1958, I, 137-45.

Gutenbrunner, S. "Namenkundliche Zeugnisse zur germanischen Urgeschichte." In *Germanen und Indogermanen; Volkstum, Sprache, Heimat, Kultur. Festschrift für Herman Hirt*. Hrsg. von Helmuth Arntz. 2 vols. Heidelberg: Winter, 1936, II, 453-70.

Kostrzewski, Bogdan. "Osadnictwo okolic Kalisza od czasów najdawniejszych do okresu środkowolateńskiego." In *Osiemnaście wieków Kalisza: studia i materiały do dziejów miasta Kalisza i regionu kaliskiego*. 3 vols. Kalisz: Wydawnictwo Poznańskie, 1960-1962, vol. 1, pp. 13-27.

Kostrzewski, Józef. "Słowianie i Germanie na ziemiach na wschód od Łaby w 6-8 wieku po Chr." *Przegląd Archeologiczny*, rocznik 22, tom 7, no. 1 (1946), 1-29.

Kostrzewski, Józef. "Ślady archeologiczne pobytu drużyn germańskich w Polsce w pierwszej połowie I stulecia naszej ery." *Przegląd Zachodni* 7, no. 5/6 (1951), 100-112.

Kostrzewski, Józef. "Stosunki plemion czeskich i słowackich z Niemcami w zaraniu dziejów w świetle archeologii." *Przegląd Zachodni*, 7, no. 5/6 (1951), 154-63.

Krahe, Hans. "Germanisch und Illyrisch." In *Germanen und Indoger-*

manen; Volkstum, Sprache, Heimat, Kultur. Festschrift für Herman Hirt. Hrsg. von Helmuth Arntz. 2 vols. Heidelberg: Winter, 1936, vol. II, pp. 565-78.

Kuryłowicz, Jerzy. "Związki językowe słowiańsko-germańskie." *Przegląd Zachodni,* 7, no. 5/6 (1951), 191-206.

La Baume, Wolfgang. "Ostdeutschland im Altertum." In Rhode, Gotthold, ed. *Die Ostgebiete des Deutschen Reiches.* 3., erw. u. verb. Aufl. Würzburg: Holzner, 1956, pp. 19-66.

La Baume, Wolfgang. "Teutons, Slavs and Prussians in Eastern Germany." In Pagel, Karl, ed. *The German East.* Berlin: Lemmer, 1954, pp. 9-16.

Lewicki, Tadeusz. "Zagadnienie Gotów na Krymie." *Przegląd Zachodni,* 7, no. 5/6 (1951), 77-99.

Malone, Kemp. "Ptolemy's Skandia." *American Journal of Philology,* 45 (1924), 362-70.

Moroń, Bogusław. " Χάλουσος ποταμός Ptolemeusza." *Slavia Occidentalis,* 9 (1930), 307-15.

Piotrowicz, Ludwik. "Goci i Gepidowie nad dolną Wisłą i ich wędrówka ku Morzu Czarnemu i Dacji." *Przegląd Zachodni,* 7, no. 5/6 (1951), 60-76.

Polaschek, Erich. "Ptolemy's Geography in a New Light." *Imago Mundi,* 14 (1959), 17-37.

Richmond, I. A. "Ptolemy's Map of Denmark; a Study in Conflicting Evidence." *Scottish Geographical Magazine,* 39 (1923), 99-102.

Rudnicki, Mikołaj. "Nazwa Odry i jej dopływów," *Monografia Odry.* Andrzej Grodek, ed. Poznań: Instytut Zachodni, 1948, pp. 10-69.

Rudnicki, Mikołaj. "Plemiona prasłowiańskie w dorzeczu górnej Noteci, średniej Warty i dolnej Wisły." *Slavianskaia Filologiia; sbornik statei.* Moscow: Izd-vo AN SSSR., 1958, vol. I, pp. 136-58.

Rudnicki, Mikołaj. "Zagadnienie pobytu drużyn germańskich na ziemiach polskich w czasie do VI w. w świetle imiennictwa." *Przegląd Zachodni,* 7, no. 5/6 (1951), 164-81.

Taszycki, Witold. "Dotychczasowy stan badań nad pobytem drużyn germańskich na ziemiach polskich w świetle toponomastyki." *Przegląd Zachodni,* 7, no. 5/6 (1951), 182-90.

Tymieniecki, Kazimierz. "Lugiowie w Czechach; przyczynek do dziejów najdawniejszej epoki słowiańskiej." *Przegląd Zachodni,* 7, no. 5/6 (1951), 113-53.

Tymieniecki, Kazimierz. "Położenie Słowian wśród ludów Europy albo tzw. pierwsze millenium. Zmiany w sytuacji międzynarodowej przed powstaniem Państwa Polskiego." In Poznańskie Towarzystwo Nauk.

Początki Państwa Polskiego: Księga Tysiąclecia. 2 vols. Poznań: PWN, 1962, I, 13-42.

Vasmer, Max. "Lugii und Mugilones." In *Sybaris; Festschrift Hans Krahe zum 60. Geburtstag am 7. Februar 1958.* Wiesbaden: Harrassowitz, 1958, pp. 189-94.

Wolf, Karl Felix. "Wer waren die Altslaven?" *Mannus, Zeitschrift für Vorgeschichte,* 7 (1915), 137-46.

Reference Works

Filip, Jan, ed. *Enzyklopädisches Handbuch zur Ur- und Frühgeschichte Europas. Manuel encyclopédique de préhistoire et protohistoire européennes.* 2 vols. Stuttgart, Berlin, Cologne, Mainz: Kohlhammer, 1966-1969.

Gebhardt, Bruno. *Handbuch der deutschen Geschichte.* Edited by Herbert Grundmann. 8th completely revised ed. 4 vols. Stuttgart: Union Deutsche Verlagsgesellschaft, 1954-1959.

Hoops, Johannes. *Reallexikon der germanischen Altertumskunde.* 4 vols. Strasbourg: Trübner, 1913-1919.

Der Kleine Pauly: Lexikon der Antike. Edited by Konrat Ziegler and Walther Sontheimer. Stuttgart: Alfred Druckenmüller, 1964- (in progress: vols. 1-3, 1964-1969).

Pauly's Realencyclopädie der classischen Altertumswissenschaft. Revised by Wissowa, Kroll, Mittelhaus. Stuttgart: Metzler *(et al.),* 1894- (in progress: 24 vols. and 12 supplements, 1894-1970).

Polska Akademia Nauk. Komitet Słowianoznawstwa. *Słownik starożytnosci słowiańskich: encyklopedyczny zarys kultury Słowian od czasów najdawniejszych do schyłku wieku XII. Lexicon antiquitatum slavicarum: summarium historiae cultus humanitatis Slavorum inde a temporibus antiquissimis usque ad exitum XII saeculi.* Edited by Wladyslaw Kowalenko, Gerard Labuda and Tadeusz Lehr-Spławiński. Wrocław: PWN, 1961- (in progress: vols. 1-4, 1961-1970).

Schrader. Otto. *Reallexikon der indogermanischen Altertumskunde: Grundzüge einer Kultur- und Völkergeschichte Alteuropas.* 2., verm. und umgearb. Aufl., hrsg. von A. Nehring. 2 vols. Berlin and Leipzig: De Gruyter, 1917-1929.

Smith, William, ed. *A Dictionary of Greek and Roman Geography.* 2 vols. London: Murray, 1873; New York: AMS Press, 1966.

INDEX

Date Due